Mass Observers Making Meaning

The Mass-Observation Critical Series

The Mass-Observation Critical Series pairs innovative interdisciplinary scholarship with rich archival materials from the original Mass-Observation movement and the current Mass Observation Project. Launched in 1937, the Mass-Observation movement aimed to study the everyday life of ordinary Britons. The Mass Observation Project continues to document and archive the everyday lives, thoughts and attitudes of ordinary Britons to this day. Mass-Observation, as a whole, is an innovative research organization, a social movement and an archival project that spans much of the 20th and early 21st centuries.

The series makes Mass-Observation's rich primary sources accessible to a wide range of academics and students across multiple disciplines, as well as to the general reading public. Books in the series include reissues of important original Mass-Observation publications, edited and introduced by leading scholars in the field, and thematically oriented anthologies of Mass-Observation material. The series also facilitates cutting-edge research by established and new scholars using Mass-Observation resources to present fresh perspectives on everyday life, popular culture and politics, visual culture, emotions and other relevant topics.

Series Editors:

Jennifer J. Purcell is Associate Professor of History and Chair of the History Department at Saint Michael's College in Vermont, USA. Using Mass-Observation diaries and directives, her first book, *Domestic Soldiers* (2010), seeks to understand the day-to-day lives of six women on the home front during the Second World War.

Benjamin Jones is Lecturer in Modern British History at the University of East Anglia in Norwich, UK. He is the author of *The Working Class in Mid-Twentieth-Century England* (2012), which was positively reviewed in *Sociology, American Historical Review, Journal of Modern History, Journal of British Studies, The Historical Journal, Economic History Review, Contemporary British History, Twentieth Century British History* and *Planning Perspectives*.

Editorial Board:

Fiona Courage, Head of Special Collections, University of Sussex in Brighton, UK

Lucy Curzon, Associate Professor of Contemporary and Modern Art History, University of Alabama, USA

Claire Langhamer, Professor of Modern British History and Director of Research and Knowledge Exchange in the School of History, Art History and Philosophy, University of Sussex, UK

Jeremy MacClancy, Professor of Anthropology, Oxford Brookes University, UK

Kimberly Mair, Associate Professor of Sociology, University of Lethbridge, Canada

Rebecca Searle, Lecturer in the Humanities, University of Brighton, UK

Matthew Taunton, Lecturer in the School of Literature, Drama and Creative Writing, University of East Anglia, UK

Published Titles:

The Biopolitics of Care in Second World War Britain, Kimberly Mair (2022)
Mass Observers Making Meaning, James Hinton (2022)

Mass Observers Making Meaning

*Religion, Spirituality and Atheism in
Late 20th-Century Britain*

James Hinton

BLOOMSBURY ACADEMIC
LONDON • NEW YORK • OXFORD • NEW DELHI • SYDNEY

BLOOMSBURY ACADEMIC
Bloomsbury Publishing Plc
50 Bedford Square, London, WC1B 3DP, UK
1385 Broadway, New York, NY 10018, USA
29 Earlsfort Terrace, Dublin 2, Ireland

BLOOMSBURY, BLOOMSBURY ACADEMIC and the Diana logo are
trademarks of Bloomsbury Publishing Plc

First published in Great Britain 2022
Paperback edition published 2023

Published in partnership with the Mass Observation Archive

Copyright © James Hinton, 2022

James Hinton has asserted his right under the Copyright, Designs and
Patents Act, 1988, to be identified as Author of this work.

For legal purposes the Acknowledgements on p. xii constitute an
extension of this copyright page.

Cover image: © Lev Savitskiy/Getty Images

All rights reserved. No part of this publication may be reproduced or transmitted in
any form or by any means, electronic or mechanical, including photocopying,
recording, or any information storage or retrieval system, without prior
permission in writing from the publishers.

Bloomsbury Publishing Plc does not have any control over, or responsibility for, any
third-party websites referred to or in this book. All internet addresses given in this
book were correct at the time of going to press. The author and publisher regret any
inconvenience caused if addresses have changed or sites have ceased to exist, but
can accept no responsibility for any such changes.

Every effort has been made to trace the copyright holders and obtain permission
to reproduce the copyright material. Please do get in touch with any enquiries or any
information relating to such material or the rights holder. We would be pleased to
rectify any omissions in subsequent editions of this publication should they
be drawn to our attention.

A catalogue record for this book is available from the British Library.

Library of Congress Cataloging-in-Publication Data
Names: Hinton, James, author.
Title: Mass observers making meaning : religion, spirituality and atheism
in late 20th-century Britain / James Hinton.
Description: London ; New York : Bloomsbury Academic, 2022. |
Series: The Mass-Observation critical series |
Includes bibliographical references and index.
Identifiers: LCCN 2021036303 (print) | LCCN 2021036304 (ebook) |
ISBN 9781350274495 (hardback) | ISBN 9781350274501 (pdf) |
ISBN 9781350274518 (ebook)
Subjects: LCSH: Religion and sociology–Great Britain–History–20th century. |
Great Britain–Religion–20th century. |
Public opinion–Great Britain. | Mass-Observation (Project : 1937–1960?)
Classification: LCC BL60 .H54 2022 (print) | LCC BL60 (ebook) | DDC 200.941/09045–dc23
LC record available at https://lccn.loc.gov/2021036303
LC ebook record available at https://lccn.loc.gov/2021036304

ISBN: HB: 978-1-3502-7449-5
PB: 978-1-3502-7453-2
ePDF: 978-1-3502-7450-1
eBook: 978-1-3502-7451-8

Typeset by Newgen KnowledgeWorks Pvt. Ltd., Chennai, India

To find out more about our authors and books visit www.bloomsbury.com
and sign up for our newsletters.

Contents

Preface		viii
Acknowledgements		xii
1	Introduction	1
2	Belief and disbelief	15
3	Death and afterwards	29
4	Religion and science	51
5	Uses of the paranormal	71
6	Moments out of time	91
7	A pagan priestess	111
8	Conclusion	133
Appendix		141
Notes		143
Bibliography		175
General Index		185
Index of Mass Observers		189

Preface

This is my third encounter with the mass observers. Nearly twenty years ago when I started work on what became *Nine Wartime Lives: Mass Observation and the Making of the Modern Self* (2010), I had already spent many years immersed in the social history of mid-20th-century Britain, but in using biographical essays to throw further light on that history I needed to find my feet in a quite different scholarly literature on the nature of modern selfhood. More than any other writer it was the Canadian philosopher Charles Taylor who offered me a map of that theoretical terrain in his magisterial *Sources of the Self: The Making of the Modern Identity* (1989). My second encounter with the mass observers, which culminated with *Seven Lives from Mass Observation: Britain in the Late Twentieth Century* (2016), depended on the same body of theory. For that book, the main challenge was to read my way into a more recent historiography in order to place my subjects' life stories in the trends and tensions of social change between the 1960s and the end of the century. My third encounter stays largely within the same chronological period, but opens up what, for me, has been an entirely new set of theoretical issues. Once again, it was Charles Taylor who came to my rescue with *A Secular Age* (2007), his profound exploration of the processes by which Western culture had moved from a condition in which it was more or less impossible not to believe in God to one where meaning-making had been pluralized and secularized and religious belief had become merely one among a number of options. Taylor is a Catholic and his account of modern secularity is shaped by his belief that the deepest human needs cannot be fulfilled without access to the transcendent.[1] I disagree, and I will explain why. But, as Taylor says of William James (whose early 20th-century classic *Varieties of Religious Experience* remains wonderfully fruitful): 'He is on one side, but he helps you to imagine what it's like to be on the other.'[2] It was Charles Taylor who showed me how it might be possible for a secular rationalist to discuss belief in the supernatural with empathy and without condescension. At the age of seventy-nine it is probably time for me to stop venturing onto unfamiliar terrain. But the mass observers keep leading me on.

My friends were often surprised when I told them I was writing a book about 'the supernatural'. As well they might be. What would I have to contribute – a lifelong atheist who had never previously, as a historian (or otherwise), shown the slightest interest in religion? I explained that I had chosen the topic partly because it seemed to arise naturally as an interesting subject from some of the individuals whose writing for Mass Observation (MO) I had been studying for earlier projects; partly because a 1996 MO directive asking its volunteers to write about their attitude to the supernatural, which attracted 279 responses, had never been analysed or written up; and, most importantly, because, unable to contemplate life without a book to write, I was looking for a new challenge. In my writing career I – a boy from a left-wing professional family – had deployed the historian's craft of disciplined empathy first by writing about working-class revolutionaries; then, swapping the class gap for twin gulfs of gender and politics, by studying right-wing middle-class women; and finally, since I retired from teaching, by exploring some of the individual lives, spanning the whole social, political and religious spectrum, revealed in such marvellous intimacy by the MO project.

But it was more than that.

Shortly after I was born my mother nearly died. Many years later, when my elder sister told me this, I wondered: Was this the origin of my father's disapproval? Be that as it may, I grew up bathed in my mother's love, but terrified of my father's anger, desperately craving his respect, and pathetically grasping at the slightest break in the air of disappointment with which this ambitious and successful scientist regarded his eldest son. And he had plenty to be disappointed about. I was slow to read, bottom of the class and clearly on track to fail the 11-plus (which I did). How far my educational backwardness was cause or consequence of paternal disapproval I will never know, but when my mother took me, aged eight, to a child guidance psychiatrist the advice was simple: 'Get him away from his father.' Being a woman of resource she found a way to do so. The one thing I could do well was sing. So, having sent me for some lessons, she took me on the rounds for a choral scholarship. King's College, Cambridge (where my father had done his PhD), turned me down flat, but Winchester, the public school, impressed by my rendering of 'In the Bleak Mid-Winter', gave me a place in their 'Quirister School' as one of the sixteen prepubescent boys they educated for free to sing as trebles in the chapel choir. So my mother's love sent me away from home to boarding school for three years (aged nine to twelve), a decision which must have been as difficult for her as it was for me.

We were atheists. My father's contempt for religion was implacable: to the Communist scientist it was unquestionable that belief in God was entertained only by ignorant and stupid people, or malevolent priests. We were atheists. But

I had become a religious professional, baptised (it was a condition of taking up the scholarship), singing in chapel every day and twice on Sundays, and struggling to make my way among a group of boys for whom religious belief was an unquestioned fact of life. The bus, back and forth each term between Winchester and home in Bristol, was a journey between two ontologies. At school I pretended to believe; at home I pretended not to. What did I believe? I have no idea. But when my closest school friend, a nephew of the Archbishop of Canterbury, came to stay I remember the agonies I suffered worrying about how to explain to him that we did not go to church on Sunday.

Back home after three years I was even more educationally backward. Making music had been thrilling, God or no God, but for the rest we were mostly taught together in a single classroom by a retired military man with little aptitude for the job. Things got no better with my father. His disappointment was confirmed termly by school reports (although these were in fact gradually improving) and daily by an exasperating neurotic habit I had acquired: 'Why does the boy hold his knife upside down?!' The remark was addressed regularly to my mother at the dinner table: for several years of my adolescence he could seldom bring himself to speak to me directly.

And then, around the age of sixteen, the boy woke up. Hormones led to girls; girls led to poetry; and from sonnets I graduated to philosophical verse inspired by John Donne, T. S. Eliot, D. H. Lawrence and Henri Bergson. Sex and spirituality were the interacting catalysts of the process by which I taught myself to write and to think. And God was also involved, if only by His denial. More than anyone else, my sixth-form history teacher, the Rev. Maurice Tucker (author of a good book on John Neville Figgis, one of the founders of Guild Socialism), who doubled as school chaplain, was responsible for my intellectual awakening, encouraging me to take him on over the merits of Bertrand Russell's atheism. The world opened up. I applied once again to King's College, this time to study history, and won a scholarship. When the telegram arrived my father, relentless in his disappointment, tried to convince me it was a malicious hoax perpetrated by one of my school friends. In the three delightful years that followed, living in college, spending more time on Communist Party politics than studying, I never once set foot inside the chapel in which, ten years earlier, I had aspired to sing. (For a full account of these years see my coming-of-age story: *Old Men Ought to Be Explorers: A History of My Adolescence*, forthcoming.)

In retirement I have returned to music, delighting in singing sacred music in a small, disciplined and secular choir. My mother would have been very pleased. But the turn to religion in my scholarly interests would have horrified my father – which, I suppose, is the point. Writing this book has been an intellectual journey, but also an emotional one – just one more stage in the unending process of settling accounts with that man. Am I waving a defiant fist by daring to take religion seriously, starting from the premise that a phenomenon so universal in human experience must arise from something more than the gullibility of the masses or the evil ingenuity of priests? Or am I, by clinging to a rationalist, secular, atheist approach to these issues, still struggling to earn paternal approval? The answer to these questions are of no interest to anyone but myself, but by rehearsing this personal history I am giving the reader fair warning of issues beyond my conscious control that will surely have coloured my handling of the mass observers' testimonies.

It is customary for academics to place brackets around the truth claims made by the believers they are studying: our job is simply to report what people say they believe and experience. The truth or otherwise of religious assertions is beyond our professional ken: 'Within the self-imposed limitations of the scientific perspective', Clifford Geertz sternly warns, 'such questions cannot even be asked, much less answered'.[3] It is, however, impossible to enter imaginatively into other people's categories of thought and systems of belief without investigating one's own underlying assumptions. Charles Taylor puts the point convincingly:

> We don't just decide once and for all when we enter sociology class to leave our 'values' at the door. They don't just enter as conscious premises which we can discount. They continue to shape our thought at a much deeper level, and it is only a continuing open exchange with those of differing standpoints which will help us to correct some of the distortions they engender.[4]

While I have been far from indifferent to the 'truth' of the various beliefs I have encountered, my focus has been on understanding, not refuting, those with which I disagree. My stance is neither neutral nor polemical. Rather, I have tried to sustain a dialogue, an 'open exchange', in which my own beliefs are as much on the table for discussion as those of the mass observers. Anthropologists know that understanding other cultures involves making the underlying assumptions of one's own culture strange and unfamiliar. I have been heartened in this approach by the gradual realization that theists and atheists, convinced materialists and spiritual searchers, often have a good deal more in common than the familiar entrenched battle lines would lead us to suppose.

Acknowledgements

Special thanks to Cathryn Steele without whose advice and encouragement this book would not have been completed. I am also grateful to my old colleagues in the Warwick History department; to Andrew Rawlinson, Chris Bostock and all the members of the Theory Reading Group of the Hauts Cantons de l'Hérault who have done so much to keep my mind alive in the depths of the French countryside; to Duncan Stewart for the loan of his Brighton flat; to the many friends who I have plagued with questions about their own beliefs; and to the keepers of the MO archive, Dorothy Sheridan, Fiona Courage and Jessica Scantlebury. My greatest debts are owed to my first reader and critic, Yvette Rocheron, and to two groups of people who must remain anonymous: the seven publisher's readers who, at various stages, read and commented on the manuscript and, of course, the mass observers themselves.

1

Introduction

I

It is a characteristic, perhaps a defining characteristic, of human brings that they seek meaning in life. Beyond our extraordinary capacity to engage in practical ways with the world about us, we have a hankering for the metaphysical.[1] Which is not to say that we are all aspiring philosophers. Immersed in the everyday routines of getting and spending, of work and play and family life, most of us most of the time appear indifferent to any larger meaning to our existence. Adolescents may agonize about existential meaning, and old people may review their lives in search of it, but by and large adult life, cluttered with the practical and the mundane, manages without metaphysics. Nevertheless the need for meaning is there in the background, as much a matter of feeling as of thought. A sense that life is meaningful, despite our inability to articulate what the meaning might be, is essential to psychological well-being. More or less consciously we work at meaning all the time, rehearsing it through the stories we tell ourselves about who we are – as individual personalities, as members of particular social groups, as human beings. We are meaning-making animals, 'suspended in webs of significance we ourselves have spun'.[2] These processes of making meaning are never finished, the webs are never complete, but it is in the spinning that we find ourselves. When meaning is absent we feel disoriented, at odds with our selves and the world, dissatisfied, unfulfilled. To the extent that it is present we feel together, whole, united within ourselves and with the world.

Sometimes the sense of meaning erupts joyfully into consciousness: in moments of intense emotion evoked by childbirth, by sexual passion, by natural or artistic beauty, by sudden revelation or enlightenment. On such occasions there is no need to put words to the meaning: it just is. At other times, shocked out of routine by some perceived injustice, some personal betrayal or defeat, by the death of a loved one or a catastrophic public event we are provoked to metaphysical speculation: Why am I here? Does life have a purpose? How should I live? But what we seek has less to do with philosophical coherence than it does with groping for words that reverberate with intuitions fashioned in obscure regions beneath consciousness.

When the mass observers write about their attitudes towards the big existential questions we can do no more than guess at the feelings underpinning their attitudes. The sense of meaning we find in our lives can never be reduced to a series of propositions. The feeling that life is meaningful is something which normally hovers on the fringe of consciousness, a product of largely unconscious processes.[3] You can reason about your beliefs, but you cannot reason your way to a sense of meaning. The sensation comes first, and the reasoning limps along behind. Wittgenstein remarked that religious believers offer proofs of God's existence in order to give themselves intellectual legitimacy, but 'they themselves would never have come to believe as a result of such proofs'.[4] Much the same could be said of the faith that some non-believers place in the sovereignty of human reason. This is a study, not of the sense of meaning itself, but of the varieties of ways in which people in late 20th-century Britain, more or less, puzzled about the big existential questions, tried to find language adequate to express sensations that were, in the final analysis, inexpressible, ineffable.

For the best part of two millennia, in the West, Christianity had appeared to offer more or less coherent answers to the puzzles of existence. If human life was embedded in a cosmos created for humankind, meaning was everywhere and everything had a spiritual dimension. However impossible it might be to understand God's purpose for humankind, faith could connect you to the divine, bathing your life, with all its ups and downs, in his care, and love. Although you might choose to disregard the metaphysical in everyday life,[5] the supernatural was all around, and God was there when and if you needed him. Today faith in a personal God is no longer in the air that we breathe. We live in a universe disenchanted by the findings of modern science, and in social orders legitimized by notions of human rights rather than divine sanction. In our secular age, the languages in which we seek to express our sense of meaning have diversified and become more problematic.

II

When the mass observers were writing in the late 20th century, Christianity was in rapid retreat. Between the 1950s and the 1970s the proportion of British adults professing belief in a 'personal God' fell from 43 per cent to 32 per cent. Thereafter it stabilized, before falling again to around 25 per cent during the first decade of the 21st century.[6] Between the 1980s and 2017 the proportion of the population defining themselves as belonging to no religion increased from a third to a half.[7] As belief in God declined, people looked elsewhere for a language in which to express their sense of meaning. But contemporary Western secular culture is built on Christian foundations, and traces of its origin are to be found everywhere. At the turn of the century most of those who defined themselves as belonging to no religion continued to embrace belief in the existence of supernatural forces. Throughout the late 20th century belief in the existence of some kind of transcendent 'spirit or life force', as distinct from belief in a personal God, held steady at around 40 per cent.[8] The diffusion of alternative, countercultural, ideas of spirituality since the 1960s helped to sustain such beliefs, and to deepen their influence on everyday life. Increasingly in the late 20th century, 'religion' came to be seen as a matter of dogma and ritual imposed on the individual from without by the authority of an ecclesiastical hierarchy. 'Spirituality', by contrast, described an inward journey, a search for the deepest meaning and significance of life authenticated not by any external authority but by each individual in their own fashion. Such journeys might involve Christian residues, ideas borrowed from esoteric and occult traditions, Eastern religions (especially Buddhism), Native American and shamanistic beliefs, or a reimagined pagan past. Alongside ongoing processes of secularization, what Britain had been experiencing since the cultural upheavals of the 1960s was, in the words of one historian, 'an enormous increase in the range of beliefs and world-views accessible to the majority of the population ... As Christianity lost a large part of its privileged position, the options in matters of belief ... were open to a degree that they had not been for centuries'.[9] This openness is apparent in the variety of ways in which the mass observers sought to articulate their feelings about life's larger existential questions.

Alongside hankerings for the transcendent, many subscribed to belief in the paranormal. In the 1990s, opinion polls suggest that around a quarter of the British population took horoscopes seriously, a third believed that dreams could predict the future and fully half subscribed to the view that clairvoyants could do so.[10] Unlike religion, belief in the paranormal was not in decline. According to Gallup polls, the proportion of people believing in ghosts more than tripled between 1950 and 1995, from 10 per cent to over 31 per cent, and polling in the first decade of the new century showed ghost belief higher still, approaching 40 per cent of the population.[11] Between 1975 and 1998 the proportion of people claiming to have actually seen a ghost tripled from 5 per cent to 15 per cent, and many others, to judge from the testimony of the mass observers, could cite such experiences reported by people they knew and trusted. What this growth reflects is probably not any increase in the extent to which people sensed the presence of the dead – let alone an actual proliferation of ghosts – but broader shifts in the culture which made it more acceptable to ascribe one's experience to supernatural forces. 'Historically', wrote Gillian Bennett at the turn of the century, 'we seem to be dealing with a major discursive shift since the mid-century: one which tends to legitimate supernatural beliefs, while religious belief is falling away.'[12]

If such a shift did occur, it may be reflected in the mass observers' testimony, most of which was written in the 1990s. Since the millennium, however, while belief in ghosts remains widespread, the appeal of a non-religious spirituality appears to have substantially weakened. A 2013 survey suggested that the number of believers in a spirituality without a personal God, which had held steady at around 40 per cent throughout the late 20th century, had halved; and amongst those who continued to believe only a minority affirmed the existence of 'a universal Spirit, life-force or energy', while most subscribed to the vaguer view that there is 'something there'.[13] Meanwhile atheism advanced. The number of people telling pollsters that they did not believe in God increased from 10 per cent in the 1960s to 27 per cent in the 1990s. By 2013, 35 per cent denied the existence of 'God or some higher power', or thought it improbable.[14] Only a minority of these people, however, described themselves as 'convinced atheists' – 8 per cent of the population, according to a survey conducted for the BBC in 2000, growing to 19 per cent according to a YouGov survey in 2015.[15] But the appeal of the New Atheism promoted in the early years of the 21st century by Richard Dawkins and others remained limited.[16]

III

As belief in a personal God declined, people looked elsewhere for answers to the existential questions that religion had traditionally sought to answer. Optimists of the European Enlightenment, believing human beings to be both rational and virtuous by nature, imagined a future in which humanity, freed from irrational superstition, took conscious control of its own destiny. However frequently disappointed, the ideas of progress and of humanity's capacity for rational collective action remain central to the modern secular imagination, not least when it comes to tackling the crisis of climate change. Modernity, however, was haunted by far darker visions. Because human beings no longer held a central place in a world objectified by science, the meaning of human existence became obscure. If, as the French biologist Jacques Monod wrote, humankind is 'alone in the universe's unfeeling immensity out of which he emerged only by chance', where was meaning to be found?[17] Some religious writers recognize the 'heroism of unbelief ... facing a disenchanted universe with courage and lucidity'.[18] A stoic acceptance that we are no more than a cosmic accident 'merits the deepest respect and, in fact, constitutes one of the most impressive attitudes of which man is capable'.[19] But few could embrace the implacable logic of Bertrand Russell's insistence that it was 'only on the firm foundation of unyielding despair' that 'the soul's habitation' could 'henceforth be safely built'.[20] More commonly, the disenchantment of the world led to nausea in face of the meaninglessness of merely contingent things.[21] The most influential picture of a disenchanted world was provided by Weber's account of a post-religious modernity in which individuals found themselves locked in an 'iron cage' of technology, instrumental rationality and bureaucratic regulation.[22] Kafka supplied the fictional apotheosis of this vision.[23]

Powerful though they are, neither the optimistic nor the pessimistic accounts of the consequences of religious decline tell the whole story. While an Enlightenment belief in the intrinsic rationality of human beings is difficult to sustain, it is manifestly not the case that non-religious people in modern societies live with a permanent crisis of meaninglessness.[24] There are sources of meaning operating independently of either religion or rationalism.

The processes by which we construct meaning are largely unconscious. Our deepest beliefs, acquired by inheritance as we find our feet in the world though childhood and adolescence, are resistant to change. Meaning, wrote William James, belongs to intuitions that 'come from a deeper level of [our] nature than the loquacious level which rationalism inhabits':

> Your whole subconscious life, your impulses, your faiths, your needs, your divinations, have prepared the premises, of which your consciousness now feels the weight of the result; and something in you absolutely knows that that result must be truer than any logic-chopping rationalistic talk, however clever, that may contradict it.[25]

As reasoners, we are drawn to evidence that confirms our beliefs, preferring rationalization to the rigours of attempted refutation.[26] The slow, patient, scientific work of analysis and empirical testing which underpins the technological basis of our culture has little impact on our beliefs or the meanings we attribute to our lives. 'Science', wrote Durkheim, 'is fragmentary and incomplete; it advances but slowly and is never finished; but life cannot wait.' Unable to tolerate such incompleteness 'the theories which are destined to make men live and act are … obliged to pass science and complete it prematurely'.[27] The human brain was not evolved to tolerate uncertainty, to accept contingency or to understand statistical probability.[28] We are constantly trying to make sense of experience, and where science or practical reason fail we fill the gap with explanations drawn from the cultures we inhabit.

Durkheim's characterization of religion as a 'premature completion' of science implied the positivist assumption that, in the long term, science would eventually come to hold sway over the whole of human understanding. But science can do little to answer the human need for meaning. It is in sociality that we spin the webs of significance that sustain us, linking our sense of who we are to something larger than ourselves. Our beliefs and our values are shaped by our membership of a family, a class, a nation and the multitude of other identities available in a pluralistic society. To the extent that we are firmly embedded in such groupings, we tend to reify them, treating them as having an objective existence independent of the people who inhabit them. In reality, beyond the most immediate face-to-face transactions of everyday life, the groups in which we invest our identities are works of the imagination, existing only by virtue of our capacity to imagine bonds of unity with unknown strangers – or even with dead ones, as in nationalist claims that 'we' have lived here since time immemorial. Durkheim understood religion as a projection of the bonds of community – cementing a larger social solidarity in face of everyday scrabbling for individual or parochial advantage by marking out in ritual and symbol a terrain of the sacred in which norms and values were embodied. The secular sacred works in much the same way. National identity is inscribed in the rights and duties of citizenship, in the stone of war memorials and the mobilizing power of patriotic emotion. A wider humanist identity enshrines notions of human rights and fosters solidarity with the global poor and with migrants displaced by war and social collapse. An ecological identity, understanding oneself as belonging to the phenomenon of life on Earth, carries with it duties of stewardship that go beyond the rights and needs of human beings. The secular social imagination creates versions of the sacred, ethical imperatives policed by guilt and shame, and embodied in powerful emotions that can operate without invoking any supernatural agency.[29] The Romantic reaction against Enlightenment rationalism which underpinned the rise of modern nationalism also spawned secular alternatives to religious sentiments of awe and wonder, aestheticizing nature and finding in music and the arts the profoundest sense of human meaning.[30]

Viewed from a religious standpoint these secular versions of the sacred appear as poor alternatives to the real thing. Stripped of a supernatural referent, social bonding, contemplation of nature or engagement with great works of art can never match the depth and richness of meaning provided by access to the grace of God.[31] Those of us who reject religious belief question this assertion, doubting that the believer's communion with an imagined God yields a more profound sense of meaning than we ourselves find in the contemplation of beauty or the solidarities of sociality.[32] Since there is no objective position from which to rule on these competing claims, it may be preferable simply to acknowledge that meaning can be found in either direction. More important is what the two approaches have in common – both sources of meaning rest primarily neither on evidence nor on reasoning, but on the power of imagination.[33] We find meaning in life only because we have the ability to see what is not, in any material sense, actually there. Alongside everyday practicalities, we all seek larger transcendent meanings. Perhaps it doesn't matter very much whether the transcendence is understood as an engagement with supernatural or with purely material forces. Either way the sense of meaning depends on the exercise of the imagination.[34]

The technical basis of human society has always rested on the exercise of practical reason and, in modern times, of scientific enquiry. But both social cohesion and the ability of societies to adapt to changing conditions depend on how we imagine ourselves, individually and collectively – on the myths by which we live.[35] Much that is mysterious about human beings springs from their capacity to work in both these ways at once – to engage with the world in practical ways and, at the same time, to tell stories about it, and about ourselves. As individuals we make sense of our lives by rehearsing and constantly updating the stories we tell about where we came from and what we have become or are becoming. It is through narratives of personal identity that we maintain a sense of agency, purpose and value.[36] And it is through a similar process of storytelling that we are bound into wider social groupings. Myths of collective identity are expressive rather than argumentative, working on the emotions rather than the intellect and their power is that of poetic imagery rather than of logical reasoning. Neither true nor false, they are not hypotheses subject to empirical falsification. They are standpoints, framing the way we see the world.

Once we accept the universality of myth-making, then some of the apparent polarities begin to dissolve. To religious conservatives and New Atheists it matters dreadfully whether or not people believe in the existence of supernatural forces. For the former, godless modernity produces a world without values, given over to egotistical materialism or swept away by destructive pseudo-religions; for the latter, humanity's progress towards enlightenment continues to be threatened by the widespread appeal of irrational pre-scientific superstition. But egotism is not confined to atheists, and irrationality is not confined to believers. What is more striking is the degree to which, in their attempts to express their feelings about life's larger existential questions, most mass observers were content to put to one side any ultimate judgement about the reality of the supernatural. The dominant tone is one of puzzlement or scepticism. Beliefs, whether in supernatural forces or the power of reason, are held with an ironic recognition of their fallibility. Ontological certainties are kept at bay with a more or less playful 'what if?'. In the chapters which follow, I examine how the mass observers handled notions of the supernatural in a variety of situations – in their responses to death and bereavement (Chapter 3); in the way they understood the relationship between science and religion (Chapter 4); in their attitudes towards apparently paranormal phenomena (Chapter 5); and in those rare 'moments out of time' when our practical engagement with the world gives way entirely to an overwhelming, if inexpressible, sense of meaning (Chapter 6). What is apparent in all these dimensions is the degree to which both attitudes and experience overlap the frontiers between believers and non-believers. The ways in which the mass observers articulate their own sense of meaning and their feelings about life's larger existential questions reveal how much is shared across the divide between those who invoke the supernatural and those who do not. In our pluralistic secular age the ontological binary fails to capture the cross-currents in the ocean from which we draw our sense that life is meaningful.[37]

IV

From its foundation in 1937 Mass Observation (MO) had set out to enable 'ordinary' people to write about their attitudes and everyday experiences. Responding to 'directives' sent out every few months – open-ended questionnaires on subjects ranging from politics to the most intimate details of personal life – the material sent in by the panel of volunteer 'observers' created a uniquely rich record of contemporary attitudes. They wrote mainly about themselves, rather than the 'masses' – the name 'mass observation' was always a misnomer. Supplemented during the Second World War by regular diaries kept by some of the volunteers, this first phase of MO has provided an inexhaustible resource for historians working on the social history of mid-20th-century Britain.[38] Although the original organization more or less disappeared in the late 1940s, its records were eventually deposited at Sussex University where, in 1981, those in charge of the archive decided to recreate a panel of volunteer writers willing to respond to 'directives' sent three times each year. Between 1981 and 2013 around 2,600 individuals sent in responses to the MO Project, as the new initiative came to be called. Half of them quickly lapsed, but around 1,100 people remained for between two and ten years, 250 for up to twenty years, and a similar number for more than twenty years, a select few writing for the whole period.[39]

For the purposes of this study I have focussed on the 279 people who responded to a directive sent out in the summer of 1996 titled: 'The supernatural: What do you believe?' The directive asked people to list everything they (or others) might regard as supernatural, and to describe their own experiences, if any, of the supernatural. Unusually, two different versions of the directive were sent out. The first, sent to those in the first half of the alphabet, was relatively brief (this directive is reproduced in the appendix). The second, sent to the remainder, included a long list of apparently supernatural phenomena. But, apart from encouraging people to provide uninformative lists of things about which they had no firm opinions, the longer version did not make any significant difference to the responses. Both versions of the directive concluded by asking those who had some belief in the supernatural to describe how this affected their 'outlook on life' in general, and how it related to their other beliefs, especially any religious beliefs that they might hold. The implication that religious belief did not, of necessity, involve belief in the supernatural was unfortunate, as several respondents were at pains to point out. Many of those who chose not to discuss their attitudes to religion in any detail did respond to other directives which dealt more directly with religion, and I have used these to supplement their 1996 responses.[40] In this way it has been possible to identify the religious beliefs (or lack of them) of all but 38 of the 279 respondents to the 1996 directive.

It might be expected that those mass observers who choose to respond to a questionnaire about the supernatural would be people who were particularly interested in the topic, but this does not appear to be the case. The response rate to this directive, about 60 per cent of those on MO's books at the time, was normal; and between 82 per cent and 92 per cent of those who did respond also responded to other directives in 1995 and 1996 on subjects as diverse as 'BSE and the "mad cow" debate', 'The countryside', 'Shopping', 'Using the telephone' and 'Unpaid work'.[41] Mass observers were ready to comment on whatever subject the organization decided to throw at them, and there is no reason to suppose that those responding to the 'supernatural' directive were untypical of the mass observers as a whole. We are not dealing with a group of people self-selected because they were unusually concerned with religion, the supernatural or the meaning of life. In this respect the mass observers were entirely 'ordinary'.

MO, however, has never claimed that its volunteers were representative of the population in general. Respondents to the 'supernatural' directive included few manual workers, a normal proportion of clerical and secretarial staff, and a very large over-representation of professionals, especially teachers, librarians and nurses.[42] Seventy per cent of the respondents were women. Older people were also heavily over-represented: half the respondents were over sixty-five, compared with 20 per cent of the adult population as a whole. Only 15 per cent were under forty-five, compared with around half the adult population of England and Wales. The proportion of middle-aged people (those between forty-five and sixty-four) was, however, more or less representative of the population as a whole.[43] Since religious belief tends to be concentrated among women and older people one would expect there to be a higher proportion of believers among the MO respondents than in the population as a whole, and a correspondingly lower proportion of agnostics and atheists.

So far as belief in a personal God is concerned this expectation is borne out – 38 per cent believed in a personal God, as against 31 per cent in the general population. Non-believers, however – and quite contrary to what would be expected of this relatively old and female group – were over-represented, at 40 per cent of the total, compared with 27 per cent among the population as a whole.[44] This anomaly might be explained by the fact that the mass observers were much better educated than the population at large. Of 174 respondents to the supernatural directive who also answered a directive on their educational history only 28 per cent had left school at the minimum age, while 20 per cent remained in full-time education until graduation and a further 12 per cent gained university degrees later in life.[45] About a third of the mass observers were graduates, and graduates were known to be disproportionately inclined to irreligion.[46] Among the mass observers themselves, however, there was no significant correlation between the level of education and the propensity to reject religion.[47] So the disproportionate number of observers who were agnostics or atheists may have more to do with the fact that the people attracted to MO were particularly thoughtful and reflective, regardless of their educational history. Whatever may be the case today, during the lifetime of most of the mass observers rejecting religion probably required more independence of thought than accepting it.

Belief in a spirit or life force, on the other hand, was under-represented – only 22 per cent compared with 40 per cent among the population as a whole.[48] This might be explained by older people being less attracted to such views than younger ones, although this does not in fact appear to be the case among the mass observers themselves. Leaving age aside, however, one would have expected the mass observers to be more inclined to such views than the general population, since they were drawn disproportionately from precisely the section of the population among which New Age ideas found their greatest appeal: professionals working in jobs which facilitate 'self-exploration, cultivation and expression'.[49] As noted above however, belief in a non-religious spirituality among the general population had by 2013 declined to around the same level as among the mass observers in the 1990s. Perhaps, as particularly thoughtful people, the mass observers were ahead of the trend.

Clearly the MO material is unsuitable as a basis from which to generalize about the distribution of attitudes among the population as a whole. The mass observers were disproportionately female, elderly and well educated. Moreover, in the absence of any respondents from Britain's ethnic minorities, there is nothing to be learned about attitudes among those raised in Muslim, Hindu or other religious cultures.[50] Nevertheless the number of respondents ensures that we can listen to a wide variety of voices from each of the three main groups – Christians, believers in non-religious notions of spirituality, and agnostics and atheists. For many of these people religious belief or its absence was fraught with ambiguity, ambivalence, uncertainty, longing or, in some cases, guilt. Opinion polls are unlikely to register such complexities. Not much hangs on what you tell a pollster, and assent to propositions about the supernatural put to people by pollsters may tell us very little about how people look for meaning in their lives. Moreover, while our everyday language is suffused with the language of the transcendent – 'soul', 'spirit' – there is little consensus about what we mean when we utter these words. The mass observers, responding to open-ended questions, were able to explore the ambiguities of their feelings and to explain what they meant by the words they used.

MO built up an extraordinary relationship of trust with members of the panel, particularly those who wrote over many years who tended to see themselves as participants in a shared enterprise of creating an archive of contemporary attitudes and feelings.[51] To that end, they wrote as honestly as they could about their thoughts, feelings and experiences. Guaranteed anonymity, they felt free to use MO to reveal their own doubts and inconsistencies and to explore their own confusions. It may have been easier to do this writing in privacy and at leisure than it would have been had they been talking face to face with an interviewer. Most of us are more confused, especially about these larger existential questions, that we would be happy to reveal to a stranger, however sympathetic. Mass observers often confessed uncertainty, but unlike the dead end of a tick in a pollster's box a mass observer's 'don't know' would normally preface or conclude thoughtful reflection on problematic issues where no certainty could be found.[52] MO's 1947 book on religion – *Puzzled People* – presented puzzlement as a problem, evidence of a rootless anomie that threatened to open the door to the kind of irrationalism that – they believed – had overtaken Nazi Germany. But if our sense of meaning is an intuitive product of unconscious processes, we should not be surprised that we find it difficult to express it in coherent rational terms. Being puzzled about ultimate existential questions may well be an inescapable part of the human condition – and probably one of the better parts.

One further advantage of the MO material is the wealth of biographical information available in the archive. Among the respondents to the 1996 directive, many were regular respondents; so it has been possible to mine their responses to a wide range of other directives in order to explore how their attitudes to religion and the supernatural might be related to other aspects of their lives. In making use of this material I faced a difficult choice. Our deepest beliefs are woven into the individual textures of our lives, and to fully understand the role played by belief – or non-belief – it would be necessary to place what people reveal about their spiritual journeys within the context of their lives as a whole. Previously I have used MO sources to write biographical essays about a handful of individuals, and I could have done the same for a few of the more interesting respondents to the directive on the supernatural. But that would have meant neglecting the great wealth of material gathered by the directive about the variety of attitudes to the supernatural. I considered doing this – and in one case I experimented with such an approach (see Chapter 7) – but in the end I decided that it would be more valuable to explore the full range of the beliefs expressed by the mass observers. Nevertheless, without attempting comprehensive biographical treatments, I have made selective use of other biographical material in the archive, most systematically of responses to two directives sent out in 1990. The first, dealing with 'Social Divisions', revealed the respondents' images of the wider society and of their own place within it. The second, titled 'Close Relationships', showed the observers' sense of themselves as part of intimate networks of kin and friendship. With such material I have been able, in many cases, to glimpse something of the interplay between respondents' lives and their attitudes to the supernatural. In order to protect their anonymity, I have used invented names for the mass observers and omitted any reference to the places where they lived. Those mentioned more than once are listed in a separate index.

2

Belief and disbelief

In modern times, argues Charles Taylor, belief in God has moved from being 'unchallenged and indeed unproblematic' to becoming 'one option among others, and frequently not the easiest to embrace'.[1] Many of Mass Observation's (MO's) Christians do not appear to have felt any need to question the faith they had imbibed with their mother's milk, and some accepted the authority of the church so absolutely that they could baldly state: 'I am a Christian and therefore the Creed expresses my beliefs'.[2] But, argues Taylor, in modern secular societies it is difficult to be a 'naïve believer', to hold uncritically to unconsidered, inherited beliefs. Unlike our medieval ancestors, we all live among people who do not share our beliefs – neighbours, work colleagues, friends, even partners: 'it is harder and harder to find a niche where either belief or unbelief go without saying'.[3] Given the gender differences in religious belief many wives must have learned to live with their husband's scepticism, and many a sceptical husband must have attributed his wife's Christian faith to the peculiarity of the feminine mind – trying to understanding which, as one atheist mass observer put it, was 'rather like doing a Rubik's Cube blindfold'.[4] From the other side of the fence Paula Harrison, a religious education teacher married to a scientifically minded maths teacher reported:

> My agnostic husband says I have naïve and simplistic views that don't make sense. … It frustrates him that that I can't seem to articulate my beliefs to his satisfaction. He asks why I believe in God and I say because I do and always have done and can't ever conceive of a time when I wouldn't believe in Him.[5]

If we are today freer than ever before to choose our beliefs, we do so amidst a cacophony of voices, deciding where we stand in the full knowledge that other reasonable and well-meaning people disagree.

The wide range of ideas and feelings expressed by Christian mass observers reflected the ferment of new religious thinking in the 1960s as both Protestant and Catholic churches tried to come to grips with ongoing secularization and explosive currents of cultural change.[6] A few, like the physics teacher Sandra Delaney, embraced with enthusiasm the liberal theology of revisionist Anglican bishops, which enabled them to 'keep only the baby' while 'chucking out all the bathwater'.[7] 'I don't agree with all the teachings of the Anglican church,' wrote Paula Harrison,

> but then it seems to me that any thinking person is going to find discrepancies and distortions in the teachings of any church they join. Like the Bishop of Durham I shall probably go to the stake for my belief that the Bible was written (and translated) by human beings and therefore is as liable to be full of misunderstandings and errors as any other book.[8]

For Cynthia Rawlinson, John Robinson's 1967 book *But That I Can't Believe* was 'a life-line … as it shows me that I can still believe in God and call myself a Christian while having doubts about many of the details of Christ's life'.[9]

Others felt free to look to other religious traditions to supplement their Christian beliefs. Gillian Latimer read widely on the margins of Christian belief, and felt that 'Christ is in all religions'.[10] As the wife of the (retired) rector of the parish church and leader of the church's 'contemplative prayer group', one might have expected her to hold conventional Christian views. On the contrary, she felt that her husband's profession gave her licence 'to explore widely – while having one foot kept firmly on the ground. He laughs and says I'd have been burned in past ages'. Her unorthodoxy stemmed from a much-loved and admired mother who, though 'a devoted and practical Christian', was also a 'free thinker'. Gillian was particularly impressed by Rudolph Steiner, whose 'anthroposophy' sought to combine the disciplined methods of natural science with the esoteric exploration of spiritual life, and Bede Griffiths, a Benedictine monk who embraced Hinduism. His book *The Marriage of East and West* (1982) explored the affinities between Christianity, Eastern mysticism and modern physics. In a similar vein Jenny Brown embraced the work of Karen Armstrong, an ex-nun, who wrote 'about western religions being overly faith-centred, demanding signing up to a system of beliefs, rather than concentrating on deep spirituality. I was brought up a Roman Catholic and remain one but in a loose, unconventional way. I see it as a useful spiritual framework but one of many possible paths to spiritual truth'.[11] Veronica Richardson could not make sense of the world without 'my central belief in God': but she had 'always had difficulty … in knowing why my religious beliefs were the right ones and everyone else was misguided'.[12] 'God is not necessarily Christian,' wrote Barbara Dilnot, a middle-aged nurse, wondering whether the Quakers or the Buddhists might have more to offer than the Anglican church in which she had brought up her children.[13] Janice Knight, another nurse, who had joined a nonconformist church in her late sixties after a spiritual voyage encompassing Theosophy and the Rosicrucian Order, took from Hindu scripture the happy thought that 'all the religions of the world are like little rivers which flow to meet the mighty ocean which is God'.[14] Subud, an organization with Islamic roots in 1920s Indonesia, gave practical expression to a similar view, seeking 'to cater for the spiritual needs of ordinary persons, whatever their personal religious beliefs',[15] and Virginia Harris, an Anglican who had gradually lost faith in the teachings of the church, found spiritual renewal in her local Subud group.[16]

For the churches religious pluralism was a risky business, 'fragilising' religion and undermining those 'plausibility structures' which in earlier times had served to sustain faith.[17] Conservatives were right to worry that the loosening of dogma advocated by liberal bishops like John Robinson might lead the more adventurous members of the flock away from religion altogether.[18] Edward Farleigh, born in 1921, had been an Anglican from childhood, but it was not until he retired from his job as a senior pensions advisor in the mid-1980s that he started to think seriously about the beliefs he had inherited, his critical faculties stimulated by a two-year course organized by the church. Ironically, by the time he collected his 'Certificate of Christian Education', he had rejected most Christian beliefs. Outwardly he remained a practising Anglican, but the creed that he silently recited in church every Sunday articulated a spirituality stripped of any specifically Christian ideas:

> I believe an Omniscient Power created the universe; The Creator is incomprehensible; do not try to fathom or describe it: doing so leads to conflict. Just contemplate the mystery with rapture, awe and wonder. The Creator's power still flows through its creation. Throughout the ages people who have touched that power have lived lives of humility, bringing harmony, healing and love. We will receive the peace for which we long when we follow their example.[19]

The old man in the pew silently professing his own post-Christian creed was symptomatic of a wider decay of Christian orthodoxy. Stella Marshall, who we will meet more fully in later chapters, certainly believed that human life had a powerful spiritual dimension, but for her the dogmas and rituals of organized religion appeared to be futile efforts 'to find meaning ... for forces quite beyond our understanding – so to follow one belief system, or one set of rules must only be for one's own satisfaction, meaningless in terms of the Whole. If my friend makes the sign of the cross, while I open my crown chakra to the light, and my neighbour faces Mecca five times daily, what difference does this make to the Universe?'[20] It was with thoughts like these that a significant minority of the mass observers rejected Christianity, with its priestly hierarchy, its dogmas and its story of a personal God, in favour of vaguer notions of the presence of the supernatural in their lives.

II

The rich variety of non-religious spiritualities which flourished in later 20th-century Britain owed much to earlier traditions –19th-century spiritualism; the 'New Thought' movement whose optimistic 'mind-cure' doctrines William James had heralded, with some misgivings, as America's 'only decidedly original contribution to the systematic philosophy of life';[21] the fin de siècle mystical revival in which occultist groups, most notably Madame Blavatsky and the Theosophical Society, recycled esoteric versions of Eastern religion for Western consumption.[22] Much New Age thinking in the 1970s and beyond replayed themes from these older traditions, often channelled through the counterculture of the 1960s. The upheavals of that decade, particularly in attitudes to sexuality, certainly contributed to the 'crisis of Christendom', but the result was not any thoroughgoing secularization.[23] While the counterculture had no time for orthodox religion, it was equally hostile to much of what passed for scientific rationality, and the materialistic, consumerist culture it sustained. The protest movements which stemmed from the 1960s may have seen themselves as thoroughly secular, but the 'post-materialist' values that underpinned them often found expression in a spiritual orientation towards life's larger meanings. Anti-nuclear mobilizations and the emerging ecological movement fostered the cultivation of spiritual resources of resistance to the fetish of 'progress' driven by scientific triumphalism. Feminists, identifying scientific fantasies of man's domination over nature as no less phallocentric than the structures of Christian orthodoxy, often found themselves drawn to a spiritual identification with a benevolent mother earth.

As countercultural ideas diffused through the later 20th century, notions of a spirituality detached from any organized religion were widely articulated. While only a small minority chose to involve themselves in the proliferating associations of spiritual worshipers, non-religious ideas of spirituality became, for many, part of the common sense of the age. Alternative and complimentary therapies boomed, the practitioners often drawn from the same educated and caring professions which feature disproportionately among the mass observers (teachers, nurses, social workers);[24] yoga, meditation and other spiritually based technologies of the self proliferated;[25] new psychotherapies pushed beyond the unconscious to the spiritual; big business paid spiritual leaders to train their staff; essential oils, crystals and other material aids to spirituality migrated from specialist esoteric suppliers to mainstream shops; and bookshops made space for an ever-expanding literature of spirituality. As William James had noted, speaking of the 19th-century New Thought movement, one test of whether a new religion has established itself is that 'the demand for its literature is great enough for insincere stuff, mechanically produced for the market, to be … supplied by publishers'.[26] However banal or ill-expressed the contents of such books, the fact that there was a market for them testified to the diffusion of ideas of spirituality.[27]

A key feature of the new spirituality was its 'epistemological individualism'.[28] The individual was the final arbiter of his or her own spiritual truth regardless of the dogmas of established authority, whether ecclesiastical or secular. There was no one path to truth, and the very variety of spiritual beliefs – each person's patched together from an eclectic mix of influences – testified to their authenticity.[29] By abandoning altogether any formal structures of religion, the spiritual truth-seekers could take further the openness and pluralism that we have already witnessed among some of MO's more liberal Christians. Mary Taylor, a cradle Catholic already disenchanted with the church at the age of sixteen, remained, in her eighties, certain that 'mankind has a need to believe we possess something that cannot die with our bodies'. This woman felt that 'the highly emotional religion of my childhood developed in me a sensitivity to spirituality which I have adapted to suit myself'.[30] A spirituality 'adapted to suit oneself' was the essence of what is often described as 'New Age' belief, whether professed by people who had broken free from dogma or those who had never been imprisoned by it. Although very few of the people considered in this chapter accepted that label, the term has been used as a shorthand for the profusion of pick-and-mix spiritual beliefs embraced by those who, while being indifferent or hostile to the authority claimed by organized religion, felt themselves to be in contact with some kind of transcendent power. 'Do-it-yourself' was their watchword. Elsie Grainger, who had grown up in the Congregational Church, left school at fourteen and now, aged forty-two, working as a care assistant for the elderly, was characteristically New Age in her very refusal of the term: 'I certainly don't belong to the so-called new agers or any group whatsoever … I'm not a religious person (in the sense that I don't follow any organised religion) but I admire parts of many religions. I have my own beliefs and I am sticking with them.'[31] In refusing the term New Age this working-class woman may well have had in mind the kind of social milieu described by Emma Fielding, artist, vegetarian and, briefly in 1990, secretary of her local Green Party: 'I know that our group of vaguely lefty-greenies-peace and love-man friends feel very much in a minority ... but we have the great advantage of knowing we are RIGHT!!'[32] The exclamation marks belie any spirit of dogmatism. 'Every week', she wrote in 1996, 'new concepts are being formulated and old certainties are overturned.' Some people, confronted by 'such an uncertain, chaotic world, ... desperately look for laws and rules to give some sort of structure to their lives', but for herself the postmodern crumbling of old certainties was exciting and liberating: 'the more I read and the more different people I meet, I realise that there are no absolute certainties, and that "reality" is only as the individual perceives it ... we have only our own experiences and judgement to go on.' What held things together for her was the hope that the values of her milieu would spread eventually to the majority: 'They say that the millennium is going to be the start of the new age of Aquarius, and we're all going to become much more spiritual, so let's hope they're right.' Unlike some others we will meet, Emma wore her new ageism lightly: 'My children think I'm totally barmy, and wait with bated breath for me to come up with this week's latest theory, so they can have a good old sulk. I don't think mummies are meant to have new ideas!' Writing on holiday in Marbella she added, self-mockingly, 'Cor this Spanish beer does induce rambling!'[33]

At its most individualistic this non-religious spirituality was well adapted to the ethos of neoliberal times, providing 'a fully sacralised version of widely held individualistic values'.[34] Individualism, however, was countered by a sense of connectedness, a holistic imagination in which each individual's discovery of their own wholeness served to embed them in a cosmic order. The very diversity of spiritual journeys bore testimony to their authenticity, and respect for other people's paths to the spiritual was founded in the optimistic belief that all were *en route* to the same destination. To be in touch with one's authentic nature was to be in touch with a spirituality diffused through the cosmos; the goal of transcendence was reached through the exploration of immanence. God, the life force, goodness – whatever the label – was to be found within each person, and it was through the cultivation of an imminent spirituality, rather than by submission to any God without, that the individual could transcend the limitations of material existence.[35] For those who could not bring themselves to believe in a personal God, the notion of a life force provided an alternative way of registering their sense of mysteries beyond the reach of a materialist understanding of the world.

Cheryl Walker, a sales assistant who described her beliefs as 'partly religious and partly spiritual', had rejected her childhood 'idea of God as a person', but thought there must be 'a Force which controls the universe … the more you think about it and try to reason it all out, the more you become convinced it is ruled by something'. But the idea left her puzzled: 'I'd love to have the time and opportunity to study this in depth as the more I've pondered over it the more mysterious it seems.'[36] Bridie Robinson, a forty-year-old arts graduate, was equally puzzled: 'My notion of the supernatural is one that is quite apart from religion. I do feel that there is a power out there but I do not know what it is nor can I harness it … If I believe in anything I believe that there are things that no human can comprehend or articulate.'[37] Alison Proctor, working as a radio monitor, aged sixty-two, had abandoned her childhood belief in God as 'someone up there' when, during a crisis in her early twenties, a friend gave her a book by Ralph Waldo Trine, a leading advocate of the American 'mind-cure movement' which so worried William James. The book, she wrote forty years later, 'changed my whole outlook on life completely'. Trine left her confident that 'we all have our place in the Universe … in tune with the Infinite'. Although God was a force 'far beyond our understanding', she felt herself to be part of this infinite, mysterious force.[38] Howard Terry, a spiritualist post office executive, was clear that 'God is another term for the life force. The life force has no personality, is androgynous, impersonal, [and] is in/within all things animate or unanimate [sic]'.[39] Felicity Davidson, a woman in her early sixties who had worked as library assistant, was still 'well known at the library for reserving books on "peculiar" subjects … because of my deep desire to learn and understand everything that happens naturally and supernaturally in the world'. She could not believe that 'the world evolved accidentally', and it seemed clear to her that the very existence of 'a natural world' implied 'that there is a supernatural one'. Nature, she thought, must 'have been created originally by some power or force, though not necessarily a God'. She was uncertain whether the individual spirit survived death, although 'there is such a strong "life force" that it would seem illogical if it totally disappeared with the ending of physical life'.[40]

III

For many people, loss of faith was a normal part of growing up. In 1991, among people in their early twenties 59 per cent said they had no religion – compared with only 20 per cent among sixteen to nineteen-year-olds.[41] Similarly, among the 30 per cent of sixteen-year-olds who had told the British Household Survey in 1970 that religion was important in their lives, barely more than a third described themselves as practising a religion eighteen years later.[42] I do not know what proportion of the ninety-seven mass observers who describe themselves in later life as atheist or agnostic had ever held any religious belief, but most of those who discussed their childhood attitudes had at one time accepted Christian beliefs, some with little conviction, others engaging passionately with the rituals of the church.

Geraldine Reynolds, brought up by conventionally believing but not practising parents, had been inspired, aged thirteen, by a charismatic parson. Her mother was taken aback when she started kneeling at her bedside in prayer, but the habit stuck and she continued to pray every evening for more than ten years after leaving school, until one day in 1954, during a class on religious education at teacher training college, she suddenly realized that 'it was all just a game of doctrine'.[43] Disbelief also came suddenly, but a good deal earlier in life, to Kathleen Sullivan. As a child she had horrified her conventionally Anglican parents by festooning her bedroom with suspiciously Popish holy pictures. It was when, around 1960, she left school and started work that the world opened up. 'Suddenly', she wrote, 'I became so much more aware of everything … I started thinking about the words of the Common Service [and] … realised that an awful lot of the things I was saying were absolutely untrue.'[44]

Dorothy Palmer had also embraced a religiosity beyond that of her parents as a child, but her route out of faith was more complex. She grew up as an only child of elderly parents in an impoverished branch of an Anglican upper-middle-class family. Money was scarce, but there were servants and a governess for her until in 1938, aged eleven, she was finally sent to boarding school, an Anglo-Catholic convent. Looking back on her early childhood she described herself as 'emotionally deprived' – bored, without friends and with a distant mother who showed her little affection. 'I had a warm and loving nature, but no idea what to do with it.'[45] The nuns provided an answer, and she responded passionately to the religious atmosphere of the school. 'I had a great deal of love to give and not enough to lavish it on – so the function of religion in my life … was I think to provide a focus for that love.'[46] But not for long. Dorothy's feelings about the approaching ceremony of confirmation probably mirrored those evoked by the shopkeeper Sally Thompson: 'the fuss, the prettiness, the once-in-a-lifetime ceremony … As a young romantic girl, the thought of being "married" in a white dress and veil was marvellous.'[47] When the laying on of hands failed to deliver the 'marvellous mystical experience' that Dorothy had been expecting, her religious passions cooled, although she continued, after leaving school at sixteen, to go to church.[48] It was only after her marriage to a man eleven years her senior, a 'wonderful lover' and a convinced atheist, that she finally abandoned religion, having found in their sex life a secular substitute for the transcendent experience she had sought as a teenager in Christianity.[49]

Several other atheists looked back on their earlier religious belief with affection. Janet Wharman, grateful to the Plymouth Brethren couple who had taken her in as a child, felt that 'religion can comfort a child and lay down a foundation of emotion security'.[50] Acting on this, she decided to send her own daughter to Sunday school, much to the horror of her colleagues in the Humanist Teachers Association. Laura Jefferies came to understand her own engagement with religion as 'a prop' she had needed at a difficult stage in her life, with which she could dispense now that she was 'happy, confident and in charge of my life'.[51] It was a thought echoed by Sam Gatley, a city banker, when, in his early fifties, he finally 'rejected all religion and became a born again atheist'. Brought up by Christian Scientist parents, he had returned to the writings of a dissident member of the sect for spiritual comfort at various points during the 'years of struggle and stress' as he clawed his way up the hierarchy of the bank. Looking back, he came to understand his engagement with Christian Science as a therapeutic practice for which he 'had no further need [now that] I felt that my life was comfortably under my own control'.[52]

Bereavement was frequently cited as a trigger for loss of faith. The six-year-old Phillip Buxton had first noticed that 'God wasn't very helpful' when he 'let my grandmother, my great-uncle and my cat all die within a short space of time', despite his nightly prayers asking God to cure their illnesses.[53] Two other mass observers said that they had stopped believing in God in childhood when their prayers for their dying fathers went unanswered.[54] For some adult believers the death of loved ones led them to question what they came to see as the false promise of religion, the expectation of eventual reunion in the afterlife. 'When my husband died', wrote a woman in the sixties, 'I could not believe that it would be the end – I felt we would be reunited in death. But my somewhat frail "faith" was totally lost. I do not believe in God anymore. I do not think there is a life hereafter.'[55] Liz Hilton, a middle-aged shop assistant, began to have doubts about the Anglican faith of her childhood during her twenties, but it was the death of her father when she was thirty-four that clinched her disbelief. Bedridden following a stroke, his mind deteriorated, and 'it struck me then that it was his physical being that made the man, not some unchangeable soul made by God … If small changes in the brain can alter personality, there can be really no soul,

[no] fixed personality to live on after death'.⁵⁶ Sleeping in the same room with him overnight to give her mother a break, and terrified that she might wake to find him dead, she 'prayed and prayed for strength, for courage, to endure whatever might transpire … and what did I feel? Nothing. No spiritual strength, no guiding hand, just pure funk. So I cursed. Silently and fiercely I cursed, and that gave me courage to stay there beside him'. After that, her religious beliefs 'withered away completely'.⁵⁷ Rebecca Hurley, born in a non-religious Jewish family, had become a Christian at school. What she retained of her faith in face of the Holocaust was struck down by the incurable mental illness of her sister and, finally, the accidental death of her own son, who drowned, aged thirty-two, in 1991: 'If there was a God', she wrote five years later, 'he knocked us down as a mugger would.'⁵⁸

Among the older mass observers, the Second World War is often cited as a reason for unbelief. Phillip Buxton was already sceptical about religion at the age of fourteen, but he loved singing in the Cathedral choir, kept his doubts to himself and accepted confirmation because 'to maintain a peaceful existence within the family I reckoned that the old Bishop laying his hands on my head wouldn't do me much harm'. Aged twenty when the war broke out, he met up with other 'soldiers who, like me, were gradually shedding their religious beliefs … Killing or maiming with weapons of war was bad enough', he wrote, but it was his participation in the relief of the Bergen-Belsen concentration camp, witnessing 'what had been done to people by others, over long periods, with intentional cruelty and barbarity', that 'made me question any kind of belief'.⁵⁹ Amanda Sorely, still at school during the war, could not accept a religion in which 'thou shalt not kill' did not apply to Germans, although she was briefly attracted by the Quakerism of her headmistress.⁶⁰ Bob Rust, a schoolboy during the war, gave up on God when he learned that the aircrew trying to kill him had 'Gott mit uns' (God with us) inscribed on their belt buckles. The liberation of the concentration camps hardened his atheism, especially when he discovered that there had been practising Catholics among the SS guards. Subsequently, serving in the regular army in the 1950s, he became known as 'Rust the Unbeliever' and was thrown out of Padre Hour for asking awkward questions.⁶¹ Jenny Baker, a young woman working in an engineering factory during the war, found it impossible to sustain the beliefs instilled by her churchgoing upbringing. The spectacle of men, supposedly protected by the same God, systematically killing one another 'finished any ideas of a goodly God taking care of people'.⁶² Her belief in 'the caring presence of God' had already been weakened by 'the terrible agony' suffered by her grandmother, a fervent Christian, who she witnessed dying of cancer. In the face of such horrors, public and private, she 'began to look at the priests in their regalia as play acting, I stopped going to Church because what they were preaching didn't fit in with real life at all'.[63]

As a young man Eric Gurney, a poet and minor civil servant, had 'sought Christ diligently', but he found himself incapable of the necessary leap of faith: 'You must abandon reasoning and blindly embrace faith. Blessed are they that can, perhaps. But I cannot ... So I am outside the kingdom ... I am not proud or at all happy about my disbelief ... But God or Evolution gave me the power of reason, and like good old Doubting Thomas, having got it I'm going to damn well use it.'[64] 'Damn well using it' was central to the identity of many unbelievers for whom 'the power of reason' was what marked them out from the common herd. Rose Evans was thankful not to believe in the afterlife because she could not abide 'the thought of spending eternity in the company of ... my unkind mother'.[65] Born in 1930 to a single mother, who, she felt, lost interest in her when she remarried and had other children, she grew up poor and Anglican in working-class Liverpool. Her mother's main sin, never forgiven, had been to prevent her from taking scholarship exams, despite abilities obvious to her teachers, and to force her to go out to work before her fourteenth birthday while her less-promising half-brother went to grammar school. Later, still in Liverpool, she came to hate the bigotry of her husband's relatives, Orangemen who marched through the streets on July 12, no less than the intolerance of Catholic work colleagues who assured her that, as a Protestant, she was doomed to burn in hell. But it was not until she returned to education in middle age, after her husband's death from cancer, that she finally abandoned religious belief. By the time she was writing for MO in the 1990s, she was an Open University graduate and an executive-grade civil servant in control of a £25 million budget. For this woman disbelief was a function of education, and belief a product of ignorance. She responded scornfully to a radio programme featuring testimony from born-again Christians, marvelling that God 'picks such social inadequates to converse with', rather than addressing himself to educated people. Working in the offices of the local council after she retired from her civil service job she 'found that the women there spent a great deal of money visiting Tarot readers, palmists, fortune tellers, spiritualists and the like. It seemed a great waste of hard earned money to pay it to charlatans, but it made them feel better'.[66] Another successful professional, director of a charity, who feared that the human condition being what it was people 'will probably always invent fairies at the bottom of the garden', explained the persistence of supernatural and religious beliefs as a product of 'a lack of self-awareness and assurance', an inability to cope 'with the fact that we are it, and there is nothing else'.[67]

For others too the credulousness of religious believers – 'beguiled into accepting nonsense if it offers them some kind of salvation, or life after death' – served to bolster their own superior grasp and maturity.[68] Harry Lewis, a self-declared left-wing 'old hippy', who, by the 1990s, held an executive post in a major charity, had 'no patience with the language of mysticism' and was 'very intolerant of those I consider stupid and gullible'. Having himself shaken off a religious upbringing, he felt that believers lacked 'the courage to face up to a definition of reality that implies taking responsibility for most things oneself'.[69] Peter Lowman, 'jobless and single and likely to be both for ever', helped out three days a week at the head office of the Campaign for Nuclear Disarmament (CND) where he was often accused of 'rationalising everything'. 'Criticised', he complained, '(never praised, note) for being rational', he dismissed belief in the supernatural as 'irrational and … merely entertainment for those who can't face reality'.[70] 'I know that I am responsible for my actions,' wrote another 'rational humanist', dismissing the notion that 'help or guidance' might be available from 'supernatural forces, whether they are the accepted face of religious teaching or the imaginary outpourings of the latest purveyor of divine revelations'.[71] A retired head teacher saw herself as part of 'a tiny minority … since I indulge in Education Permanente'. Born to a Catholic family in Nazi Germany she became British as the bride of an occupying solider after the war. Going one step beyond Kant, she had worked out 'my own critique of PURE REASON … there is no god bar the good within me (and others)'. 'Life has taught me', she wrote, 'that I am living my life REALISTICALLY and need no invented spookies … no god/gods/priests'.[72]

Not all the atheists were so self-assured. However determined they might be to live by the light of reason, many of MO's disbelievers confessed to wavering in their disbelief. As we will see throughout this study, thoughts and feelings akin to those fostered by religion frequently flourished beneath the carapace of atheistic reason, and many disbelievers expressed opinions and reported experiences which others would describe as pertaining to religion or the supernatural. There were 'naive believers' among the mass observers, and naïve disbelievers as well. Most, however, confessed to doubts and uncertainty. When it came to questions about the meaning of life most people were puzzled. 'The modern individual', writes Peter Berger, 'exists in a plurality of worlds, migrating back and forth between competing and often contradictory plausibility structures, each of which is weakened by the simple fact of its involuntary coexistence with other plausibility structures.'[73] Christians lived with atheists, and some of them recognized the mythical nature of the foundational Bible stories, and were open to influences from other religious traditions. Those searching for spiritual truths outside the framework of any religion nevertheless borrowed freely from established religions. And some atheists and agnostics, as we will see, laid claim to the word 'spirituality' itself, reluctant to concede to the believers exclusive possession of areas of human experience for which they could find no language that did not carry unwelcome overtones of the supernatural.[74]

3

Death and afterwards

To understand life we need to understand death. And vice versa. The meanings that people attribute to their lives are closely connected to the meanings they attribute to death. The difficulty of contemplating our own mortality and that of our loved ones is, of course, a major source of beliefs about the supernatural. But what is striking about the evidence supplied by the mass observers is the degree to which attitudes to death overlap between the Christians, the non-religiously spiritual and those with no belief in the supernatural. The main differences in attitudes to death have less to do with belief or non-belief in the afterlife than with the ways in which people, irrespective of their attitude to the supernatural, orient themselves to life itself. Three distinct approaches are apparent in the mass observers' discourse of death, each one expressing a different orientation to where meaning was to be found in life. For most people the bonds of family were central; others, more self-centred, invested meaning above all in their individual journeys; and a third group are distinguished, for want of a better term, by a more philosophical outlook on life. All three orientations – familial, individual and philosophical – are apparent among Christians, among the spiritually minded and among the disbelievers. When it came to the question of death, attitudes to life were more important than attitudes to the supernatural.

I

As we have seen the death of a loved one persuaded many believers to abandon faith in God. But for many others the Christian promise of life after death served to assuage their grief. It was difficult to imagine the afterlife. Received images of 'sitting on clouds, playing harps' held little appeal.[1] 'Whatever lies ahead I have no intention of playing a harp', wrote a churchgoing science teacher, adding indignantly, 'and if there's no library I'm heading straight back here!'[2] The most concrete image offered by the mass observers was of a place where one would be reunited with the deceased. 'Heaven to me means clouds and meeting people who have gone before you … I have thought about an afterlife and I wonder if I will meet my little brother again or my Dad or even my two little dogs (The tears are running down my face as I write this.).' Gwen Halliday, who wrote this, was married with six children and working as a cleaner. She no longer went to church. Brought up 'in the fear of the Lord' amongst a close-knit community of Wesleyan Methodists in a Welsh village, the family had moved, following the death of her brother when she was ten, to Devon where they found the middle-class ethos of the parish church cold and unwelcoming. Religion, for Gwen, was closer to home: 'I would call our family a Christian family … We are a very kind family and we all willingly help each other, we do not put on each other and all feel secure within our family.'[3] But while you could be a good Christian without going to church on Sundays, baptism remained an essential condition of eventual salvation.[4] Gwen looked to the church to legitimize rites of passage, and she was indignant when it refused to do so. She took pains to have all her children christened (despite a local vicar who refused to christen babies whose parents did not go to church) on the grounds that 'if there is a life after this one I would not like to get there and find my children could not be reunited with me because they were not christened'.[5] A Catholic woman, whose life had been devoted to making her 'little patch as loving, caring and happy' as possible, expected to meet 'in Heaven … all those who were dear to me on earth'.[6] Like Gwen, this included her pets, and the church did not demur 'My late priest said he believed animals you loved went to heaven and I have no reason to question this belief.'[7]

These stories echo the findings of Gillian Bennett's ethnographic study of a group of elderly Christian women in Lancashire in the 1980s, for whom traditions of belief in the afterlife gave permanence to loving family relationships, providing a reassuring sense of continuity. Investing life's deepest meanings in their familial roles, they were 'reluctant to give them up even when death intervenes'.[8] David Lloyd, an Anglican vicar, agreed: 'To the extent that people have any idea of an afterlife it is … simply in terms of seeing "loved ones" again … God not really coming into it!'[9] Among his flock, he suggested, family reconstitution displaced spiritual union with God as the ultimate purpose of existence. As Sarah Williams found in her study of popular religion in working-class London, 'the afterlife was seen as an attribute or an extension of the present life, rather than the present being seen as a preliminary to the future state'.[10]

An afterlife peopled by family members served many of the mass observers as a myth appropriate to the centrality of family in the values by which they lived. It is, Durkheim insisted, from our membership of society – in its most rudimentary form, the family – that we acquire a 'sensation of the divine'.[11] In her study of 'belief in belonging', Abby Day argues that the stories people tell of encounters with deceased loved ones express an essentially anthropocentric view of the supernatural: it is dead human beings, rather than God, who provide access to the transcendent.[12]

A sensation of contact with the spirits of loved ones often occurred at the moment of death itself. Gwen Halliday, growing up Wesleyan in South Wales, remembered childish talk about death with her siblings: 'We all wanted to die first so that we would not have to be here when any of the family died.' One brother, aged twelve, a year older than her, 'got his wish':

> I was sitting up in bed … My dead brother came into the bedroom. He was dressed in white but he was in like a blue haze. He smiled at me, I was not frightened and when I went to speak to him he just disappeared. My brother died in my grandmother's house which was about half a mile away from our home.

'It was the worst thing that happened to me in all my life', she wrote. Nevertheless his 'lovely smile' remained a treasured and a reassuring memory.[13] Like Gwen, a factory worker felt that a similar apparition – his one and only paranormal experience – had profoundly affected his life:

> As I went into a twilight sleep my father's face appeared looking down on me – I awoke with a start looking round the dark quiet bedroom. Soon I was dozing off, when his face appeared again I cannot recall how many times this occurred – but when daylight arrived I was sound asleep.

Woken by telephone, he 'rushed downstairs shouting to the wife [up and about long since] "That's about Dad"'. He had had a heart attack and died a few hours later:

> I know in my heart he came to me that previous night … He was a man's man – quiet – but I think he loved us, more than he showed. As a result I make sure my children and grandchildren know how much they mean to me. I wear my heart on my shoulder. We kiss 'hello' and kiss 'goodbye'. So I think it takes this sort of experience to make one appreciate living.[14]

Several other mass observers report similar apparitions occurring at the death of a loved one, but some presentiments of death were weirder. Paula Harrison, a religious education teacher, felt she had shared something of her paternal grandmother's death agony. As a student, away at university, she was woken up one night with 'a horrible feeling … the atmosphere in the room had changed. It was … very oppressive, an almost malevolent air'.

> I had the definite feeling that there was a presence and I didn't like it. I pulled the bedclothes over my head and lay there wishing whatever it was would go away. And suddenly it did, just like that, as if someone had switched off a light. The luminous hands on my bedside clock said ten past two. My uncle arrived next morning to tell me that my grandmother had died in her sleep at ten past two.

'If it was my grandmother paying a last visit', she wrote, 'you'd think she'd want to leave me with a pleasant memory.' But the old lady had been terrified of death, and it was that terror, Paula suspected, that she had somehow communicated to her granddaughter. Paula's great-aunt, on the other hand, departed with better grace:

> My parents, brother and sister and myself were travelling somewhere when suddenly the whole car was filled with perfume. We all immediately recognised it as the very distinctive scent my great-aunt used and I remember my mother saying, 'She must be dead', though there'd been no reason to suppose that she was likely to die in the near future. But sure enough when we got home we had a phone call to say she had died suddenly. It was a strange thing to happen, but we took it that this was my aunt's way of saying goodbye.[15]

Whatever happened at the moment of death, however, Paula Harrison was convinced that 'all those I've lost over the years continue in another form and that they still do care about and watch over me and the people I love'.[16] Among the elderly Lancashire women interviewed by Gillian Bennett,

> it is the common opinion that the spiritual world permeates the mundane one. The dead are thus witnesses of the lives of those they have left behind, and may perpetuate their role of parent or spouse as mediators between two worlds, continuing to interest themselves in the small concerns of daily life and if necessary coming to the rescue, armed not only with their former love but also with their present superior knowledge.[17]

For these women the presence of dead loved ones was the single most important aspect of their supernatural beliefs:

> They embody all the qualities that figure most prominently in their moral and philosophical value scale. They are intensely intuitive experiences; they

graphically symbolize the power of love and its triumph over death; they are based on interpersonal communication, often of an internal telepathic kind; and they render the world a safe and protected environment.[18]

Many mass observers felt the continuing presence of dead relatives – 'only in the next room', wrote one, imagining her demented mother and disabled father suitably restored to the prime of life.[19] Very occasionally this continuing presence was experienced more as a haunting to be exorcised than a comfort to be cherished. Julia Kirby, a cradle Catholic, was pestered by her mother's spirit for ten years after her death until one day when she was counselling a distressed sibling on the phone, she thought, 'I am the mother now, it's my problem. With that I felt a rush of air pass me and exit through the window.'[20] But for the great majority the experience was positive. Marion Phillips, a Quaker, sometimes felt that her dead father 'was somehow near enough to share things with' and she 'talked to him in my mind. This is not the same "feel"', she explained, 'as remembering him'.[21] Jenny Baker, who had given up religion during the war, nevertheless believed 'that the mind lives on after death'. She had never seen a ghost, but she met her relatives in her dreams, and talked with them 'even though I know at the time they are dead. This doesn't happen frequently but when it does, I know that there has been a happening, and I can describe it in every detail, and remember the conversations for years after'.[22] An elderly farmer's widow who, after rejecting her churchgoing upbringing had taken an interest in psychical research, regularly saw her husband 'sitting at his desk as I passed by the window … raising his hand as he would have done in real life'.[23] A middle-aged woman working as a carer, and desperately lonely after the deaths of both her parents and of her fiancé, was never afraid when visited by their ghosts: 'I feel it's a special meaning in my life and that it's nice and special that the ghost shows itself to me.'[24]

The notion of the 'guardian angel', which had a theological rationale in Catholic doctrine,[25] was almost invariably linked to the continuing presence of dead relatives, although one spiritual explorer's guardian angel was a Red Indian. And guardian angels gave not just comfort but also practical help at moments of need.[26] Several respondents invoked the spirits of dead parents or grandparents intervening to save them from car accidents or other misfortunes.[27] William Reilly wrote of an experience he had when his son was diagnosed with an incurable disorder of the central nervous system:

> I suddenly became aware of a warm sensation in my outstretched palms and I felt, although I saw nothing, the presence of my late Mother. I was overcome

with an extraordinary sense of well-being and a sudden conviction that my son would respond to treatment and lead a normal life once more. And that is what happened.[28]

Cyril Kennedy's mother had been bedridden throughout his childhood and she died when he was nineteen. Many years later, in a moment of extreme anxiety over a promotion at work which he had not sought and did not want, she appeared to him:

> I was driving to the office and was caught in a traffic hold-up in Vauxhall. I noticed masses of flowers being put into a laden hearse outside an undertaker's – one tribute spelt out the word MOTHER in flowers and I thought it was more likely that they had called her Mum or perhaps Ma, so why go to the expense of spelling out a longer and more formal word. Suddenly as the traffic began to inch slowly forward I saw my mother's face quite clearly looking down at me from just above the windscreen and I half said, half cried, 'Oh Mum, tell me what to do.' The tears were streaming down my face and I am not one who sheds tears easily. By the time I reached the office about 20 minutes later I had resolved to hand back the promotion … I thought I might get the sack but the chairman was so impressed with what he called my bravery that he congratulated me and I was looked after in a way from then on.[29]

Elsie Farrow, still working as a civil servant at the age of seventy, felt that it was her grandmother who looked after her rather than her husband, who had died in middle age. A Christian, but also a spiritualist, she explained this anomaly on the grounds that 'there is work to do' in the spirit world, and 'I am sure he is toiling and has given her the job'.[30] Paula Harrison gave detailed descriptions of what she and her sister described as periodic 'tours of inspection' by their grandmother 'to check how we're getting on'.[31] Mark Charlton, a young store manager, also thought he was looked after by his grandmother. For many years before her death he had visited her weekly confiding 'my ever increasing anxieties as adulthood approached' and especially his 'frustration and depression at not having a place of my own and the agonies of having to live with my parents and brothers'. Desperate though he was for a 'space to call my own home to start to discover who I really was', his attempts to escape the family home came to nothing because his income was too small to rent 'anything larger than a postage stamp size room in a grotty area'.

> A while after my grandmother's death a strange thing happened. Out of the blue I received a telephone call from a friend whose mother's next door flat had become vacant. It was above a shop in the area I was brought up in, was

spacious, two bedroomed, the rent was ridiculously cheap and the landlord was very particular to whom he rented the property but was prepared to consider me as he remembered me from my childhood when I had visited his shop regularly with my grandmother ... The moment I entered the flat ... I knew that it was all more than a coincidence and that my grandmother had had some influence from where ever she was. I felt her reassuring presence so strongly in the flat where I continue to live and no matter what happens in my life I always feel her spirit or energy here. Things sometimes disappear, or seem to move place, occasionally doors open and close with an eerie will of their own. I don't feel spooked. I just think she's reminding me that she's still around, which even now I'm in my mid thirties is a great comfort.[32]

In all these cases the presence of a dead relative was understood as a manifestation of the supernatural. But similar sensations were also experienced by people with no belief in life after death. Margaret Thompson, a biologist with a 'fervent disbelief' in the supernatural, explained her own experience in materialist terms: the sense of presence was caused by 'a continuing response of the ... nervous system to triggers, like familiar sounds and smells', which fades with time.[33] Bob Rust, an atheist lorry driver who had inherited his trade from his equally atheist father, felt for many years after his father's death that 'he was keeping an eye on me; in the fog: in the winter when the roads were bad. Even when something was starting to go wrong with a vehicle or a load, although there was no physical indication, I got and still get a strong feeling that I must stop and look round the vehicle'. Unlike those whose experiences are described above, however, Bob did not assume that his father's help necessarily had a supernatural origin. 'It could be', he wrote, 'that I unconsciously absorbed so much of his knowledge that I sense tiny changes subconsciously.'[34]

Confronted with the loss of loved ones some disbelievers felt nostalgia or envy for the comforts offered by the religious faith they had rejected, or never entertained. Clara Davies, a middle aged typist, longed for the kind of religious faith 'where everything is cut and dried there is a suitable answer for every mortal occurrence – this leaves no room to doubt life's grand pattern for us all with a wonderfully satisfactory outcome in eternal life if we are good here on Earth'.[35] The 'mortal occurrence' for which she sought solace was the death of her ten-year-old son, who had run out of the house after she forgot to bolt the door and been killed by a passing lorry. By the time this occurred, the strict Christian faith in which she had been brought up had faded away, but in later years she found herself wondering whether premonitions she remembered having had about the disaster had been sent by a guardian angel whom she had failed to heed. Rebecca

Hurley, who had also lost a son, envied those whose faith gave them comfort in bereavement.[36] Rebecca's anger – she felt she had been mugged by God – was echoed by Jane Fox, a 66-year-old social worker whose loss of her childhood Methodist faith left her dismayed at the thought 'of leaving everyone, of their lives going on without me. ... I would much prefer to be hovering somewhere watching my family, seeing still what they are doing and maybe being able to influence them ... I am angry that my life has to come to an end, that I can't always be here.'[37]

Coping with the pain of bereavement, a few of the atheists were tempted to hope that they might be wrong. Eric Gurney, a poet and minor civil servant, refused to 'abandon reasoning and blindly embrace faith', but he confessed that for many years after the death of his wife he 'used to go into the room [where she died] and tell her the news and wait for any – any – sign. Nothing.'[38] Harry Bolton, a retired decorator and aspiring writer, had long since rejected religion when in his early fifties he renewed contact with his first girlfriend, lost through the disruptions of war, only for her to fall ill and die within six months of their mutual rediscovery. It was a story he told several times to Mass Observation (MO), working it up into a tale of almost mythic significance. The war was responsible for many lost loves, the remembrance of which provided for people of Harry's generation a delicious, sad and secret pleasure.[39] In Harry's case the secrecy was necessary because he was married and had to hide from his wife the devastation he felt when his first – and still unconsummated – love was cruelly ended so soon after it had been rekindled. It was with this in mind that he wrote: 'If such a reunion with a loved one [could] happen on this earth, in whatever spiritual form, then it would convert me to a belief in religion and its promise of an afterlife more surely than a thousand years of a parson's preaching.' But the fact that he was contacted neither by the girlfriend's spirit, nor, much later, by that of his wife to whom he remained happily married for more than fifty years, seemed to him irrefutable proof that life after death was a delusion.[40]

In making his disbelief hostage to his passions, Harry would have met the disapproval of Sally Noonan – another septuagenarian atheist – who sternly insisted that any thought of contact with the dead was 'as unhealthy as it is irrational'. The bereaved, she recommended, should abjure imaginary conversations with lost partners, sustain 'normal' sociability and rely on time to sooth their grief.[41] But Sally was still happily un-widowed, and her all-too-rational advice would have cut no ice with Hugh Fairbrother, an agnostic typesetter. As a child he had questioned the hellfire religion preached at Sunday school – 'I could not see the logic ... how could a body burn for ever without turning into insensible ashes?' – and rejected it altogether by the time he was serving as a young naval rating during the war. Painfully aware of his own educational disadvantage – he left school at fourteen – he worried that others much better educated than himself seemed to have no difficulty in accepting religious ideas. Although he often found himself 'wondering why I cannot come to the same conclusions as everyone else' – including his own wife who was a churchgoing Christian – and felt 'uneasy living with my beliefs', he nevertheless concluded (aged eighty-nine) that he 'would be even more uncomfortable with any of the ... religions known to me'. Twenty years before he wrote this, his disbelief had been put to the test when, following the death of his wife, he had for some years felt a powerful sense of her continuing presence in the house:

> Being a dreamer I often sit in my living room contemplating or organising something in my mind and I often feel her presence on the settee ... I have experienced the same sensation in bed and felt the bed sagging with her weight often turning over to say something, I have even spoke [sic] before realising I was on my own. For some reason it does not upset me, on the contrary it leaves me with a nice warm feeling inside.[42]

He knew it was ridiculous to believe that it was possible to communicate with the dead, and would have agreed with the Catholic sceptic who, seeing her son in his room soon after he had left for university, concluded that 'ghosts are in the grieving eye'.[43] Nevertheless he confessed to MO (but to no one else) that he had been prepared to 'waive [his] scepticism just in case my only love is trying to contact me. This will be the main reason for living in my house for as long as I am able'.[44]

> I felt I owed it to her to at least try praying in case she was trying to contact me and I tried it many times without any success. It has not altered my beliefs only made me a little sadder that she left this world convinced we would meet again.[45]

If bereavement could persuade a disbeliever like Hugh Fairbrother that it might be possible to receive messages from the dead, it should be no surprise that spiritualist ideas appealed to many who were more attuned to the supernatural. Among the 40 per cent of mass observers who discussed their attitudes towards spiritualism, more than half were inclined to dismiss it as nonsense, 30 per cent believed in it and the remainder were unsure.[46] Most of the believers were Christians, almost half of whom accepted the reality of spiritualism, compared with a third of those embracing a non-religious spirituality. There were also five atheists or agnostics who believed that it was possible to receive messages from the dead.

It was of course easy to dismiss spiritualism as 'a cruel deceit', so much 'hogwash' purveyed by 'charlatans preying on grief'.[47] Some of the best-known mediums had been exposed as frauds, and disbelievers marvelled at the 'stupefying banality' of the messages purportedly conveyed by the deceased.[48] 'Why don't the dead ever say anything of interest?', demanded Paula Harrison, the religious education teacher: 'Why do they all seem to make bland statements about being well and happy, but give no hint of what the afterlife is like? Perhaps', she added mockingly, 'they have to sign gagging clauses.'[49] Christians, like Paula, had an additional reason to steer clear of spiritualism, since dabbling with the psychic was a dangerous pastime, liable to stir up evil forces. While most mediums might be well meaning, explained Elsie Grainger, a spiritually minded care assistant, they were 'often the victims of pranks played by mischievous spirits'.[50] Even when mediums appeared able to channel knowledge that could only have come from the deceased, their real sources might well be not 'our dead friends but … evil spirits who are pretending to be these people'.[51]

Other Christians disagreed. In 1995 there were more than five hundred spiritualist churches in Britain, with a combined congregation of around forty thousand attending services much like those of regular churches – hymns, prayers, Bible readings, a sermon – but with the addition of 'a short time when the speaker/medium … gives what are known as "message"… describ[ing] someone they "see" – you may immediately recognise the description as a relative/friend you have known, or you may not'.[52] Doris Spalding, who wrote this, had been an occasional attender at spiritualist churches since her 1950s childhood: her parents were 'of the Spiritualist Faith'. She was also a member of her local parish church, and she saw no contradiction between the two. In both kinds of church 'the marvellous, kind, caring, people I have met … [have] enabled me to overcome many hurdles through my life and enjoy so much each day whether at home or in my work environment'. She had no time for 'fortune tellers, séances and similar' and she felt that the sensationalized way the supernatural was portrayed in the media – as 'witches or similar' – undermined popular understanding: 'Whereas if they were present at any of the lovely, enlightening services and events I have been privileged to be present at, I am sure they would come to a more happy feeling about what is called the Supernatural.'[53] It was her spiritualist faith, she wrote, that 'has sustained and "kept me going" many times in the weeks and months following a close relative's or friend's passing.'[54]

There were several other spiritualists among the mass observers. Elsie Farrow, had received messages from her father-in-law in the Spiritualist Centre, but not from her husband who, she concluded rather sadly, must have been so occupied with other work in the spirit world that he had left the job of watching over her to her grandmother.[55] Janice Ranger, who had worked on the factory floor before becoming a secretary, was brought up by Christian spiritualist parents, and her aunt was a medium. As an adult she happily combined spiritualism with membership of a Pentecostal church, much to the distress of her pastor who 'got quite hot and bothered when I said … in my opinion Jesus Christ was the first Spiritualist as he died and then reappeared to his Disciples and friends'.[56] Sally Thompson, a shopkeeper, had a more anxious relationship with spiritualism. Although by her sixties she no longer went to church regularly, she knew the vicar well and he was aghast when he learned that one of her daughters had become a medium in the local spiritualist church: they were, he said, 'playing with the devil and all things evil'.[57] Sally told him not to be so narrow-minded, but she had doubts of her own. In her teens, her mother had often taken her to a spiritualist church, and Sally's interest in spiritualism revived when, in her early forties, she went with her father to a spiritualist church where the medium told her she was 'smothered in a gold light'. Her father promised to contact her after his death, and she blamed her own lack of receptivity when, at first, nothing happened. Eventually however her persistent attendance at various spiritualist churches was rewarded with messages from both her parents. Despite this she remained sceptical: 'somewhere in my heart', she wrote in 1994, 'I liken "mediums" to fortune tellers' and in 2013, aged eighty-three, she was doubting whether the afterlife existed at all. What held her scepticism in check, more than anything else, were the messages her spiritualist daughter brought from the other side: 'I bless her cheerfulness …I do not think that my daughter would tell lies, [so] communicating with the dead must be possible.'[58] For Sally, as for the other spiritualists, spiritualism was a family affair.

Howard Terry, who spent his working life in the post office, rising from postman to executive, had been brought up Catholic by his Irish mother, but the more lasting influence was that of his paternal grandparents earnestly 'investigating spiritualism at the turn of the century'. In his forties he joined the Spiritualist Association of Great Britain (SAGB), whose mediums offered 'only the best and highest so that those on both sides of the veil can progress in a truly spiritual sense'.[59] Like Elsie Farrow, he believed that death was the gateway not to eternal rest but to an afterlife of spiritual growth fostered by joyful work in the service of others. Howard and his wife regularly visited mediums, in search not for 'maudlin' messages 'from Auntie Flo or Uncle Charlie', but for spiritual knowledge and advancement. We live, he insisted, in eternity, and our other, spiritual existence is 'as close as the skin on the back of your hand'. Heaven 'intermingles with our existence here' – which was just as well, since, writing at the end of the Thatcher years, he expressed a pattern of discontent with contemporary society common among working-class Labour voters, combining fury at Thatcher's cultivation of inequality and the rule of money with an embattled rejection of liberal tides of sexual permissiveness, feminism and multiculturalism.[60] While the Christian churches purveyed an anthropomorphic image of God, designed 'to pass the message to those less gifted people of limited intelligence', spiritualists understood that 'God is a power akin to an electrical current with the ability to manifest itself in any shape or form … It flows through everything on this planet … it is intelligence absolute'.[61] And, unlike Christians awaiting the day of judgement, spiritualists did not abandon themselves to the will of the higher power: they believed that when we die our earthly lives are judged 'not … by God but by ourselves – we see ourselves as we really are warts and all.'[62]

II

Howard Terry's spiritualism had little time for family reconstitution. Contemptuous of 'maudlin messages from Auntie Flo', he focussed instead on an individual spiritual journey. He was attracted by Buddhist ideas of reincarnation, because 'no man or woman can learn all there is to learn in these three score years and ten'. Before one could hope to become a perfect spirit at one with God, it was necessary to gain 'the complete gamut of experience' by progressing through many lives. Belief in reincarnation was common among believers in a non-religious spirituality, and it often catered to an individualistic sense of the continuity of selfhood in contrast to family-centred notions of the next life.

According to opinion polls about a quarter of the population believed in reincarnation at the end of the 20th century, a substantial increase since the 1960s.[63] Reincarnation appealed because it addressed directly the problem of perfectibility, the fact, as David Lloyd, the Anglican vicar, put it, that God's 'creativity is spoilt and limited if there is no chance for us to fulfil all we might be (which none of us get near to doing)'.[64] For Lloyd, as for most Christians, decisive progress towards perfection could only be imagined for all but saints as something which would occur after death released the soul from its material embodiment.

But reincarnation brought the process down to earth. Gillian Latimer, the heretical rector's wife, liked the idea of life as 'a training school … the soul comes back till lessons are learned'.[65] Elsie Grainger, who worked as a care assistant for the elderly, was firmly convinced that 'when we leave this body we have to account for all our actions in this life, anything we need to learn we will have to come back to learn. Until we have learned everything we as individuals need to know we cannot advance, spiritually'.[66] Fiona Evans, a middle-aged medical sociologist and enthusiastic psychical explorer, had 'a very strong sense of being in this world for a specific purpose … to learn some specific lessons'. 'Right now', she wrote in 1996, she was 'busy trying to straighten up a lot of bad karma' and 'just *hoping* that this will be my last trip.'[67] Hilary Cameron, a 62-year-old plumber's wife working as a shop assistant, believed that 'the better you conduct yourself, in the way of love, compassion, forgiveness and loving your enemy, the higher up the "spiritual ladder" you climb. Eventually you gain the right to become a "divine spirit"'. For this woman, not only was 'each life a test', it was also a test 'that we knowingly undertake': the returning spirit was free to 'pick out which life or challenge you wish to take'.[68] Howard Terry, the spiritualist post office executive, did not go quite that far but it was a staple of spiritualist belief that it was ourselves, not God, who made the judgement.[69]

For Christians, reincarnation was a difficult notion.[70] One Catholic woman toyed with it, but bowed to authority: 'It doesn't form part of my belief system.'[71] Alistair Bevan disagreed, arguing that reincarnation 'has not in fact ever been totally ruled out for Christians but is one of those matters … never gone into'.[72] Pauline Connell, an elderly but very active woman who described herself as 'a professional in the sphere of Christian ministry',[73] acknowledged that, while she was personally sympathetic to the idea, she was 'not supposed to believe in reincarnation, [and] I cannot, and do not, preach that as a fact'.[74] Gillian Latimer, straining to reconcile her imaginative explorations with her Anglican faith, suggested that, in biblical times, reincarnation had been such a commonplace belief that the authors of the Bible saw no need to mention it.[75]

Bill Woody, an active Christian, looked to reincarnation to explain the dramatic shifts in his own fortunes and outlook. As a child in the 1970s he had resented his working-class background and 'longed for wealth and importance'. He left school at sixteen in the year Thatcher won the election, worked for a time in a bank, and then, borrowing money to buy a fish-and-chip shop, set out to become a millionaire. Other shops followed, but by 1991, struck down by leukaemia and spiralling interest rates, he was bankrupt. By the time he wrote (briefly) for MO in 1996–7, describing himself, aged thirty-three, as a 'former supermarket owner', he had spent five years as a house husband bringing up two young daughters and doing an Open University degree while his wife went to university and trained as a teacher. It was an astrologer who, shortly after his illness, had provided Bill with the key to understanding these events. The reason he had felt so out of place as a working-class child was, she explained, that in his past lives he 'had held many positions of great importance and responsibility which I had often abused'. Thus punished for his previous sins, reincarnation gave him the opportunity to make amends. At first, 'hell-bent on becoming a millionaire', he had not taken it, but fate gave him a second chance 'to learn the true meaning of Altruism'. Now a member of the Labour Party, active in the local church, and known in the village as 'a bit of an advice centre' (helping people fill in the mystifyingly complex forms required to claim disability and other benefits), he had repudiated his earlier materialistic ambitions, although he remained confident that he could have achieved them if illness had not intervened.[76]

The idea of reincarnation had most appeal among those whose spiritual leanings were unrestricted by religious dogma. Stella Marshall, a retired social worker whose spiritual journey is fully told in *Seven Lives from Mass Observation*, observed in 1996 that the idea of reincarnation 'has gently seeped into our way of thinking – working forward from the Beatles and the Maharishi, no doubt', although she herself did not come across it until the early 1970s when she took a course in comparative religion.[77] At Sunday school in the 1960s, Elsie Grainger had been told not to be cheeky when she asked how God prevented heaven from becoming overcrowded with so many generations of dead people to accommodate. Reincarnation, she later concluded, provided an obvious answer.[78] 'It would seem economical for a creator to re-use souls,' remarked Pauline Connell.[79] A retired insurance agent, who felt that his dead father watched over him and guided him out of danger, was able to reconcile this with his belief in reincarnation on the grounds that 'souls are not reused automatically straight away and perhaps while they are "free" they have the power to influence events in the living world'.[80] Other spiritual quantifiers worried about a different problem: how to reconcile reincarnation with population growth. A young computer consultant wondered whether the 'life force – some sort of energy … that goes into a pool on the death of an individual and part is taken by a baby being born' – might be spread too thinly: 'perhaps the greater nastiness in the world today is accentuated because there isn't enough energy to go round and so individuals are lacking something important'.[81] To others it was clear that there must be a pool of previously unused souls (or freshly created ones): a fact which conveniently explained why only certain people had memories of their previous lives.[82]

Such 'memories' seemed to many to provide evidence of reincarnation, especially compelling when offered unprompted by children who 'have started to talk, at an early age of their "other mother" or "other father" and have described in detail a place to which they have never been in this life'.[83] Several of Stella Marshall's friends reported their children giving such accounts 'in matter of fact tones', noting that these stories were 'particularly worthy of consideration in under-fives whose ideas would be less likely to be affected by external sources'. One small boy informed his mother: 'When I was a girl I used to live in that house', pointing to a house he could never have visited.[84] Perhaps this 'memory' had more to do with the fluidity of gender identity than with reincarnation, as is also suggested in the confession offered by a gay middle-aged newspaper executive who, wondering 'in my innermost thoughts whether I've been here before', recalled his previous self as 'a girl of about 16 or 17 who had a brother a couple of years younger who was subsequently killed in WW2. ... Or perhaps I was the boy'.[85] Another function of such memories is suggested by Kirsty Parsons, a childless spiritual healer who kept a 'reincarnation notebook' noting intimations of past lives 'most particularly in ancient Egypt'. Among other things, she convinced herself that in a former life she had experienced the 'deep love and the fulfilment of motherhood, although these joys have eluded me in this life'.[86] Gloria Blake, a middle-aged woman, saw reincarnation as 'a kinder version of hell where you have a chance to repent ... we keep coming back till we've improved ourselves – if you've led a bad life then you get sent back immediately and spend your next life suffering so that you learn to do good'.[87] For Mary Jones, social worker and evangelical Christian, the ethical implications of reincarnation were more dubious. She wondered whether she had been born 'in comfortable suburban England rather than the back streets of Calcutta ... because I lived a "good" life last time' – a thought which registered simultaneously guilt about her privilege and the possibility that she deserved it.[88]

Belief in reincarnation brought perfectibility down to earth, but at the same time it powerfully asserted the primacy of the spiritual in human experience. 'We are spirits manifest in human form reincarnated so that we may work our way towards perfection', wrote Sheila Faraday, a spiritual healer.[89] Kirsty Parsons expressed a similar thought: 'The spirit returns time and again to inhabit a physical body, the purpose being to learn lessons and develop in ways that are only possible in the material world.'[90] Mark Charlton, the young department store manager who knew that his deceased grandmother was looking after him, insisted that 'that we are spirits having a human experience rather than humans occasionally having spiritual experiences'. As such, family was ultimately of less importance to him than his individual spiritual journey. His belief in reincarnation added 'a richness and comfort to my life and makes sense of much of my own personal experience'. He had thought a lot about the ramifications of the idea. While it was true that most people had no conscious memory of their previous lives, he believed 'that the "transferred" spirit does possess a deeply encoded memory, or store, of wisdom, judgement, morality etc. and possibly adverse emotions, such as anxiety or memory of particularly bad experiences in one of its previous lives. How a person uses or learns from this encoded knowledge is connected to the effort or importance any individual places on the exploration of their spiritual self'. When Eastern philosophies 'promote the concept of seeking answers from within', it is to these 'deep subconscious legacies' from former incarnations that they are urging us to pay attention. Central to his own experience was a platonic relationship with a woman he had known since childhood, 'a bond of love and trust' whose 'intensity and depth', he suspected, reflected a close relationship between their respective spirits in some previous life. Although the relationship, about which he writes movingly, was brutally disrupted by her premature death, their spiritual liaison continued:

> Naturally I miss her physical presence immensely [but] her spirit is truly always with me and I know for certain that she now fulfils the role of guardian angel to me. So much has changed in my life since her death, I've made decisions and acted with far greater confidence and courage and many of those decisions have paid off and brought me a far more successful and enriching life. I sort of tune in to her energy and let it guide me.[91]

Stella Marshall, always willing to explore, and particularly impressed by her friends' accounts of their children's remarks, attended several 'regression workshops' where people tried, under hypnosis, to get in touch with their past lives. While 'some participants reported vivid experiences, some inspirational, others violent, terrifying, distressing', Stella herself felt only 'vague dreamlike drifting sensations'. Being in 'an altered state of consciousness' had been, she wrote, 'pleasant and relaxing', but 'always I came out at the same door as in I went … Alas, uncommitted'.[92] Rose Worley, a retired professional woman, had more success:

Both my daughter and I have had such induced experiences, and my daughter 'remembered' being a boy in Holland in the 17th century, going to sea, and dying of a fever. I was with her when she was undergoing this and it all seemed very real to her and to me, at the time. It was not like a dream, because it was consistent and in sequence. I also had an experience in a group when I 'remembered' standing on the bank of a canal and knowing that my mother had been drowned there. I looked down at my feet and saw heavy black boots, I had been a farm labourer.[93]

But she too remained sceptical about the reality of these induced 'memories'.

Belief in the afterlife as an opportunity to renew bonds with deceased loved ones was characteristic of people whose sense of themselves was strongly invested in their familial roles. Some of the Christians, particularly those with less investment in family life, rejected this anthropocentric view, insisting that it was not family but one's individual, private and personal relationship with God that ultimately gave meaning to life. Mary Jones, a psychiatric social worker and an evangelical Christian, was clear that 'being with loved ones who have died seems to be irrelevant compared with being with God'.[94] Jenny Brown, an aspiring writer and a liberal-minded Catholic, imagined the afterlife as 'some mystical state of communing with other souls and God and enlightenment as to what one's earthly life meant'. It was only the prospect of an afterlife, allowing 'the realisation of a soul's full potential in a higher plane of existence', that made it possible to accept the limitations of spiritual progress during one's life on earth.[95] Sarah Hodges, who had married into the Catholic church, abandoned it after she divorced and in old age become a practising Anglican, had a similar view, looking forward to entering 'a spirit world with many levels where with God's help we will continue to learn and grow in faith until we are fit to enter heaven'.[96] She would no doubt have shared Jenny Brown's refusal to contemplate the possibility that she might simply cease to exist, a prospect which 'fills me with horror ... every instinct in me revolts at the idea'.[97]

III

Belief in life after death could serve either a family-centred view of life or one more focussed on the journey of the individual soul towards perfection, perhaps through a series of reincarnations. Faced with bereavement, even some who saw themselves as atheists or agnostics were tempted to revise their views or, at least, to wish that they could do so. But for many others neither a family-centred nor a more individualistic notion of the afterlife held any appeal. Doubting the reality of any kind of life after death they sought philosophical reconciliation with the fact of human mortality.

The third, philosophical, group among the mass observers did not consist solely of people who rejected belief in the supernatural. Despite the centrality of life after death to Christian doctrine many believers had their doubts. In 1998 the British Social Attitudes survey reported that 75 per cent of those inclined to believe in a personal God thought the afterlife either certain or probable, while 25 per cent either dismissed the idea altogether or found it improbable.[98] A very similar division of opinion was apparent among the sixty-nine Christian mass observers who discussed the question, with 77 per cent believing the afterlife was certain or probable; 17 per cent doubting or denying its existence; and the remaining 6 per cent hovering between the two positions. Among MO's Christians the kind of salvation anxiety that had driven Weber's Calvinists to invent capitalism was notable by its absence. Since hardly anyone believed in hell, religion no longer pressed itself on every waking moment with the same urgency.[99] If the alternative to everlasting bliss was mere oblivion, rather than eternal agony in the fiery pit, it became a great deal easier to accept that no one really knew what, if anything, might happen when the body died. From being the pivot of religion, the promise of eternal life had become, for many, a matter of speculation.[100]

Julia Seymour, a retired teacher and a practising Anglican, insisted that her conception of God as 'immanent in nature and beyond nature' had 'nothing whatever' to do with 'the accretions of superstitious centuries … [or] the superstitions of irrational people who, to lighten the burden of their uncertainties, create mythical explanations which have no firmer foundation than we now know the various creation myths to have'. So far as the afterlife was concerned, there might be some kind of 'spiritual immortality' but 'neither I nor anyone else knows what that means … (and) anyone who says he knows is a liar or deluded'.[101] David Lloyd, the retired vicar whose business it had been to promote such 'superstitions', privately confessed:

> If I'm honest my thoughts/beliefs [in this] area are bit of a muddle … I preach and pray at funerals about a life to come – and do so with conviction and firmness. But there is always part of me which recognises that I could be wrong … as an individual I feel uncertain, because there is the danger of wishful thinking. As the philosopher C. D. Broad said 'One can only wait and see, or alternatively (which is no less likely) wait and not see'.[102]

Similarly philosophical was Helen Pennyweather, a middle-aged Methodist school teacher: 'I would like to believe in [the afterlife] but I don't think I do really ... on the other hand that doesn't really worry me too much.'[103] What did worry her was that other members of the congregation, preoccupied, she believed, with the Day of Judgement, 'would be shocked if they knew what I really think about these things'. She kept her doubts to herself, confiding them only in the privacy afforded by MO.[104] As did a number of others who felt guilty about questioning established doctrine, worrying that their doubts about the afterlife displayed a lack of faith.[105] One wonders how many churchgoers – and vicars – were similarly evasive.

In so far as the afterlife was imagined as a site of family reunion, several of the Christians had good reason for finding the prospect far from reassuring. Liz Howard, a middle-aged teacher and occasional churchgoer, toyed with the idea of the afterlife when her father died, but not because she wished him eternal bliss: 'at this moment I really hope beyond hope that my father ... has gone to hell ... I hope if there is an afterlife he suffers a lot.' But she did not really think that there was one: 'It's all a lot of nonsense.'[106] For Cynthia Rawlinson, a retired radiographer active in her local parish church, disbelief in the afterlife was confirmed – paradoxically – by her own dead mother:

> The subject of life after death was one which my mother was inclined to doubt. She was a rather forbidding person, given to scolding in preference to loving. I was amazed when she agreed with me, (I was over twenty at the time), that perhaps there wasn't an afterlife. A few nights after her funeral in 1988 I had a vivid dream: she was striding towards me in her usual tweeds and low-heeled shoes, saying: 'You are perfectly right, there's nothing here.' [107]

Her parents, who had decided that they could only afford one child, wanted a boy and had been dismayed when she arrived. 'My Mother's attitude to me for the next 50 years appeared to [be] one of vengeance. Mild but noticeable.' Sent 'home' to boarding school from colonial Ceylon, Cynthia had been 'a solitary person all my life'. Her first marriage was unhappy, and her second marriage left much to be desired. 'At each stage of life no one has been at all close to me ... a text book recipe for an introverted, self-centred being. As such one grabs at and clings to hints of "outside help."' It was not for the hereafter that she needed her belief in 'a Power beyond myself which/who watches over my life', but as 'a very necessary ... prop and stay to help me through this world'. And if there was, after all, a life to come she would certainly not have wanted to share it with her mother.[108] Nancy Darling, a Scottish Presbyterian, who had been unhappily married to a patriarchal Elder of the Kirk, decided she would prefer to 'dissolve into nothingness' rather than join him in heaven. 'It would … be … a bit of a crush anyway,' she added mischievously, 'as he had two other wives!'[109] In contrast to the women who embraced the prospect of the afterlife as a reassuring continuation of their devotion to family life, this woman felt that she was 'not very good at close relationships' because they involved 'a loss of freedom and that is *very* important to me'. At the age of seventy-two she hoped that when she died it would be 'the end'. Having lived a happy life, she felt no need for more.[110]

A similarly philosophic acceptance of their own death was apparent among many of the non-believers. Garry Edwards, a devotee of Spinoza, believed that 'as individuals we are of little importance in the scheme of things':

> We come into the world for a short time and leave it to return to the nullity we were before conception. As such we can enjoy, admire and even worship creation (e.g. one's feelings of contentment when in the mountains or on the sea – or even being lost in a book) but one should not expect any such feelings from God/Nature or the Supernatural in return.[111]

Several atheists and agnostics drew comfort from their sense of being a tiny part of a vast cosmic process without feeling the need to attribute any supernatural purpose to the whole thing. 'Our bodies', wrote Samantha Geraghty, 'are composed of atoms, and hence subatomic particles, that have existed since the beginning of time.' She had spent thirty years working as a computer programmer in California, where she became involved in green activism. While expressing her respect for the New Age ecofeminist writing of Margot Adler, Starhawk and others, she resisted their appeal to a transcendent spirituality and defined herself as 'a secular humanist'.[112] 'Care for the environment', she wrote, 'is not a religion for me, but in some ways it takes the place of a religion.'[113] 'I have been stone, dust of space', she explained, citing the Irish poet, Michael Hartnett, to express her own sense of oneness with the cosmos: 'I will be here: I have always been here.'[114] Harry Bolton, the retired decorator, aware that human beings 'for all our sophistications … (are) just a mere link in the life chain on this planet', took comfort in the thought that 'nothing really dies' since 'recycling is in the natural order of the universe'.[115] Rachel Harriman, who we will meet in Chapter 6, expressed a similar attitude towards her own mortality:

> Our personalities and capabilities and potentials are so huge, but in reality we are just tiny beating hearts fluttering insignificantly for a split second on Earth. I have always felt very secure in this insignificance.

She wanted to be buried in cardboard so that her rotting corpse could help a tree to grow: 'That is not macabre – it is what should happen if we identify with our Earth.' The truth of reincarnation was not that 'the same soul flits from one body to another', but that death is essential to give birth to new life.[116]

But not all the disbelievers were so accepting. Several atheists, with no belief in the afterlife to fall back on, expressed horror at the void to come. A young professional woman who 'never had much of a religious faith' found herself 'panic-stricken' by the thought that death could occur at any time.[117] Mark Darling, a 31-year-old chemist, who had lost his faith in childhood when his prayers failed to save his sick father from death, felt anxious about the fact that 'you cease to exist and the world carries on. The thought that there will come a time when I am not around is weird, incomprehensible'. It would be much easier, he wrote, 'to believe in heaven or an afterlife ... I wish in a way that I could, as it would be much more comforting than believing in "nothingness".'[118] Several other young disbelievers worried about the apparent meaninglessness of a life with no hereafter. 'Things, surely, can't be so simple that we just merely cease to exist on death', wrote a 32-year-old computer consultant, before adding: 'But, then, why shouldn't we just cease? In looking for the meaning to life, we forget sometimes that there may not be one!'[119] An actor who, following 'a quickly exhausted religious fervour at puberty' adopted a jokey tone to write about the Christian beliefs he had abandoned insisting that 'the world doesn't pose a question to me', nevertheless acknowledged that 'there is clearly need for some sense, however nebulous, of a direction, a purposive force in our lives'. At the age of thirty-five he had, however, no idea how to pursue this thought.[120] Adrian Fraser, an atheist computer programmer, suffered recurrent anxiety attacks. On the point of falling asleep, horror at the thought of death and oblivion 'flood(s) my mind like vertigo ... I scream and shout and sometimes scramble out of bed to crawl across the floor on my hands and knees. This all takes place in a couple of seconds of panic, then I come round and usually go back to sleep fairly quickly.' Adrian, to whose vivid imagination and intense intellectual curiosity we will return, wondered whether these attacks continued because, at some level, it gave him pleasure to stand on the edge of the abyss. He experimented with hallucinogenic drugs, and he loved to frighten himself with ghost stories and horror movies.[121] It may be significant that these existential terrors were expressed only by the young – all the people quoted in this paragraph were in their early thirties, perhaps an age when awareness of one's own mortality begins to surface. Older atheists might waver in their denial of the afterlife under the stress of bereavement, but they expressed no terror about prospect of their own death.

The mass observers' attitudes to death reflected their orientations to life – orientations I have labelled as familial, individualistic or philosophical. That, in itself, is unremarkable. What is significant for my overall argument is the fact that these different orientations transcended the divisions between believers in a personal God, adherents to a non-religious spirituality and those who rejected any notion of the supernatural. When it came to the understanding of human mortality, beliefs about the existence or non-existence of the supernatural were less important than orientations towards the meaning of life. Confronted with death, imagination trumped ontology.

4

Religion and science

Science is central to modern secular society, and the great majority of mass observers, whatever their views of the supernatural, had a positive attitude towards the practice of scientific enquiry. Indeed, as volunteers in a project of social research, many saw themselves as actively participating in this practice. When, in 1996, Mass Observation (MO) asked them to discuss their attitudes towards the 'supernatural' the focus was on discrete paranormal phenomena. The directive did ask respondents to discuss the implications of their views of the supernatural on 'any religious beliefs you may hold', but there was no equivalent question about the relationship between attitudes to the supernatural and to science. For many respondents this was the elephant in the room, and they went out of their way to explain that science was at least as important as religion in influencing how they understood apparently supernatural phenomena. Nowhere is the shifting and ambiguous meaning of key words more apparent than in the discussion of these issues. However much people might disagree about the significance of 'death' or the 'afterlife' the concepts themselves were relatively clear and undisputed. But what people meant by 'science', 'religion' and the 'supernatural' was as varied as their beliefs about the proper relationship between these entities.

As in their thinking about death, the mass observers' views about the extent to which science could make sense of the world did not simply reflect their belief or non-belief in the existence of supernatural forces. Drawing on the long and complex history of relations between science and religion, believers followed divergent strategies in their pursuit of an accommodation between these different paths to knowledge. Some thought that no accommodation was called for, while many others were content to live with what they acknowledged as an unresolved conflict between the findings of science and their own intuitions. A few, less tolerant of philosophical incoherence, looked for ways to combine spiritual exploration with the practice of science. Meanwhile, among the non-believers, by no means everyone was confident that, in the absence of what they took to be the irrational superstitions of religion, the practice of science held the key to understanding the place of humanity in the cosmos.

I

For some Christians the relationship between science and religion was unproblematic. Science used reason and empirical observation to explore nature and the material world, while religion supplemented reason with the faculties of intuition, emotion and feeling to explore the realm of the spirit. Like the palaeontologist Stephen Jay Gould they assumed the existence of two distinct realms of knowledge, neither having significant consequences for the other.[1] Sandra Delaney, a physics teacher, explained that 'science has little to do with the divine mystery … so to me there isn't any conflict'.[2] Len Smith, a Methodist mechanic whose story is told in *Seven Lives*, was clear that the 'spiritual experience' underpinning religion was entirely unaffected by advances in scientific knowledge.[3] For Christine Hartman, a Catholic civil servant who found a 'beauty in logic, and in the study of Science',[4] the important conflict lay not between religion and science, but between both of them and superstition. 'Of course, as a Christian, I believe in the supernatural,' she explained, 'it is the whole basis of religion': but that was something entirely different from the weird and wonderful beliefs and practices listed in MO's directive.[5] She put her faith in 'a Creator who controls the Universe, not by any whims, but according to Natural Law. Science is all about trying to understand that law beside which the popular idea of the supernatural – the occult – seems shabby and ridiculous'. (Although she did allow that for 'those who cannot accept orthodox religion' such ideas might go some way to meet 'their need of some spiritual aspect in their lives'.)[6] Julia Seymour, whose firm Christian belief had 'nothing whatever to do with … the superstitions of irrational people', was in no doubt that 'almost everything' listed in the 1996 directive could 'be shown to have a rational or psychological explanation rather than to imply the existence of supernatural forces'.[7] For Gordon King, a Methodist who had worked as a senior manager in the food industry, it was important to insist that God 'does not change or overrule the laws on which the universe has been founded … he abides by his/her own natural rules'.[8] Experiences which appeared to defy the laws of nature testified, he believed, not to the interventions of a capricious God, but to the limitations of human understanding. As scientific knowledge increased, the realm of the supernatural would shrink. Brian Gregory, a retired clergyman, did not share Christine Hartman's excitement about science, but he was, like her, keen to draw a sharp line between religion and popular superstition. She would have approved the distinction he drew between the *super*natural and the *supra*natural, the latter being the province of religion, and the former all too frequently in evidence in popular religious sensibilities. Several of the other Christians took a similar view, though few as vehemently as the autodidact toolmaker Ted Watkins: 'I do not believe in ghosts, ghouls, hobgoblins, vampires, spirit séances or any of the pseudo-paranormal products of man's neurotic imagination.'[9]

It was intrinsic to religious belief that there were limits to scientific explanation. Man was not destined to become God; ultimate mysteries would remain; humility was called for. 'I think that we humans are like ants on an ant heap when a human walks by,' wrote Sandra Delaney, the Christian physics teacher:

> They can have no conception of his mind, plans etc. with their little brains. We are as ants are to humans in our understanding of God; we just haven't got the brains to understand. ... I do believe in God. To try to understand Him we create pictures and stories, but in truth it's all quite beyond us.[10]

Phil Ponsonby, a retired engineering executive, was happy to 'acknowledge the superior intellects of those who develop their theories about Big Bangs and the like, but I earnestly believe that they can never know the answer to the ultimate Mystery, of how and why it all began'.[11] As one retired teacher remarked, astrophysics had long since pushed heaven into 'a totally different dimension ... not even the most devout theologian still thinks of heaven as "up there"'.[12] No one believed literally in the biblical creation myth, but, as with heaven, the notion of the Big Bang simply pushed the ultimate mystery of creation into another dimension. 'Scientific theories take us back almost to the beginning of time,' wrote Gerald Brewster, an East Anglian bank manager, 'but no human mind could make up a theory which can explain how something started from nothing ... we all know in our heart of hearts that that was supernatural.'[13] Ted Watkins, an autodidact toolmaker whose Christian belief, acquired in middle age, was the result of an extensive intellectual journey, relied, in the end, on 'spiritual faith rather than factuality' – the 'sage beneath his Bo tree' came closer to understanding the universe than modern science or philosophy. What, he asked, can we understand about 'God, the trinity, space, time, eternity or the Beyond ... (are you there Prof Hawkins?) ... absolutely nothing'.[14] Brian Gregory, the retired clergyman, believed that advances in scientific understanding would always do more to raise new questions than they did to answer old ones: 'All generations live at the centre of a circle of ignorance which gets larger as knowledge expands.' Like other proponents of rational religion, Gregory had no time for the paranormal phenomena listed in MO's directive, but he worried that his belief 'in the spiritual but not in the psychic' made him 'an oddity' among his fellow Christians.[15] 'Oddity' is too strong. But he was certainly in a minority among the Christian mass observers most of whom, as we will see in Chapter 5, entertained beliefs in the paranormal which the proponents of rational religion dismissed as ignorant superstitions.

II

The most celebrated battles between science and religion had changed the frontiers between these two ways of knowing, but there was no consensus about the outcome, and many believers had little difficulty in reconciling scientific advance with religion. Jenny Brown, a liberal-minded Catholic, was reassured to note that while 'some scientists say their discoveries prove the non-existence of God, others say the complete opposite'.[16] Atheists might believe that Darwin had put paid to God, but the pitched battles of the Victorian era were far from decisive. In the early 20th century many religious thinkers had found ways of reconciling the theory of evolution with belief in God. Teilhard de Chardin reworked Darwinian evolution, not as a mindless struggle for existence but as a mechanism for spiritual progress. Far from being undermined by Darwinism, he argued, Christianity 'can now embrace, and indeed, fulfil it'.[17] Julia Seymour objected to an ill-judged passage in MO's 1992 directive on nature and the environment, which she saw as posing 'a fallacious dilemma between Darwinism and a creative deity'.[18] While she was perfectly happy with the theory of evolution as an explanation of how man had evolved from 'the primeval soup', she was also sure that there was a spiritual element in his make-up 'which is not wholly explicable in terms of the chemistry of the brain … even if this is only the ability to enjoy beauty or to explore the possibility that God exists'. Abstract concepts 'such as love, justice or beauty' were already 'implicit in the moment of the Big Bang', but it was only through the process of evolution that beings evolved who were capable of understanding them. The coming of monotheistic religion, for her, marked the moment when human beings had evolved sufficiently beyond the law of the jungle to be able to enter into a conscious relationship with a personal God.[19] She would have agreed with Marion Phillips, a Quaker schoolteacher, who rejected the possibility that human spirituality could have arisen in the absence of a creative deity because 'I don't see that a river can rise above its source'.[20]

Most believers lacked the sophistication of Julia Seymore, but intuition told them that evolution alone could not explain the whole picture. 'Will we really ever know how Nature was created?' asked an elderly Jewish woman: 'My head tells me one thing, but my eyes and heart another.'[21] In their explicit acknowledgement of divergent meanings supplied by the head and the heart – reason and intuition – these mass observers exemplify the fragilization and pluralization of belief that Charles Taylor sees as characteristic of modern times. Religious believers, he argues, are no less enmeshed than non-believers in the secular imagination of modernity.[22] The classic argument from design remained convincing, even among those who knew, as one observer put it, that such proof of God's existence had become, since Darwin, rather 'old hat'.[23] 'It is not always easy to believe in God,' wrote Christine Hartman, a practising Catholic with a scientific training,

> but the amazing diversity of plant and animal life banishes my doubts. I do not disbelieve Darwin's Theory of Evolution, but when I see (usually on a TV Natural History programme) the variety of ways each individual species has developed of reproducing, feeding, protecting itself or catching its prey … I know beyond all doubt that Darwin's theory cannot explain it all and that it must be the work of some Supreme Being.[24]

William Reilly, a retired civil servant and also lapsed Anglican, found it 'hard to accept that mere evolution has produced the extraordinary complexities of all forms of life, and that what we call "Nature" is not a grand design for regulating the resources of the world'. Darwin, he conceded, might have 'logic and reason' on his side, but he remained convinced that the 'order and regulation of all living species, of physical and climatic conditions and the precise adaptation of all living things to suit the physical and climatic demands of their environment' could only have arisen as the creation of 'some kind of supreme force'.[25] Another retired administrator, with no definite religious beliefs, felt that 'the world, its animals, plants and humans, are so well formed in an intricate procession of development, so inter-related that it cannot be the result of an accident'.[26] 'The main religious significance of nature to me is in the sheer complexity of it,' wrote a woman who had converted to Catholicism after an Anglican upbringing: 'I do not believe it all came about by either a big bang or evolution, without a guiding hand.' 'One has only to consider how wonderful everything in nature is,' wrote Sarah Hodges, 'it could never have all happened just by chance.'[27] Ada Roberts marvelled 'at the changing seasons, the growth of plants, the sunshine, the rain. I marvel at Harvest Festival, when Spring breaks after a particularly cold winter, that everything seems to "come to life". I just don't see how nature can just happen and carry on without some supernatural force'.[28] Edward Farleigh, who despite being a practising Anglican had rejected most of his Christian beliefs, nevertheless felt that 'the magical glory of the whole Universe' left no doubt 'that there must be a purpose to the creation … one has only to look at a tropical sky at night'.[29] A retired florist – whose calling matched her beliefs – put the point simply: 'If you look at a daffodil bulb and then see it blowing in the spring winds as a beautiful yellow flower, how can you not believe in God who is creation?'[30]

The argument from design did not necessarily imply the existence of a personal God. Gerald Brewster felt that God was 'the one alien it is hard to disavow completely', not only because scientific theories could not penetrate before the Big Bang but also because they could not explain why 'we are surrounded with a wonderful environment and a wonderful existence of our own'. None of this, however, persuaded him to believe in 'a personal God who is interested in everything I do and watches me and everyone else closely at the same time and keeps a record, an account book of everyone's actions'.[31] Phil Ponsonby, the retired engineering executive, had given up churchgoing in his twenties. While he continued to believe that some intelligence must have created the universe, he reluctantly abandoned the idea that the creator was still in control: 'It may have grown bored with the whole thing and gone off to create another Universe with another set of bricks.' Despite the light-hearted tone, he confessed to profound terror at the thought of the immensity of space and the 'absence of any reference points to which I can connect'. For fifty years – speaking to the much-loved father who had died when he was nine years old – Phil had longed for some evidence of the supernatural. But contact came there none, and this confirmed his belief that God was dead, or departed elsewhere.[32] Garry Edwards, an amateur philosopher inspired by Spinoza, shocked his local vicar by explaining that while 'we can enjoy, admire and even worship creation … we have no right nor reason to expect that our worship/appreciation of life should attract special consideration from the Deity'.[33] Florence Brewer, a retired teacher, marvelling at 'the way living things fit together down to the smallest creature and plant', took human insignificance one stage further: the 'grand plan', she wrote, was not made 'specifically for mankind':

> I can believe that whales, communicating as they do, have the same sexual, maternal, hungers and pains as we, and see themselves as *the* life form; or on

the other hand ants or bees, who are also social creatures, why are they not just as important as we two legged thinkers? They create structures, complicated as anything we make, they have a better grip of mathematics and design than most of us.[34]

Gloria Blake, reflecting on the possibility, implicit in James Lovelock's theory of Gaia, that the biosphere might be better off without human beings, remarked that 'if nature is controlled by a God ... it could be that it will all be taken away from us if we abuse it too much'.[35] Such a punishment was hardly conceivable for a Christian. The idea of a God who could simply abandon humanity, a God who might even prefer ants, belonged to a spirituality far removed from Christian tradition.

III

If the argument from design survived the onslaught of Darwinism, this had more to do with the capacity of believers to hold contradictory ideas in separate parts of their minds than with sophisticated arguments about 'creative evolution' advanced by theologians and philosophers.[36] Another innovation of 19th-century science, however, was seized on by several mass observers to justify their religious beliefs. Whatever the differences between science and religion, there was scope for fruitful interchange between the two areas of thought. Newton, after all, had puzzled his way to gravity, a force acting at a distance, by contemplating the supposed behaviour of angels.[37] Similarly, the 19th-century formulation of the first law of thermodynamics by scientists including William Thompson and James Joule owed a good deal to their conviction that nothing that God had created could be destroyed.[38] While none of the mass observers made the association between angels and gravity, the first law of thermodynamics was cited by several Christians as a justification for their belief in the afterlife. Veronica Richardson, a retired university lecturer married to a doctor, had been 'brought up scientifically to believe that nothing can be created or destroyed, and to see this applied to souls too'.[39] Bill Woody, a churchgoing young man, understood the law of the conservation of energy as providing decisive proof of the afterlife: 'It's a scientific fact [that] matter cannot be destroyed and that all the energy and activity in our brains goes on to another level.'[40] Liz Howard, the Scottish teacher who had wanted her father to go to hell, was rather less sure: 'Our life force ... can't just disappear forever – something happens, but what? ... What happens to all the energy in our bodies? Energy doesn't just die too ... maybe our spirit does live on in some form. That's what I believe just now, but it changes as I read and learn more.'[41] Given the influence of religion on the origins of the first law of thermodynamics, there is something delightfully circular about these appeals to the conservation of energy to establish the truth of religion.

Among the mass observers the most extensive effort to attach the prestige of modern science to the legitimation of belief in supernatural forces lay in the study of apparently paranormal phenomena. David Lloyd, the vicar, combined his religious duties with long-standing membership of the Society for Psychical Research, established in 1880 by scientists resisting the materialist disenchantment of the world threatened by Darwinism. He was convinced by their researches of the existence of phenomena (including ghosts, poltergeists) which 'are hard to explain except on the spirit communication hypothesis, reluctant though I am to believe it ... the evidence would convince any reasonable person ... [and] some of it does seem to offer very good evidence for survival of self'.[42] For others it was near-death experiences, investigated and established by what they took to be scientific procedures, which provided 'a foretaste of the afterlife' (Jenny Brown)[43] or, more conclusively, 'overwhelming evidence of survival after death' (Paula Harrison).[44] It was this 'evidence' that eventually persuaded Thomas Partridge, a retired teacher and practising Catholic, of the reality of the afterlife:

> It would be nice to be able to write that my change of attitude has been brought about by a greater understanding of the teachings of my church: but that is not the case. I think my change of attitude has been due to the mounting evidence that death is not the end. I refer to the near-death experiences, which have now been reported in such large numbers, and have even been experienced by professed atheists such as the late philosopher, Professor A.J. Ayer, that they cannot be ignored.[45]

The relationship between psychic investigations and religious belief was, however, far from straightforward. Several of those fascinated by the paranormal feared that psychic research might lead them in directions incompatible with religious practice. Alistair Bevan, an ex-teacher who had written novels about the supernatural, confessed himself 'not at all sure ... where superstition begins [and] religion ends'. Despite making 'an intellectual distinction between belief in God as Creator of the Universe and belief in "supernatural forces"', and viewing the latter as 'merely superstition', he nevertheless found himself drawn towards it. He was a practising Christian – 'and no doubt I need to practice', he added modestly, 'because I'm not very good at it' – but his fascination with the supernatural went beyond his writerly imagination. He had no doubt about the existence of ghosts and he had himself experienced both astral travel and, he suspected, demon possession. Nevertheless he continued to see these beliefs and experiences as something quite separate from his religious life.[46] David Lloyd, the vicar who confessed his own uncertainty about the existence of an afterlife, made a similar distinction between 'two strands of thought' – the religious and that of the paranormal investigators. While both strands pointed towards the 'survival of the personality after physical death' they did so 'in very different and to some extent conflicting ways'. He also suspected, as did Bevan, that it was his 'speculations about the survival of the mind (which is not the same thing at all as Christian life after death)' which did more than his religious beliefs to inform the way he imagined the afterlife.[47]

Like Bevan and Lloyd, Gillian Latimer, the freethinking rector's wife, also combined her Christian faith with an interest in the paranormal. As a child she had absorbed a wide range of ideas about the supernatural. While aware that much that had been thought supernatural in the past could now be explained by science, and that the paranormal offered 'a very good field for wishful thinking and fraud', she was nevertheless 'amazed' that so many people, 'blinkered and arrogant', closed their minds to what experience surely told them – that 'there was something out there to be tapped'. She herself had one or two paranormal experiences including a vision in which she felt radiantly transported to another dimension, bright and clear: 'I think I had a very brief glimpse of the etheric world that is all around us but cannot necessarily be seen.' She also had news of her dead mother from a psychic friend. All this, however, sat uncomfortably with her religious beliefs: 'the psychic path … can be very fascinating,' she wrote, 'but to my mind [it is] a dead end … It has nothing to do with our spiritual development – which is more difficult and not very exciting.' Attending meetings of the Churches' Fellowship for Psychical and Spiritual Studies under the leadership of the Rev. Dr Martin Israel, she felt that she 'could trust him as he was on the spiritual path and not the psychic and a most understanding, balanced man'.[48] When Martin Israel died in 2007, the obituary in the *Church Times* noted that he had rescued the Churches' Fellowship 'from a pseudo-Spiritualism, so that it could become firmly linked with mainstream Christianity, and could be a lifeline for people of psychic sensitivity who wanted to remain in the Christian faith'.[49] This was precisely what Gillian Latimer sought.

Some of those who embraced a non-religious spirituality were less hesitant, looking beyond the scientific investigation of psychic phenomena to a thoroughgoing spiritualization of science itself. Florence Brewer, the retired teacher who played with the idea that whales, bees and ants might have a greater claim to God's consideration than human beings, cited the work of the popular existentialist writer Colin Wilson as exemplifying the kind of interdisciplinary approach of which she approved: combining 'experiments in hypnotherapy, homeopathy, faith healing' with insights from 'computers ... archaeology, technology, etc., each bringing bits of factual material which joined to other bits from a different sphere begin to make sense of previously unexplainable events.'[50] In a similar vein Emma Fielding, the New Age mother whose young children resented 'mummy's new ideas', thought that 'to really work, science has to stop being just science but [become] a mixture of other disciplines too ... a better way would be to include the supernatural in physics – e.g. time going in loops which would explain clairvoyance'.[51] Edward Farleigh wondered whether praying for someone else might help them because 'merely thinking of someone with love and compassion causes a transmission of hope and comfort in some telepathic way direct from one person to the other. Not divine intervention but a physical phenomenon of which we are so far unaware'. In his early seventies he was keeping himself 'busy and confused' trying to understand a book on the *Quantum Self* which argued that quantum physics provided the basis for a selfhood at one with the cosmos, reconciling Western individualism with Eastern mysticism.[52]

The most sophisticated ideas about the spiritualization of science were those advocated by Fiona Evans, a medical sociologist energetic in her pursuit of 'a balanced approach between the intuitive and analytical faculties'.[53] Born in 1951, she had been scarred by the death of her father in a road accident – her grieving mother had offered the three-year-old no explanation of her father's disappearance, and the child blamed herself. In adolescence she suffered a crisis of anorexia, intensified, she recalled, by her attempt 'to force myself into a religious mould which just wasn't the right shape for me'. In her twenties and thirties, still struggling to come to terms with the trauma of her father's disappearance, she had a series of relationships with older men, culminating in a brief marriage to a man terminally ill with cancer, a marriage which 'changed me psychologically and emotionally and allowed me to begin to get in touch with unexpressed grief from earlier losses'.[54] Looking back in 2007, aged fifty-six, she felt comfortable with 'a take on life, which is definitely more "spiritual" [than] "religious"'.[55] Contrasting herself with a born-again Christian of her acquaintance, she imagined a meeting with him in the afterlife:

> He is in what looks like a very large goldfish tank, pacing up and down reciting bits from the Bible. I'm outside, knocking on the glass and yelling 'Hi, I'm here!'

He is totally oblivious to my presence, and is in quite a lonely place, while on my side of the glass, there is a very rich crowd of interesting people.[56]

Fiona was good at surrounding herself with interesting people. Fascinated by the supernatural ever since reading H. G. Wells as a teenager, she described herself as 'a bit psychic and very interested in spiritual issues'. In her efforts 'to develop [her] spiritual self', she consulted mediums, studied astrology and went on retreats with a pagan guru who channelled messages from 'the Ascended Masters, the Angelic Collective and the Elementals and Old Gods'.[57] All too aware of the ridicule that a secular culture attached to people who 'sit … around being spiritual, developing our ESP, twitching our divining rods and going into altered states of consciousness', she did her best to approach her psychic explorations in a scientific spirit. Dismissive of the 'message from Auntie' procedures of 'platform mediums', her preference was for 'trance mediums' who 'operate on a higher spiritual vibration and bring through ascended masters' who could give her 'spiritual guidance on how to live my life'.[58] Similarly with astrology, she had no belief in its predictive powers, but pursued it rather as 'a useful tool in gaining personal insight and self-awareness'.[59] While never doubting the existence of a transcendent spiritual dimension, she knew that paranormal occurrences did not happen 'independently of the people experiencing them'. When it came to ghosts, for example, she insisted that 'we should pay as much attention to the perceivers as to the perceived, and always use Occam's razor to whittle away the alternative explanations first'.[60] While it was clear to her 'that some people experience events which cannot be explained in terms of currently accepted scientific paradigms', she was confident that 'if we continue to bring physics and mysticism together in the way we are beginning to do, we will eventually find a more popularly acceptable explanation for events which we currently call "supernatural"'.[61]

She had joined the Society for Psychical Research in 1976, but was frustrated by its elitism which, she alleged, 'discouraged ordinary people … from getting actively involved in psychic research'. In 1981 she joined the newly formed Association for the Scientific Study of Anomalous Phenomena and after the death of her husband ten years later she and her new partner set up a local organization under its auspices to cater for 'people with an enquiring mind and an interest in unexplained phenomena'. She organized field trips to explore 'ancient sites, crop circles, dowsing, folklore, ghosts, healing, ley lines, old churches, sacred wells, UFOs, anomalous animals and challenging issues'.[62] Alongside this activity Fiona held regular meetings in her flat, some addressed by outside speakers. A talk on physics and extrasensory perception was given by Gwyn Hocking, a professor of chemistry who was later to become secretary of the Theosophical Society.[63] But it was Peter Fenwick – 'a scientist (medically trained) who has been prepared to stick his head above the parapet and challenge existing paradigms' – who made the greatest impression.[64]

Fenwick, a neuropsychiatrist who writes about near-death experiences and reincarnation memories, has served as president of the Scientific and Medical Network (SMN).[65] Since its foundation in 1973, by a group of British scientists concerned 'to reconcile scientific investigation and scientific models of reality with the spiritual dimension of life, and so to open dialogue between scientists and spiritual luminaries of all backgrounds', the SMN has attracted academics from across the physical and natural sciences, doctors, psychologists and philosophers.[66] E. F. Schumacher and Arthur Koestler were early members, and Fritjof Capra, author of *The Tao of Physics*, perhaps the most widely read exposition of a spiritual approach to science, is an honorary member.[67] According to Capra the late 20th century was witnessing a paradigm shift in which the scientific and spiritual imaginations, divided since the 17th century, were again becoming allies, not enemies.[68]

Although not a scientist herself, Fiona was anxious to put her skills as a social researcher at the service of those brave scientists who were prepared to risk the 'antipathy and scorn' of their colleagues by challenging established paradigms. Encouraged by one of her friends, a sociologist studying spiritualism, she 'drafted a research proposal for some work on the ways in which [some scientists] manage to maintain their interests in esoteric (or, to some, "barmy") topics while continuing to work in scientific environments'. She had in mind, particularly, the men she had invited to her flat to present, to a sympathetic audience, 'findings … their peers would pour scorn upon'. The project, it seems, did not get funding, but its very conception is nicely illustrative of the circuits of knowledge and belief linking non-religious spirituality among the mass observers with the esoteric fringe of the scientific establishment represented by men like Peter Fenwick.

Fiona was not the only mass observer to be touched by the work of the SMN. Had she been awarded funding for her project she might have found herself uncovering, among the scientists whose courage she so admired, an elitism at least as great as that she disapproved of in the Society for Psychical Research. Peter Leggett, one of the founders of the SMN, was a mathematician who became the first vice chancellor of the new University of Surrey. In his search for 'a new metaphysic, based on experiment and experience, embracing psychological insights and some practices of the East and the scientific disciplines and knowledge of the West', Leggett was one of a group of intellectuals in positions of influence who, in the tradition of Madame Blavatsky and the Theosophical Society, constituted themselves as members of an esoteric order tasked with guiding humanity from behind the scenes with the help of ancient wisdom entrusted to them by occult forces.[69] Leggett claimed to be guided by a Master – possibly Djwhal Khul, a Tibetan master first named by Madame Blavatsky in the 1880s – whose wisdom was dispensed only to people deemed 'capable of understanding and acting on the message for the spiritual enhancement of the race'. He received this guidance as a member of 'Light and Science', a small and secret circle of men of influence, which met regularly in a private house with a medium to channel the words of the Master and a scribe to write them down.[70] Another member of this circle was the Rev. Dr Martin Israel, who was the president of the Churches' Fellowship for Psychical and Spiritual Studies and much admired by Gillian Latimer, the rector's wife whose explorations beyond orthodoxy we discussed earlier.[71] Although Leggett was also active in the Churches' Fellowship, his more influential role was as the vice chancellor of the University of Surrey in the late 1960s, and it was in this capacity that his concerns intersected with another of the mass observers.

So far as I know Stella Marshall – whose full story is told in *Seven Lives* – never met Leggett, but she was greatly influenced by humanistic psychology, a discipline introduced to Britain in the early 1970s at the University of Surrey because, as vice chancellor, Leggett put his weight behind a maverick philosophy lecturer, John Heron, whose project of bringing Californian practices of humanistic psychology and co-counselling to Britain struck a chord with Leggett's mission to promote the 'spiritual enhancement of the race'.[72] Stella, who as a divorced single mother was busy acquiring the higher education that her parents had denied her, was an early member of Heron's 'Human Relations Training Laboratories', an involvement she continued with one of Heron's disciples after she moved from Surrey to Yorkshire at the end of the 1970s to take up a job as an adoption worker in Bradford. Her effectiveness as an innovator in the world of professional social work, discussed in *Seven Lives from Mass Observation*, owed a good deal to her engagement with humanistic psychology, and particularly its emphasis on the dynamics of interpersonal relationships explored in encounter groups, psychodrama, transactional analysis, gestalt and other therapies.

Stella's own approach to the relationship between science and spirituality is reflected in her view of 'body auras' as 'an area where folly, imagination and science meet headlong'. While fraudulent psychics might pretend to see auras, she herself had occasionally done so, and children, she suspected, often saw them until they were socialized out of it:

I understand biophysics, biochemistry, atomic physics and other disciplines presently offer acceptable scientific accounts of how the exchange of material, heat, light, fluid, takes place, non-stop, between ourselves and our environment. There is no longer any reason to suppose that the body has the precise boundaries we previously imagined.[73]

Similarly with spiritual healing, about which she recommended 'a very delightful, un-sanctimonious book ... cheerful, unpatronizing, unreligious'.[74] Having once regarded such practices as 'superstitious nonsense', she now saw the idea that 'the body can be "treated" divorced from the mind and spirit' as a delusion promoted by the secular rationality of Western scientists 'intent on classification and division'. Not that she dismissed the achievements of analytic reason: 'Much as I believe in other dimensions of being', she wrote, 'I have to accept that ... yesterday's supernatural is today's science ... Some phenomena which may seem to provide evidence of the supernatural may be explained scientifically tomorrow, or the next day'.[75] Like the founders of the S MN, she looked to the spiritual to complement, not to discredit, the procedures of Western scientific rationality.

Stella had been fascinated by 'the lure of the arcane' ever since her wartime childhood, when she and some friends set up a 'Ghost Society' and enjoyed frightening themselves 'with twilight visits to churchyards, lovers' lanes, old beach huts – anything dilapidated, dark, isolated, or ancient'. Responding, aged sixty-five, to the 1996 directive on the supernatural, she told stories of clairvoyance, and was open-minded about reincarnation, spiritual healing and the omnipresence of the spiritual in the natural world. In the end, however, 'the web of being of which we ourselves form an infinitesimal part' was probably 'beyond our understanding ... We can't see the whole ... our lives are woven into a giant tapestry, thread by thread, but ... all we can see on our present plane is the tangle at the back of the tapestry, like a darn'. Perhaps, she added optimistically, 'in some other time and place we may go round to the front, and see the glory of the pattern'.[76]

In her later years she became rather more sceptical:

From astronomy, cosmology we learn we dwell within an infinitesimal dot, one among 120 billion galaxies – we are crumbs, microbes. ... If there is an afterlife, if there is a God, if there is some meaning or purpose, we cannot grasp it. It is far, far beyond the capacity of our rigid, limited earthbound minds. Like tadpoles in a pond for whom the concept of frog-ness is inconceivable.[77]

Distressed by man's capacity for evil and the apparent meaninglessness of life, 'not a day goes by when I do not vex my head with these questions'. Now, aged seventy-eight, she found peace – indeed 'blissful relief' – not in the enchantments offered by purveyors of spiritual wisdom but in the altogether more detached and speculative procedures of a fortnightly philosophy class provided by the University of the Third Age. Here, substituting intellectual curiosity for existential angst, she knew 'without a shadow of doubt the participants are as full of questions as myself. For two hours I know that there is no right answer waiting to be discovered and take comfort'.[78] In the end, for this open-minded and intelligent woman, puzzlement seemed the best option.

IV

To many of those who rejected belief in the supernatural, puzzlement seemed an insufficient response. Belief in the primacy of reason was central to their identities and they looked to the practical reason of scientific enquiry to explain the nature of the world and of the creatures (including themselves) who inhabited it. 'Analysis and scientific evidence are the cornerstones of civilisation,' wrote a young teacher, herself emancipated from the 'superstitions' of a Catholic childhood.[79] Helen Sharp, the 'pragmatic', middle-aged daughter of a vicar, had been unable to find any 'spark within me' for the family religion. For her it was axiomatic that there was a rational explanation for every occurrence: 'Where there appears to be no explanation for an event, I believe this is only because we do not have enough information, knowledge or skill to find one.'[80] Responding to MO's questions about paranormal phenomena most atheists and agnostics were clear in rejecting any notion of the 'supernatural': 'if it occurs it is part of nature, though we may not understand it.'[81] Margaret Thompson, who wrote this, was a biologist, a Communist (until 1984), a peace activist whose participation in direct action spanned sitting down with Bertrand Russell in the Strand in the early 1960s to 'embracing the base' at Greenham Common twenty years later. At university in the late 1940s she had rejected adolescent religiosity in favour of a 'fervent disbelief' in the supernatural informed by 'the scientific way of considering nature and experience. When I began to understand things by observation, correlation, comparison and wherever possible testing, I soon realised that an external "god" or "guiding force" is not necessary for the emergence or existence of the world or the universe.'[82]

Jill Forrest, a thoughtful 23-year-old bank worker with no 'religious beliefs, or any particular sense of a powerful force guiding our destiny', approached the directive on the supernatural as 'a learning experience for me, learning about my opinions and feelings as I write'. Resisting the 'natural human tendency' to 'place a structure and an explanation on events', she believed – a belief which she confessed frightened her – 'that the world is not an ordered place at all, but in fact a mess of chance events ... there is no master plan'. After reviewing what she knew about the various paranormal phenomena suggested by MO, she concluded that she had no belief in the supernatural 'as a separate force, or entity. I do not claim that there are or aren't supernatural occurrences; but I classify these as events outside our current understanding'. While 'as a human being, a naturally curious animal, I might like to consider possible explanations [of these phenomena], it is not of vital importance to me to find answers. I do not have to find an explanation for the Supernatural in order to maintain my beliefs about our world'.[83] Strange phenomena that now seemed inexplicable would eventually succumb to the advance of scientific investigation, as had happened in so many areas of human experience since the 17th century. In the meantime, as an exasperated chemist, Mark Darling, tried to explain to his all-too 'creative and imaginative' wife and her superstitious friends, nothing was gained by supplementing ignorance with 'fanciful explanations'. Until 'hard evidence' was available, it was best to remain sceptical.[84] Confronted with puzzling experiences, Mark, like Jill Forrest, invoked the principle of doubt which lay at the origins of modern empirical scientific practice: the secrets of nature could only be unravelled one at a time, and in the meantime it was perfectly legitimate neither to believe nor to deny every sailor's tale of exotic monsters.[85]

Among atheists, the practice of science has sometimes appeared to provide an unproblematic basis for social and individual perfectibility.[86] But scientific advances – bioengineering, artificial intelligence, the discovery of human-like consciousness in other animals – raise as many existential questions as they resolve, and atheists could be as puzzled as anyone else about life's larger questions. In so far as MO's unbelievers looked to science to resolve life's larger existential questions they were destined to be disappointed. Robert Crane no doubt spoke for many when he complained of the inability of scientists to

> explain the universe in terms that are comprehensible to the vast majority of human beings ... there is no point in trying to understand it ... When I was a child I used to look up at the sky and try to imagine where it went to. Eighty years later I have long ago given up such fruitless puzzling. We know no more about it than we know about time.[87]

The night-time anxiety attacks suffered by Adrian Fraser, the computer programmer, could be seen as an extreme manifestation of his openness to such 'fruitless puzzling'. With characteristic intellectual panache, he interpreted a childhood memory of inconsolable distress over a dropped ice cream as a dawning realization of the concept of infinity, a concept that still made him nauseous: 'A replacement didn't help – I had suddenly realised that I would *always* have had *one less* than I could have had. Infinity minus one. That was what really upset me.' For a time, as a militantly atheist teenager he had been brashly confident that 'science would set us free from the dark ages of superstition and the supernatural'. But as he found out more about contemporary science – especially the fact that the generally accepted model of the universe predicted two-thirds more matter than could be detected – his optimism began to fade: 'Fields such as particle physics and chaos theory seemed to generate infinite quantities of woolly blather, of little human relevance or value. My impression is of people theorising with little more to go on than they might have had a thousand years ago.' Despite this, however, he still accepted that 'the rational, scientific model of the universe [is] the best we have to go on, I just no longer believe that it is anywhere near being complete'.[88] Harry Bolton, the retired decorator whose atheism had been reinforced by the post-mortem silence of his lost wartime love, expressed the same qualified scientific world view: 'whether science can give us all the answers to understanding the universe, I know not, but we have nothing more.'[89] Margaret Thompson, conceding that 'although we will go on understanding more and more as our techniques of exploration become ever more sophisticated we will never understand everything', added, tolerantly, 'If some people want to call this ever-receding last bit "God" or the equivalent, this doesn't worry me'.[90]

As an Anglo-Catholic teenager in the 1930s, Robert Crane had struggled, and finally failed, to convince himself of the existence of God. Fifty years later he fulminated against 'the illogicality of the godbotherers ... [who] like the White Queen ... believed as many as six impossible things before breakfast'.[91] Having retired early from his managerial post in the NHS, tired of being 'buggered about' by higher authority, he was happy to devote himself to his editorship of a cycling magazine. In 1990, alongside the Green Party, Greenpeace, Friends of the Earth and the Campaign for Nuclear Disarmament, he was also a member of the British Humanist Association.[92] His own beliefs, however, were a good deal less disenchanted than his secularist rhetoric might suggest. Fakery and fraudulence notwithstanding, Robert was inclined to accept the mysterious reality of many paranormal phenomena – telepathy, ghostly apparitions, poltergeists, premonitions, clairvoyance, spiritual healing. 'I suspect that the answer to all this', he wrote, 'may lie in what Bernard Shaw called the life force – some sort of enveloping electrical or magnetic atmosphere that some people with unusual minds can "tap into."' For Shaw, the notion of the life force had offered an escape from the bleak purposelessness of Darwinian evolution. God, the creator, did not exist, but evolution itself was a creative force propelling humanity towards the emergence of godlike powers.[93] Robert Crane's use of the term was very much more tentative and, despite the attribution to Shaw, he appears to have been deaf to the central message of creative evolution: 'I see no reason', he wrote, 'to believe that there is any purpose to life on this planet.'[94] But perhaps the very boldness of this statement betrays a continuing desire to find some 'reason to believe'? Behind the brusque humanist rejection was a man in search of meaning, as is suggested by his membership of the Rainer Foundation, established to celebrate the mystical poetry of Rilke. Guardian angels were so much sentimental 'guff', he told MO, but, one might speculate, Rilke's angels, much beloved in late 20th-century New Age circles, provided Robert Crane with a more acceptable, poetic, route to the ineffable.[95]

At first sight the mass observers' attitudes towards the supernatural appear closely aligned with the ways in which they understood the relationship between science and religion. Almost everyone accepted that modern science had done much to demystify the world, but while believers sought to reconcile scientific advance with abiding spiritual truths, non-believers looked to science to refute and dispel what they took to be the irrational superstition underpinning religious belief. On closer examination, however, a more complex picture emerges. Some believers were as hostile to what they took to be 'superstition' as were the non-believers. A sense of one's own distinction as a rational person raised above the folly and ignorance of the multitude was by no means confined to those who rejected any notion of the supernatural. Many believers, uncomfortably aware that science threatened to destabilize some of their core beliefs, chose to put reason to one side and to sustain these beliefs instead on the basis of intuition. But some of the unbelievers were equally conflicted, disappointed that science could offer no answers to life's deeper mysteries. Some of the Christians toyed with the possibility that psychic research conducted on scientific lines would bridge the gap between science and the supernatural, but they were uneasy about attempting to combine the psychic with the spiritual. A few, like Fiona Evans, believed that the gap could be abolished altogether by the spiritualization of science itself. But it was Stella Marshal's puzzlement which probably came closest to representing the sentiments of most of the more thoughtful mass observers, whether religious, spiritual seekers or unbelievers. Chapter 5, which examines how the mass observers responded to apparently paranormal events, reveals a similar mix of dogmatic rationalism, intuitive credulity and open-minded intellectual curiosity.

5

Uses of the paranormal

I

For Richard Dawkins, the high priest of the New Atheism, the prevalence of paranormal beliefs in modern society is a scandal. Much of the blame, he thinks, belongs to the entertainment industry, that 'misbegotten child of the sense of wonder'. Feeding the populace on an impoverished diet of bad science fiction, pseudoscience and 'Tolkeinian faked-up myth', the media systematically purveys 'an anti-rational view of the world which, by virtue of its recurrent persistence, is insidious'.[1] On this, if nothing else, Derek Torrens, a Methodist computer programmer, agreed with Dawkins. He was dismayed by the media's 'active encouragement … to belief in the supernatural':

> Throughout life one is bombarded on all sides by evidence of the supernatural in factual programmes on television and articles in newspapers and magazines and in movies, books, plays and all forms of entertainment, whether high, middle or low brow.[2]

There is clearly some truth in this. The popular appetite for the supernatural is fed relentlessly by the entertainment industry, from the daily diet of newspaper horoscopes to TV drama with a supernatural edge. Responses to the 1996 Mass Observation (MO) directive, which included an explicit question about media coverage, left no doubt about the influence of such material. The X-Files, showing twice a week on television at the time, was a particular favourite: 'Although a lot of the episodes are just too silly to be believable', wrote a 'fairly sceptical' young woman working in music publishing, 'some do make you think "I wonder if …"'.[3]

As we have seen the grief of bereavement provided a rich terrain for the cultivation of belief in the paranormal, and such beliefs, and the experiences they facilitated, played an important role in many individual lives. Among the elderly Christian women interviewed by Gillian Bennett, everyday conversation and exchange of experience served to keep alive traditions of belief in extrasensory perception, telepathy, premonitions and precognition: being 'a little bit psychic' was part and parcel of their intuitive and family-centred belief system.[4] The cleaning woman, Gwen Halliday, clearly conformed to this pattern, associating the love and empathy she lavished on her large family with a 'sixth sense' she had witnessed in the farm animals she had worked with as a young woman: 'All my life I seem to know what other people are thinking … maybe I'm more animal than human.'[5] A similar overlap between ideas of a specifically female capacity for empathy, family responsibility and what many referred to as 'psychic sensitivity' is apparent among some other mass observers, but for them such psychic abilities were seen more as a curse than a gift. Thus Barbara Dilnot, a Christian, thought she had inherited an ability to see into the future from her mother, despite the fact that her mother, believing this ability to be evil, had done her best to suppress it. As a young nurse, Barbara found herself knowing things that would happen on the ward in advance. It was a 'gift' that she hated and she was thankful when it disappeared during her twenties. From childhood, however, her daughter had 'known things' and, now in her late twenties, was still liable, in midst of normal life, to be suddenly taken by a daydream which revealed 'what is happening to a friend or relative'.[6] Clare Harman, a middle-aged Anglican, believed in the supernatural because 'I have to. I have second sight'. It was a skill that came unbidden and which she had never tried to cultivate. 'I hate it, I won't deliberately use it and tell no-one what I know through it.' Her maternal grandmother, her mother and her sister shared the same distressing ability.[7] Laetitia Jevons, a magistrate, was confused and troubled by dreams in which she foresaw the future, an ability which, she suspected, came from 'the other side'. As an orphaned child she had been smacked for bothering her adoptive parents with stories of her prefigurative dreams. These dreams left her feeling that she had 'no control over my life'. Did they mean that free will was an illusion? That what she or other people had not yet decided to do was in fact preordained? As a regular churchgoer she asked the vicar for advice, but he appears to have had the same problem.[8] Rose Evans, a successful civil service executive, had no time for religion, disembodied spirits or any of the other manifestations of the supernatural listed by the MO directive, with one exception: 'the women of [my] family have the great misfortune to dream events that are going to happen and to know when one of the others is in distress. … It is a faculty I could well do without.' Much of what she foresaw was trivial, but her sense that her daughter was near death in childbirth turned out to be accurate. While she herself could 'offer no explanation' for these dreams, her complaint that 'often one is left after a terrible nightmare worrying about problems that never arise' suggests that what she had inherited was not so much an ability to foresee the future as a tendency to fear the worst.[9] Gillian Bennett's Christians seem to have been more comfortable with their psychic gifts than these mass observers, but perhaps what underpinned their common capacity to foresee the future, whether understood as 'gift' or as 'curse', was a level of concern and anxiety rooted in a specifically female engagement with, and sense of responsibility for, the well-being of the family.[10]

And not only the family. Among MO's Christians, belief in the paranormal catered to profound currents of anxiety. Of the fifty-eight Christian respondents to the 1996 directive who expressed a clear opinion, forty-one subscribed to paranormal and occult beliefs, and a further seven had an open mind on such issues. A few of them cited paranormal phenomena as evidence of the existence of a benign spirit world, but the most common Christian response to the paranormal was revulsion, fear and horror. Again and again the Christian mass observers wrote explicitly about the importance of their faith in forbidding them to 'delve into', 'dabble in' or 'meddle with' such paranormal phenomena. These people had no doubt about the existence of the spirit world, but they believed it to be evil. Julia Kirby, a cradle Catholic who worked as a tourist information officer, deplored 'the fashion for the occult' in TV entertainment. 'People really don't know what they are summoning up,' she wrote, 'I reach for my crucifix (yes really). I think the devil himself is capable of popping out of the screen.'[11] Simon Hadley, a primary school teacher active in his parish church, was more relaxed about fictional ghosts – 'so long as they don't encourage people to dabble in the occult'. But he was indignant about MO's directive on the supernatural: 'It is silly, dangerous and irresponsible to encourage people to think and write about the "supernatural" … Spiritual activity can be worship and prayer, in which case the atmosphere will be peaceful and calming, but it can also be spiritualist activities where people try deliberately to get in touch with evil forces.'[12] Lilly Jevons the churchgoing magistrate, who was much impressed by a medium's knowledge of her parents' lives, reminded herself that 'the Bible tells us we should keep away from mediums as they are not talking about our dead friends but to evil spirits who are pretending to be these people.'[13] 'It says in the Bible', reported another churchgoing Anglican, 'not to try and contact the spirits of the dead because there are evil spirits the same as good ones.'[14]

Such attitudes were not confined to the laity. Sally Thompson, the shopkeeper who combined Christian worship with spiritualism, earned the wrath of her Anglican vicar: 'You are playing with the devil and all things evil.'[15] That the church took seriously the presence of evil spirits was apparent in the practice of exorcism, described by several grateful recipients of the service. Ethyl Smyth, a widow in her seventies writing in 2013, believed herself afflicted with a poltergeist in her rural cottage:

> I called my vicar and asked for the cottage to be exorcised. She spent an hour with me and she said she would contact the Bishop. ... The next visit was the vicar, a trainee and a cannon who came and we had four pages of pray [sic]. She sprinkled salted water in all 6 rooms and the hall. She was her [sic] an hour. We all had Holy Communion. I gave a donation. There has been peace since she came.[16]

While these rituals may have been a kindly show put on to help a confused old lady, another mass observer reported that her local vicar had no doubt about the reality of the poltergeist he attempted to exorcise from her daughter's house. When his attempts failed, he accepted that 'if things went on it might be helpful to call in a medium ...though he preferred the church's method of dealing with it'. Whether the medium had more success we are not told.[17] Pauline Clark, an elderly Baptist, felt very uneasy in her bungalow, which had previously been occupied by a spiritualist who held séances there: 'I think something supernatural happened here many years ago ... I think such things are possible, but forbidden in Scripture,' she wrote, neatly summing up the attitude of so many Christians. She called in the minister, whose prayers proved effective, exorcising the atmosphere of evil and leaving the house 'tranquil and peaceful'.[18] And even Brian Gregory, the clergyman who so deplored popular superstition, had himself conducted exorcisms on two occasions – one of them involving devil worship and the apparent involvement of a politician whose name was a household word. While he was clear in his own mind that he was dealing with psychological, not actual, demons, his readiness to deploy the rituals of exorcism can have done little to advance the cause of rational religion among his parishioners. As one otherwise sceptical working-class woman in Coventry observed, 'the church obviously believes in evil spirits as they take part in exorcisms so I suppose we shouldn't discount them entirely.'[19] Traditions of magic, it seems, were alive and well within the late 20th-century Christian churches. Hell might have left the stage, but Satan still lurked dangerously in the wings.

II

Belief in the paranormal could serve to express emotions of grief, anxiety and fear of evil. But other, more positive, feelings were also at work in the ways in which the mass observers made use of the paranormal. Despite their fears, many of the Christians had at some stage in their lives attended a séance, visited a clairvoyant or played with a Ouija board. Dabbling with supernatural forces might be dangerous, but it could also be fun. The 1996 directive asked believers in the supernatural to 'describe how this is important to your outlook on life? How does it affect your behaviour?' Many responded that their belief in, and in some cases their experience of, supernatural phenomena was unimportant and had little effect on their lives. Which brings us back, perhaps to entertainment. For many people, engagement with the supernatural was a form of play, and play, they felt, could not be seen as 'important'. But play can have a serious purpose.[20] Why, in a society dominated by scientific thinking and instrumental rationality, did so many intelligent, thoughtful and often well-informed people take pleasure in notions so at odds with the reigning orthodoxy? Again and again the mass observers cite Hamlet's rebuke to his sceptical friend: 'There are more things in heaven and earth, Horatio, than are dreamt of in your philosophy.'

The common factor underpinning the plethora of supernatural beliefs revealed by responses to the 1996 directive was a positive desire for mystery. 'We have very fertile imaginations and easily deceive ourselves,' wrote a male civil servant: 'As the world gets more technological and intimidatingly impersonal people are more inclined to dwell on the supernatural.'[21] The mass observers wanted things to wonder at, things to feed the imagination and take them into liminal, uncanny spaces. They enjoyed the excitement of glimpsing a world untamed by reason, science, technology, a world beyond the dull compulsions of everyday routine. Tales of the supernatural – believed, half-believed, entertained with an ironic shrug of the shoulders – provided a site of resistance to the disenchantment of the world.[22] In exercising their capacity for enchantment, the mass observers were not merely relaying ancient traditions of belief, revealing a childish gullibility or parroting messages from the mass media. They were also expressing a healthy resistance to the instrumental rationality of modern society. Playing with the paranormal can be good for the soul.

'Opiate for the masses,' expostulated Mathew Forrester, an elderly retired insurance executive, 'ridiculous to anyone of normal intelligence, but obviously pander[ing] to a sense of getting away from boring reality ... a need for a bit of fun in their drab lives'.[23] Others, confessing their own fascination with the supernatural, were rather less condescending: 'I can't explain why I like reading about the supernatural,' wrote one middle-aged woman, 'I think it is because it is something outside of everyday life, it is imagination.'[24] Adrian Fraser, the computer programmer whose horror at the idea of death erupted in night-time anxiety attacks, got over his childish fear of ghosts in puberty. But he continued to seek out ghost stories. 'I found these as fascinating as they were scary, and although they always led to a fresh bout of disrupted nights, the fascination remained ... I don't believe in ghosts, but I still fear them a little.'[25] Discussing his pleasure in reading ghost stories, a middle-aged atheist suggested that they 'give satisfying form to the unanswerable; to thoughts and feelings, even experiences, which are common to all imaginative people, but which cannot be rendered down scientifically into "nothing but" something else'. The best work in this genre (he cited Walter de la Mare, M. R. James and Algernon Blackwood) 'draws upon the unconscious mind, in the manner of poetry, offering an antidote to daily living in an increasingly mechanistic and predictable society'.[26] Marion Phillips, the Quaker, thought that 'the word "supernatural" is really a way of saying that there are things about which we still know very little, that we all love a good story and need more stimulus than the daily round offers'.[27] She drew a clear line between religious awe and what she called 'the spectral', which provided her with 'an element of adventure in a commonplace life':

> I used to believe in the supernatural and be very frightened by it, whilst being fascinated by and unable to resist creepy stories ... [The spectral] is very atmospheric, almost stagey. It likes the dark, and it likes fringe, almost subliminal suggestions; an almost inaudible rustle, a movement on your peripheral vision, 'what was that'. ... I have lived in very humdrum circumstances myself and often had to top up my zest for living by reading about 'Black Shuck', the 'Loch Ness Monster', 'Flying Saucers' or Andean 'Lost Cities' ... we all love a good story and need more stimulus than the daily round offers. [28]

'Maybe I like being frightened,' wrote a middle-aged housewife;[29] and Jill Forrest, who had no doubt about the power of science to account for apparently paranormal phenomena, nevertheless felt that 'the "supernormal" will always be an area of interest because ... human beings are curious animals. Things which have no obvious explanation are intriguing, exciting and maybe frightening, but in the way of a rollercoaster, mixed with excitement'.[30] This mixture of fear and excitement is richly illustrated by the mass observers' stories of encounters with the paranormal.

Ghosts

Ghosts, apart from those associated with bereavement, belonged largely to the ludic. More than a fifth of the respondents (sixty-one people) thought they had seen, heard, smelt or otherwise felt the presence of the ghost of someone with whom they had no previous acquaintance. Most of these ghosts appeared in houses, but others cropped up at sites associated with traumatic death – a murder, a gallows, a plague pit, road accidents and battlefields, or, in one case, a mountain top. Edward Howes, an atheist, had no belief in the supernatural, but he could not account for the apparition of an elderly couple (she in high heels, he in suit, collar and tie) sitting on a rock on the top of Great Gable. Walking in the Lake District with a group of friends, all young, fit and well equipped, he could not understand how the couple had got there or how they could possibly get back from the mountain before nightfall.[31]

In the great majority of cases these encounters had no lasting consequences. What they provided was a frisson of fear – more or less pleasurable – and, for those so inclined, confirmation of the existence of a something beyond the brute materiality of the everyday world. Felicity Davidson, fascinated by the supernatural since her teenage years, confessed a reluctant scepticism, disappointed that she had never personally encountered any incontrovertibly paranormal phenomenon. 'With my lifelong interest', she remarked, 'I'd hope any sensible ghost would chose me as a likely person to appear to, but no luck so far.'[32] When, twenty years later, no ghost had deigned to appear, she acknowledged that 'I don't know if I ever believed in such things'.[33] But she had gained much pleasure over many years by playing with the idea.

Among lorry drivers, stories of ghostly apparitions were a staple diet of transport café conversation helping to cement group identity among men whose work, most of the time, was stressful, boring and lonely. Bob Rust's repertoire of travellers' tales included ghost lorries appearing out of the mist at the site of ancient crashes, old men sitting on walls to warn drivers of accident black spots and a limping soldier in a lonely lay-by near Edgehill, the site of a famous civil war battlefield.[34] Acknowledging that there was a curious illogic in believing in ghosts while, as an atheist, rejecting any notion of the afterlife, he advanced his own theory that 'the electrical energy which occurs in one's brain and makes the difference between being alive and dead is somehow captured in the surroundings at the point of sudden, violent death'.[35] Other respondents, reaching for similarly materialist explanations, suggested that the shock of traumatic death was somehow recorded in the fabric of the buildings where it occurred, that they were 'a kind of "negative" on a light wave, only seen under the right conditions'[36] or that they were 'made up of particles which travel faster than the speed of light [and] can therefore travel through time'.[37] For most, however, the stranger ghost was an unquiet spirit, not yet at rest.

Poltergeists

A few people thought they had experienced poltergeist activity – objects thrown around the room, or moved mysteriously from one place to another – and many more believed that it occurred. Despite understanding the essentially ludic nature of her own interest in the supernatural, Marion Phillips believed the poltergeist phenomenon to be real and was inclined to accept the commonly advanced explanation that it was a product of electricity generated by disturbed adolescents.[38] Rose Worley, mixing poltergeist with friendly ghost, told a long story about some woolly hats lost and mysteriously found, which (according to a clairvoyant she consulted) turned out to be the work of a friend who had died fifteen years earlier.[39] Others saw poltergeists as 'mischievous but not malevolent'.[40] For one office worker the fact that 'papers and documents mysteriously disappear from desks only to reappear some time later' was clearly evidence of a poltergeist at work.[41] One young woman, who kept an open mind about the supernatural, nevertheless believed that it was a poltergeist – affectionately known as 'Polly' – who was responsible for moving objects about in the family house; and another family blamed 'Phred' for the unaccountable movement of things.[42] Being atheistic rationalists my wife and I cannot blame a poltergeist for these irritating misplacements, but instead of blaming each other we invoke an unnamed 'Somebody'.

Ouija Boards

Ouija boards provided a common source of paranormal entertainment, and several of the mass observers had played with them in their youth. Some were unconvinced, others terrified. Among the latter were Paula Harrison (later to become a religious education teacher) and her sister, who, responding to a schoolgirl craze for Ouija boards, made one of their own and attempted to contact a dead ancestor. 'To our horror the glass began to move and because we knew that neither of us were responsible, we gave up there and then.' But, they believed, they had meddled with evil, and they were suitably terrified when the ghost of the ancestor subsequently turned up in their bedroom: 'After that, doors opened inexplicably, objects moved, things disappeared and reappeared and, worst of all, there was the sound of footsteps on the stairs. The footsteps were the worst because they followed us up the stairs, but if we stopped the footsteps didn't.' Eventually the girls managed to convince themselves that it was all in their imagination, until, years later, their mother confessed that she had heard the footsteps too, and seen the ghost, but had not told them at the time in order not to frighten them.[43]

Peter Burnham, an atheist computer consultant, gave a detailed account of a Ouija board session organized by a fellow student during his student days:

> There was a lot of giggling to begin with and nothing much happened. It was a 70s block of ex-council flats. Nothing out of the ordinary. There were about ten of us crammed into the tiny kitchen. We had pieces of cards with the letters on and a cheap red wine glass bought especially for the occasion. Gradually the glass began to move in circles on the table and we quietened down.[44]

For a time nothing was spelled out 'and we were starting to get a bit bored'. Then a soldier who had died in the Falklands came through. When someone asked if he missed his children, 'the glass rushed to the No card, someone else commented "You bastard", and the glass fell over!' When the session resumed the glass spelled out 'an unusual male name', the words 'car' and 'death' and a year in the 1950s. One of the students went pale and left the room: the glass (he later explained) was accurately describing his elder brother's death.

> After that we were very subdued. In fact, several people cried off and left just four of us. We very quickly got back the guy who died in the Falklands. When asked if there was a message he replied positively and then started spelling out my name! I moved my finger off the glass very quickly, I can tell you. There was never a proper message from him. We established, through asking questions, that he'd known my dad many years ago and knew me as a baby ... A lot of what appeared like gobbledygook came next – a couple of digits different to my dad's old [army] service number, as I found out later.[45]

Robert Crane, a humanist with a penchant for the paranormal, related a session in which the glass appeared to react violently to an adulterous affair although none of those concerned were actually present. 'I know that this incident proves nothing', he concluded, 'but it does make yer think, don' it?'[46]

Angels

Angels might be thought to belong to the religious imagination. But the detailed accounts of angelic visitations offered by two of the respondents have more in common with stories of the paranormal than with religious experience. In both cases the conviction that something supernatural actually occurred is qualified by an ironic aside, leaving open the possibility that what is being told is an elaborate exercise in ludic make-believe.

One stormy day in February 1989, Jenny Brown, aspiring writer and liberal Catholic, was fetching her daughter from school, when the wind caught them:

> I held my daughter tightly with one hand and clutched any handholds I could with the other: lamp posts, walls, fences. We got to a point when there was nothing to hold onto … To turn round would have been like fighting against a tidal wave. … I couldn't breathe, my legs were being lifted up from under me. 1 felt convinced that we were going to be dashed to pieces. I was getting to an almost calm feeling that death was inevitable. There was no one anywhere near us. Then suddenly there he was: a young man in a leather jacket appeared from nowhere. 'Let me help you.' he said calmly and authoritatively. Placing firm reassuring arms around us, he led us over the main road and saw us round the corner where it was more sheltered. 'You'll be all right now.' I didn't have a chance to thank him. He was gone as suddenly as he had appeared.[47]

Writing of the supernatural in general, Jenny Brown argued that 'even if 90 per cent of people's accounts are exaggerated wishful thinking – a desire to spice up the ordinary events of life – there are probably 10 per cent which can't be accounted for'. One might suppose that 'spicing up the ordinary events of life' was a very good description of her story of an angelic rescuer. Even while placing the event among the 10 per cent of genuinely supernatural occurrences she could not resist a hint of the ludic: 'I am convinced that it was an angel – a guardian angel in a leather jacket!'[48] Is it fanciful to see leather jacket – and its exclamation mark – as a knowing wink to her readers, inviting us to understand her experience as a fortunate but perfectly natural event wilfully misinterpreted as an angelic visitation?

Paula Harrison, the religious education teacher whose local church had been hijacked by a happy-clappy vicar, was inclined to dismiss guardian angels as 'a relic of some long-forgotten religious belief'. Yet she believed that on one occasion she had met a messenger from God, an angel fully embodied (again) as a young man, this one with 'long blond hair, blue eyes, wearing denim jeans, a white T-shirt and denim jacket and … carrying a small blue rucksack'. In the early 1970s, having completed her teacher training, she applied for a job in a small Midlands town. On her way to the interview, wandering round the bus station with no idea which bus to catch, the young man appeared as if from nowhere and told her, 'This is the bus you want.' She got on, checked with the driver and sat down. The young man followed, but she was puzzled that as he walked past her seat there was no reflection in the glass panel behind the driver which acted like a mirror. When she turned her head to follow his progress down the aisle, he was nowhere to be seen. Assuming he must be lying down on the back seat, she got up to look but there was no one there. 'Being on the way to an interview', she continued, 'I had more pressing concerns than vanishing men, so I returned to my seat and read my notes.' Not knowing where to get off the bus she had asked the driver to tell her. He forgot, and she would have missed her interview had the young man not reappeared, touched her on the shoulder and said, 'This is where you get off.' When she turned to say thank you he had, again, vanished. She was offered the job but turned it down – 'that was in the days', she wrote in 1996, 'when you could do that sort of thing and be sure of finding something else.' While she had 'absolutely no explanation for what happened', she had no doubt that the visitation had occurred and that it must have had some purpose, though what that was she could not imagine. 'Why should God or anyone be concerned about me and not about thousands of others? Perhaps other people have experiences but dismiss them or don't even notice.' But again there was an element of playfulness in her account, which had clearly been polished in multiple tellings. For MO she prefaced her story with the remark that 'I often tell people jokingly that I once met an angel, but perhaps I did'.[49] Or perhaps not.

III

More or less playfully, the mass observers used paranormal beliefs to assuage their desire for mystery, to give themselves something to wonder at. But for some of them the play extended into a more considered challenge to dominant secular modes of thought. Among people of little social status, belief in the supernatural – often maintained despite fear of ridicule by conventional educated opinion – could operate as an assertion of their right to make their own meanings in a world that afforded them little respect.[50] 'One thing is for sure', wrote a shop assistant: 'We each have a freedom of thought – nobody can deny us the right of our own beliefs [and] these can change with our own experiences through life.'[51] A similar assertion of independence energizes the testimony of Vera Roper, a working-class woman who left school at sixteen and had stopped believing in God aged twelve when, despite her prayers, her stepfather died on the operating table. In the 1960s she went through two marriages, the second one as a battered wife, from which she escaped only when her husband was jailed for theft, after which social security benefits and a part-time job enabled her and the children to start a new life. Eventually she set up home with a new partner, and in 1987 when she started writing for MO, she was working as a waitress. Her sense of class identity was strong – middle-class professionals were overvalued: 'People say that you need the managers and the clever people but I do not agree. Among any group of working-class people there is someone who is more than capable of learning to manage and because they are working class they will do a better job.' Middle-class people also lacked the domestic virtues of the respectable working class: 'I have been in homes of teachers etc. and they are nothing short of disgusting.'

While her childhood belief in the Christian God never returned, 'over the years I became convinced that there is something else other than birth and death'. In her late twenties her curiosity in matters supernatural was triggered by a Sunday newspaper serialization of Eric Von Däniken's *Chariots of the Gods* (1971), which used evidence from ancient structures and artworks to argue that the Earth had been visited by alien astronauts. Ezekiel's winged creatures with wheels, which during the Second World War had been seen by at least one mass observer as revealing biblical foreknowledge of aerial warfare,[52] now bore witness to the presence of spacemen at the dawn of civilization. Thus stimulated, her imagination roamed – with the help of wider reading, TV documentaries and a psychic friend – to encompass ghosts (and, after having decided they existed, she saw one); spiritualism (she had not visited a medium, but was convinced by her psychic friend's account); life after death ascending through successive plains towards perfection (she read an account by a medium who had been given details from the other side by a deceased Catholic priest); and reincarnation (bolstered by her own sense of affinity with a variety of past eras, and proved beyond doubt by a BBC documentary). In all this she distinguished herself from religious 'bigots' or the merely foolish: 'I look at things in a sensible way' without believing 'all the rubbish I read'. She prided herself on having 'read the facts and made up my mind'. It would have been easier, she added, 'to say I don't believe, that takes no effort, no thinking, and I like to think'. Vera was intensely class conscious and, whatever ontological anxieties it helped to assuage, her idiosyncratic pursuit of 'something else other than birth and death' clearly served to reinforce her self-respect in face of the 'managers and the clever people', and the domestically incompetent teachers she so resented.[53]

A similarly imaginative defiance informed the testimony of Bruce Carpenter, a middle-aged Methodist miner's son, who had worked as a nurse. What Jesus meant by 'in my house there are many mansions', he explained, was that when we died we were transported (in UFOs) to other planets 'for our souls to be "encased" in other bodies in another universe'. Presumably aware that his readers at MO might find these views strange, he added: 'Science and the people who have science jobs think they know it all. If a thing does not tie in with known laws it can't be. They don't know it all. Many times they are wrong.'[54] Clarice Roper, a young mother home-educating her children half a mile from the nearest road in a remote Scottish island, found it reassuring 'to see things in the world that cannot be explained'. Science seemed to her to be inseparable from masculine arrogance and she was 'comforted to know that men do not know everything about the world and how the world works'.[55]

This hostility to science was unusual. While the paranormal provided many of the mass observers with avenues for independent thinking, few wanted to distance themselves completely from the most prestigious source of knowledge in the modern world. If Clarice stood at one end of the spectrum, Fiona Evans and the scientists she encountered in the Medical and Scientific Network stood at the other. Ranged between these two extremes, many other mass observers embellished their supernatural beliefs with scientific speculation. The convinced atheists, like the Christian rationalists, might be secure enough in their beliefs to dismiss talk of the paranormal as so much 'irrational superstition', but for a very broad spectrum of people between these two extremes engagement with what they took to be scientific thinking served not to undermine but to fortify their belief in the reality of supernatural forces.

Harry Lewis, a charity executive, had 'no patience with the language of mysticism' and denied any 'need for supernatural explanations'. But he was fascinated by the idea of telepathy and was convinced that 'our current western definition of what is within "nature" as opposed to what is "super"-natural is critically limited and narrow-minded'. He was particularly impressed with Rupert Sheldrake's notion of 'morphic resonance', a theory condemned by most biologists as feeding a popular appetite for pseudoscientific adventures in the supernatural.[56] Reading such work 'in the spirit of intellectual scepticism and rebellion that I have cultivated about taking anyone's word for anything', Lewis enjoyed his freedom to speculate (if not to believe), unrestrained by the 'narrow-minded' protocols of conventional science.[57] A middle-aged woman working as a technician had no time for religion or the supernatural, but she did not entirely rule out the possibility that ghosts 'might just be a glimpse of a dimension that we are normally blind to in which the soul can time travel'. Not that she believed in souls or in life after death, but 'if someone discovered a different level of existence that the mind could move to I would not think it impossible. … If this were so I do not think a God would be involved, it would just be an extension of the laws of physics, only different'.[58]

Human curiosity being what it is, apparently supernatural events were bound to provoke imaginative speculation beyond the frontiers of experimental method. But there is nothing unscientific about a readiness to speculate, and there was no necessary conflict between such speculation and the maintenance of a scientific outlook. 'It is not that I lack imagination', wrote Jill Forrest, explaining her rejection of supernatural explanations, 'but that I can imagine a million reasonable explanations [for paranormal phenomena] to every strange spooky one.'[59] Unperceived electromagnetic fields or unheard low-frequency sounds might be responsible for some phenomena commonly perceived as paranormal.[60] Adrian Fraser, the computer programmer, had studied psychology as an undergraduate, and he was well aware of the ways in which 'the creative ability of the unconscious mind' might account for many apparently supernatural phenomena.[61] Perceptions of the presence of dead loved ones clearly owe a great deal to the psychology of grief and mourning.[62] Hallucinations induced by grief, drugs or wishful thinking were commonly cited as an explanation of ghostly appearances or out-of-body experiences. The work of neurologists like Oliver Sacks has enormously extended our understanding of the power of the brain to play tricks – and thus of the unreliability of conscious perception as a guide to what is actually there.[63] As Coleridge had put it when asked if he believed in ghosts: 'No, Madam; I have seen too many myself.'[64] Much that was cited as evidence of the paranormal rested on the tendency of the human brain to perceive order in randomness, meaning in coincidence, faces in inkblots.[65] The trick of light; the unexpected shadow on the wall; the creaking of old buildings; the voice in the head; the more-than-usually vivid dream; the half-waking hallucination – to the believer all these phenomena bore witness to the paranormal. 'Seeing is believing,' said MO's ghost believers over and over again, upholding a positivist common sense in defiance of a century of psychological and neuroscientific research. More to the point is the observation of the poet Andrew McNeillie that 'some things must be believed to be seen'.[66]

The frontier between scientific and pseudoscientific speculation is unmarked, and it would be a bold person who could confidently predict which speculations are without foundation and which might eventually be vindicated by new scientific discoveries about the nature of the world. Karen Brunding had too much experience of premonitions to discount them, but she offered her own, potentially scientific, explanation: they 'must be due to the knotted nature of time which gets kinks which cause two points to touch and pass information across'.[67] John Davies kept a dream diary in an attempt to authenticate a similar explanation for premonitions expounded in J. W. Dunne's book, *An Experiment with Time*, which his father had given him as a child.[68] Eric Gurney, the retired civil servant who was 'going to damn well use' his powers of reason, was convinced that poltergeists existed, but felt that there must be some scientific explanation – they were 'far too earthy to be spiritual'.[69] Probably, suggested Mathew Forrester, an ex-Methodist agnostic who dismissed the paranormal as 'opiate for the masses', such activity was the product of some 'strange physical force ... outside our current scientific knowledge'.[70]

The history of modern science is replete with the discovery of strange physical forces, and the extreme strangeness of the behaviour of matter as theorized by 20th-century physics could be used to legitimate more or less any speculation. Curiosity about phenomena apparently inexplicable within existing paradigms has played an important role in the progress of science. Without a taste for the anomalous, it is all too easy not to notice that which cannot be explained by currently accepted ideas. Adrian Fraser subscribed to *The Fortean Times*, a journal founded in 1973 to report what the American autodidact, Charles Fort, had described (in 1919) as 'damned facts' – observations normally dismissed as lies or hallucinations because they appeared to be incompatible with established scientific ideas. Fraser knew that Fort was 'often attacked for relying on anecdotal, self-reported evidence', a criticism, he could not resist remarking, which was frequently directed, by 'certain severe and orthodox sociologists', at MO itself. But just as MO's scattergun probes into British culture have served to alert historians and social researchers to ambiguities and complexities in popular attitudes inaccessible to more orthodox research techniques, so too the 'kind of anomalous, subjective material' sought out by Charles Fort was 'well worth recording. At worst, it's folklore. At best, you may trace the first signs of something new which could turn the whole world upside down'. And that, for Adrian Fraser, was the attraction: 'the vertiginous fascination of the possibility that *everything I know is wrong!*'[71]

The delight with which Fraser contemplated the abyss was not necessarily incompatible with a scientific approach, but it does suggest that his engagement with the anomalous may have been driven as much by a positive desire for mystery as by any search for scientific explanations. If people wanted scientific explanations of apparently paranormal phenomena there were plenty to be found in psychology, neuroscience and other established disciplines. The pleasure many mass observers took in futuristic speculation about forces as yet undiscovered by modern science cannot be understood simply by the absence of more down-to-earth explanations.

Telepathy provided a particularly fertile site for speculation beyond the frontiers of established science, as it had ever since the term was invented in 1882 by the spiritualist and psychic researcher Frederic Myers. Neatly linking notions of human em-pathy to emergent technologies of communication (tele-phone, tele-graph), Myers's coinage held out the promise of a scientific explanation for the common experience of intra-subjective communication apparently occurring independently of the five known senses.[72] 'I do believe in telepathy,' wrote a Catholic woman, 'If I think a lot about someone they usually telephone';[73] and many others cited the experience of thinking of someone just before they phoned as evidence of telepathy. The other experience most commonly cited was mind-reading between partners or close family members. In the days before the mobile phone, Bob Rust, the lorry driver, always found a hot meal waiting for him at the end of a run because his wife could sense his unpredictable homecomings. And when, on one occasion, he thought about something he had forgotten to ask his wife to do before he left home, she 'heard' his thought at exactly the moment – they subsequently worked out – when he had it.[74] As a teenager Paula Harrison, the religious education teacher, had such a close connection with her sister's thoughts that they found it impossible to play the game of Battleships 'because we always found each other's ships too easily'.[75] These examples are relatively trivial, but telepathy was also invoked to explain remote knowledge of the injury or sickness of loved ones. Fiona Evans felt a sudden sensation of tunnel vision while working in her office at the moment when her partner was involved in a car accident.[76] A middle-aged nurse had felt her sister's abdominal pain in childbirth.[77] As a young man Sam Gately, the city banker, had a serious accident in the middle of the night while on manoeuvres with the Territorial Army. Before he lost consciousness he was convinced that he was dying. At the same moment his mother 'was awoken suddenly by the conviction I was in serious danger or perhaps dead. She was so agitated that she awoke my father. They spent much of the night awake drinking tea until receiving news of me in the morning'.[78] The synchronous knowledge of the death of a loved one, discussed in Chapter 3, was also commonly attributed to telepathy.[79]

The concept of telepathy had been designed to open up a paranormal phenomenon to scientific exploration, and most of those who discussed it thought that, rather than being evidence of the supernatural, it might turn out to be a natural phenomenon which science had not yet understood. As Robert Crane pointed out, 'we are only on the fringes of knowledge of what the human brain can do'.[80] It was in this spirit Mark Darling, the chemist who was so irritated by his wife's 'superstitious' beliefs, nevertheless accepted that he experienced telepathic communication with her. 'There could be a quite rational explanation,' he suggested: 'Since the brain works by electrical signals perhaps it generates radio waves, which we can tune into if we are particularly close to someone.'[81] Edward Farleigh, the retired pensions advisor whose studies for a 'Certificate of Christian Education' had served to undermine his Christian faith, kept his options open. Since 'we know perhaps less than we think about the workings of the mind ... it is just conceivable that some kind of thought-wave transmission could take place in certain favourable circumstances'.[82] 'I firmly believe that the mind is incredibly powerful,' wrote Jill Forrest, a young rationalist working in a bank, 'maybe the explanations ... lie within the grasp of current science, and [telepathy] will pass from the world of the supernatural to the world of science.'[83] If science did eventually unlock the mystery of telepathy it would, wrote Gerald Brewster, a bank manager, provide a powerful tool for 'the super-race which humans will one day become'.[84] Others were more inclined to see telepathy as belonging to the human past than the future – 'an instinct which modern man has ceased to use and exercise on a regular basis'.[85] Elsie Grainger, the care assistant, thought that animals, babies and young children had retained such abilities, but that most adults had 'lost this gift'.[86] Fiona Evans, whose interest in the scientific exploration of the psychic was discussed in Chapter 4, believed that telepathy was 'probably a skill human beings had and used a great deal at some time in history but which has been lost as other forms of communication have developed. I believe we all have the ability to be "telepathic" but that many of us block it out'.[87]

Whatever the merits of such speculations they all neglected the fact, pointed out by several of the sceptics, that more than a century of experimentation had failed to establish that telepathy actually occurred. Among the eighty-three mass observers who commented on telepathy, only thirteen seriously doubted that it occurred, most of them atheists. Many of the experiences commonly attributed to telepathy might be more simply explained, argued the sceptics, by coincidence (and our neglect of all those occasions when we thought of someone and they did *not* phone us); familiar thought patterns among close relations; unconscious non-verbal communication 'betraying and picking up information through body language, tone and tiny changes of expression';[88] or false memories of simultaneity in the aftermath of traumatic events. By neglecting such explanations in favour of forces as yet undiscovered by science, the believers in telepathy, playing on the frontier between science and pseudoscience, kept the door open to the supernatural. The scientific study of the paranormal, as launched by Myers and the Society of Psychical Research in the 1880s, had been rooted in anxiety, stemming from the impact of Darwinism, about the power of science to disenchant the world. Myers hoped that telepathy would provide a more rational explanation of communication from the dead, thus proving the existence of life after death.[89] Using the tools of science, the objective was to shore up rather than undermine belief in the existence of a spiritual realm beyond the material world. A century later the mass observers' belief in the reality of telepathy reflected the same desire to attach the prestige of modern science to the re-enchantment of the world.

For some rationalists the widespread belief in the paranormal was conclusive evidence of the irrationality and ignorance of the masses. But such a blanket dismissal obscures the variety of purposes that belief in the paranormal served for the mass observers, most of whom were neither ignorant nor irrational. Whether or not paranormal phenomena are works of the imagination, they helped many of the mass observers to articulate and to handle profound emotions of grief, anxiety and fear of evil. And other, more positive, feelings were also at work. More or less playfully the mass observers looked to the paranormal to provide an antidote to the dominance of a merely instrumental rationality in modern society. The paranormal gave them space to speculate, and while some of the speculation was conducted in a spirit of hostility towards science (and scientists), for the most part the mass observers tried to find a *modus vivendi* between the delight they took in the mysterious, uncanny and unexplained and their acceptance of scientific enquiry as the most reliable path to positive knowledge. You don't have to believe in the supernatural to enjoy a ghost story, and for some playing with the paranormal was entirely consistent with adherence to a materialist ontology. More commonly the games were played with varying degrees of belief in the reality of paranormal events, often accompanied by a desire to stretch scientific modes of thought to encompass the widespread feeling that there were 'more things in heaven and earth' than conventional science allowed. However illegitimate by the strict protocols of scientific enquiry, playing with the paranormal provided a space in which to cultivate feelings of mystery and of wonder that the everyday routines of modernity too often denied. And, as we will see in Chapter 6, it was wonder that spoke most directly to the sense of meaning, regardless of ontological disagreements about the existence or non-existence of supernatural forces.

6

Moments out of time

I

William James, in his classic account *The Varieties of Religious Experience* (1902), argued that religious *experiences* were real, and that they had transformative effects on the lives of those who experienced them. Religious *belief*, on the other hand – especially as codified and orchestrated by churches and theologians – was a secondary matter, a rationalization, a tidying up, a corralling, disciplining, routinization of primary experiences which arrived unbidden, astonishing, from a country unregulated by reason: the vast new territory of the subconscious being opened up by psychological thinking at the turn of the century. Maybe religious experiences came from God – James thought they probably did – but, if they did, God worked through the subconscious. For the psychologist, the study of religion was the study of sudden, fleeting, but, sometimes, life-changing eruptions of subconscious forces into consciousness. What James set out to investigate was the phenomenology of religious experience, the thing in itself, not the theological accretions which religious leaders wove around it.

James's assumption of the pre-discursive nature of religious experiences is not easy to verify.[1] We only know of such experiences because people report them, and in reporting them they draw on pre-existing ideas about their meaning. Nevertheless the testimony of the mass observers suggests that these 'moments out of time' do have common characteristics, characteristics which transcend the particular frameworks, whether supernaturalist or naturalist, within which they are recounted.

Since the 1960s, the growing interest in a spirituality distinct from its incorporation in particular religions has given new relevance to James's approach to 'religious experience'.[2] James had based his conclusions partly on an exhaustive survey of the writings of religious mystics, and partly on accounts of religious experiences in contemporary America collected by another psychologist, Edwin Starbuck.³ Britain's Starbuck was Alister Hardy, a marine biologist, who began collecting accounts of religious experience in the 1920s. In 1979 he argued, on the basis of an analysis of more than 3,000 such accounts, that 'transcendental experiences' similar to those described by James were widespread.⁴ Between the 1970s and the end of the century, David Hay (another British zoologist by profession) supplemented Hardy's work with a series of surveys and interviews which served to demonstrate, he argued, that 'spiritual awareness is a necessary part of our human make-up, biologically built into us'.⁵ Even atheists, his surveys showed, had religious experiences, although they did not describe them as such.⁶

Hay was emboldened in this claim by responses collected by the British writer and journalist Marghanita Laski from her friends and acquaintances in the early 1960s, almost all of whom – including many with no religious belief – answered affirmatively to the question: 'Do you know a sensation of transcendent ecstasy?'⁷ Laski, herself an avowed atheist, followed William James in seeking what was common in such experiences regardless of the belief systems through which they were interpreted. Her characterization of these experiences echoed James's findings: they were 'joyful, transitory, unexpected, rare, valued, and extraordinary to the point of often seeming as if derived from a praeternatural source'.⁸ Such experiences erupt spontaneously, a bolt from the blue. For a brief moment they stop you in your tracks, suspending the flow of everyday time, replacing 'the mental functions concerned with differentiating and classifying' with overwhelming feelings of awe, wonder and oneness with the cosmos.⁹

II

Such experiences were common among the mass observers, whether understood as glimpses of a spiritual reality beyond earthly existence or as sensations generated by purely material processes in the human brain. Mary Taylor, the ex-Catholic with 'a spirituality which I have adapted to suit myself', found an echo of her own experience of 'a moment to glimpse all in harmony' in the epiphanies described by James Joyce in his *Portrait of the Artist as a Young Man*. 'Perhaps', she wrote, 'all of us have experienced this at least once in our lifetimes.'¹⁰ Gillian Latimer, the rector's ecumenical wife, reported a vision in which she felt radiantly transported to another dimension, bright and clear: 'I think I had a very brief glimpse of the etheric world that is all around us but cannot necessarily be seen.'[11] Responding to Mass Observation's (MO's) directive on the supernatural, Marion Phillips sent some reflections prompted by reading Rudolf Otto's *Idea of the Holy*. University-educated, married with two grown-up children, she had worked as a schoolteacher and was now active in retirement in Oxfam and Greenpeace. A practising Quaker, though having been brought up as an Anglican, she now 'sat loose to dogma' and would 'no longer expect to be able to understand or to make a creedal statement'.[12] Her description of the 'fear of the Lord' echoes one of the defining characteristics of mystical experience in the accounts analysed by William James – paralysis of the will and complete powerlessness:

> It is like fear, but there is no sense of assault and no resistance one can consciously call up – indeed one appears to be incapable of any kind of action at all. It is obviously totally beyond comprehension and possessed of absolute power, yet in some incomprehensible fashion – well, the nearest I can get is that it does not seem to matter if it turns out to be the air you can't breathe and the end of you.[13]

A visitation like this cannot be summoned. You can surround yourself with 'all the ritual props' of Christian worship but 'it just is not there'. 'The altar is built', she wrote, quoting a writer of Christian fantasy novels, 'but the fire descends elsewhere.'[14] 'It can seize hold of one', without warning, triggered by something as trivial as a walk in the country.[15]

It was in fact walks in the country that were most commonly cited by the mass observers as triggers for transcendental experiences. As modern societies became dominated by Weber's 'iron cage' – the instrumental rationality of science, technology and bureaucratic organization – Romanticism had invested nature with a sense of the sublime. For Byron 'high mountains are a feeling',[16] the kind of feeling that Turner put on canvass, registering the transformation of Alpine wilderness from 'an object of horror into a place of pilgrimage'.[17] Wordsworth found 'a sense sublime' in the beauty of the Wye valley, transporting him beyond 'the dreary intercourse of daily life' to realms of joy and 'elevated thoughts'.[18] Alone on the fells, Ruskin shivered from head to foot with 'instinctive awe, mixed with delight'.[19]

A chorus of such testimony was evoked by a question posed by MO, in the course of a 1992 directive on 'Nature and the Environment': 'Does the idea of nature carry any particular religious significance for you?' A school secretary, admitting that her faith was 'fairly childlike', found in the natural world 'the confirmation (to me) that there is a God'.[20] For one middle-aged woman 'the beauty and grandeur of the natural world is a reminder of God. When out walking, especially on my own, in the local countryside, on the beach or hills, I feel a nearness to the maker in whom I believe.'[21] Recalling the Sunday walk to church during her childhood, Emma Trelawney, a middle-aged magistrate, remembered 'looking up at the sky through the tall trees and branches and thinking it was God's cathedral – the birds were signing for him and the wild flowers showed his glory and wonder – and the wild animals were the congregation. I still feel that deep inside.'[22] Solitude enhanced such feelings. Gloria Blake, whose sense of the spiritual was vague and undefined, described witnessing a sunrise beside the sea: 'I climbed up a small rock face and when I reached the top I had the wonderful feeling that there was no one else existed because of the complete silence and I felt totally at one with nature. I suppose that was the nearest I've ever had to a religious experience.'[23] In the mountains or by the sea, Garry Edwards, a devotee of Spinoza, found himself 'feeling an intimate part of nature with a joy unmatched in everyday life.'[24] When Janet Moody, a retired teacher and environmental activist, held rocks and crystals in her hands she felt herself linked to the origins of the Earth.[25] A lapsed Scottish Presbyterian, living in Surrey, thought that it was 'the humbling effect of the forces of nature – storm, flood, earthquake, lightening – that instil in mankind the sense inadequacy and belief in an all-powerful deity'. For herself it was 'the display of Nature's power or beauty [that] gives me a feeling of awe which is very close to a religious experience.'[26]

Although MO's question framed such experiences as 'religious', they probably owed more to Romanticism than to the church. Religious ritual itself, although designed to enable participants to feel a sense of connection with a transcendent spirituality, may have been less effective than natural beauty in evoking feelings of awe and wonder. Very few of MO's churchgoing Christians offered descriptions of their experience of worship, and those who did tended to stress something altogether calmer and quieter. Evangelical enthusiasm had little appeal among the mass observers. Paula Harrison, the religious education teacher, was indignant when a new vicar replaced traditional communion with fundamentalist hellfire sermons and guitar-playing evangelicalism aimed at the young: 'I feel that my church has been hijacked and part of my life forcibly severed.' Her account of what had been lost gives a vivid picture of the quiet virtues of traditional Anglican worship:

> The vicar was a delightful uninspiring man who when he met you at the church door on a Sunday morning never remembered your name or indeed whether you were a regular worshipper or not, but always gave you a cheery welcome.

The services were short and traditional; the congregation was small, around forty at the main services, and at the early communion the same dozen women faithfully turned up. I attended church most weeks and enjoyed the sense of peace. I went to commune with God, to give thanks, to remind him who I am, to tell him my problems, to ask for help. I felt better for it. [27]

For many churchgoers worship was, as one middle-aged woman put it, simply 'part of life',[28] sustaining a sense of the transcendent without requiring any more strenuous or direct encounter with divinity. Edna Thomas had escaped from a pious Irish upbringing aged eighteen to train as a nurse in 1950s London, and subsequently married, divorced and married again. Through all this she retained her faith, describing herself as on the liberal wing of Catholicism. Writing in the 1980s she confessed that 'I have had no great lightening moments. One could say I am lazy'. But churchgoing continued to fulfil 'some deep-seated need'. For Edna it was the 'culture of Catholicism', known since childhood – the ceremony, the incense, the music, the copies of great paintings – that enabled her 'to step outside [her]self', and sustain contact with 'the awe and the mystery' of God.[29] While for this woman the richness of Catholic ritual made up for the absence of any 'great lightening moments', the less ritualistic practices of Protestant worship left some churchgoers wondering whether they were genuinely in touch with their maker. Clare Harman, a middle-aged journalist active in the local church, had never wavered from the Anglican faith of her childhood and could not 'picture a life without a religious framework'. But she worried that her faith had never 'been boosted by some intensely personal experience'. Confronted with born-again nonconformists in an ecumenical Bible-reading group she found herself wondering 'if I've got a proper (devout?) faith at all'.[30]

The value placed on public worship could stand in inverse proportion to the ardour of faith. A woman in her late sixties who had been a member of the Anglican church all her life found 'strength and consolation in prayer and the rituals of the … Church', but she knew that she was only just hanging on to her sense that 'there is something above and beyond me and the world', and suspected that her 'very tenuous religious beliefs' were rooted in the 'primitive uneducated feelings' of childhood, and were 'rationally and logically' indefensible.[31] Some of the more vivid evocations of the power of religious ritual came from people whose belief in the doctrines of the church was even more tenuous. Edward Farleigh, as we saw in Chapter 2, continued to 'worship at the Cathedral and play an active part in its work' long after he had abandoned his Christian faith.

'The Eucharist', he explained, 'is a magical piece of theatre – like a Renaissance painting':

> I still go to Matins on Sunday as I enjoy the music, the poetry of some of the Old Testament has been part of my life and many of the sermons are thought-provoking. The Cathedral is a lovely place to sit and meditate.[32]

Hilda Barrington acknowledged that in our 'largely post-Christian time[s] … many of us contain vestigial traces of thinking formed during enforced church attendance in childhood', but she regretted that 'the church has by and large taken the numinous out of its services'. On one occasion the lunchtime concerts she attended at St John's in London's Smith Square

> turned out to be Sung Eucharist. This, apparently, is one of three times in the year, in that diocese at least, when the King James Bible is used. To hear those words is a rare experience now. They are still familiar and awe-inspiring. At fifteen I found their force overwhelming and the particular nature of the ritual scary. … I don't have belief (I don't think I ever did) but for me some moments in church services are manifestations of that supernatural I'm not proof against … My acquired scepticism is just hung on to against a background of accessibility to the supernatural.[33]

Religious ritual could also retain its magic even among atheists whose 'accessibility to the supernatural' was entirely blocked. Rachel Harriman, whose writing for MO tells a remarkable story of maturation (emotional, intellectual, political) from a wild youth spent in serial relationships with abusive men, had an unquenchable zest for life. The spirituality that she acknowledged existed 'only in our minds while we're alive', a 'spirituality' which gives us 'an intangible communication with others which we express with our senses and words – in art, literature and music and just expressing our thoughts and feelings'. There was no concession to religious belief in the delight she derived as a member of a choral society – 'a joyous celebration of sound and architecture, intellect and friendship'. Although she sometimes felt that 'I should not be singing this religious music when I don't believe in God', the spiritual uplift to be derived from choral music, as from the gothic cathedral, was, she insisted, no less available to the atheist than to the believer. Such stupendous creative achievements transcended their religious origins, and there was nothing paradoxical in her desire to have Bach's Mass in B minor sung by choral friends at her humanist funeral.[34] Music could provide compelling access to the most profound, mysterious and life-enhancing levels of human experience: 'music heard so deeply that it is not heard at all,' as T. S. Eliot put it: 'You are the music while the music lasts.'[35] For some among the 19th-century bourgeoisie the concert hall had replaced the church; and today, in many places, the church itself is more likely to be filled by audiences for classical music than by religious worshippers. Music gave access to the ineffable, for the atheist as much as for the believer.[36]

A sense of the transcendent power of the arts was precious to Margaret Thompson, who recognized that her 'fervent disbelief must preclude me from ever experiencing anything supernatural'.[37] As a biologist she found a 'deep emotional significance' in the complexity of nature, and she was no stranger to what she called 'ecstasy'.[38] Her escape, during her undergraduate years in the late 1940s, 'from superstition, religion, heaven and hell' had been facilitated by a romantic attachment to a fellow student, who not only introduced her to socialism, atheism and physics but also took her to art exhibitions, films, opera, theatre, ballet. Looking back from the 1990s she recalled the excitement and optimism of her student days, immersed in a milieu which transcended the alienating logic of C. P. Snow's 'two cultures':

> The physiology lecturer, a Communist, held musical evenings in his home, three of the science lecturers were accomplished water colourists and the debating and orchestral societies were run by engineering students.[39]

Her most intense pleasures, then and later, owed nothing to religion or the supernatural, registering instead the kind of materialist spirituality which Rachel Harriman defined as 'existing only in our minds while we are alive'. For Margaret, moments of 'ecstasy' occurred 'sometimes with music. Sometimes with art or scenery. Most often with lovemaking, not necessarily including sex. Especially with my first and last lovers'.[40]

Such ecstasies, of course, were not unknown to religion. Although none of the mass observers practised tantric sex, several of them exemplified Weber's view of eroticism as an important means of escape from instrumental rationality, 'a gate into the most irrational and thereby real kernel of life'.[41] Stella Marshall, discovering the joys of sex in late middle age, felt that in her lovemaking she gained access to 'a parallel world where time doesn't exist – perhaps it's more important than what we call the "real" world'.[42] Dorothy Palmer, a retired social worker, had finally abandoned her faith when she found, in her sex life, a secular substitute for the transcendent experience she had sought as a teenager in Christianity.[43] 'The illusion of two fusing however briefly into one', she wrote, 'is the height of bliss … I [had] a sacramental feeling about love-making … a feeling that it was a sacred, almost mystical, act of union'; although, she acknowledged in parenthesis, 'not exactly in the religious sense'. Her feeling of having attained something almost mystical remained with her long after she had lost respect for her husband and the marriage had failed.[44] Rachel Harriman, who had never entertained religious feelings, placed sexual love at the very heart of her materialist spirituality:

> Some people get high on adrenalin, some on E, I have always needed the love drug and I think have been naturally blessed with a lot of potential for it!! ... Love is what ... makes life have meaning, it lifts the spirits and puts one higher than the angels. Love is essential for living, it makes everything beautiful. It makes me smile, and sing inside, it gives me butterflies and makes me tread lightly ... When you love someone you think about them all the time, you commune with them in your mind. ... Love is all consuming and utterly wonderful. Without it, you are lost, devastated, desolate and alone.[45]

It is clear from the context that she was talking about sexual love.

Marghanita Laski's informants, when asked what it was that triggered their feelings of 'transcendent ecstasy', offered a list which included religious worship, solitude in scenes of natural beauty, works of art (especially music), sexual pleasure, the first hours of a newly born child, and, amongst the artists, writers and scientists who were disproportionately represented among her friends, intuitive moments of creative inspiration or scientific insight.[46] Several of the mass observers also wrote about the mysterious process by which creative 'feelings and ideas seem to come from nowhere'.[47] A Methodist with a scientific education offered his own complex explanation: 'We have souls that can be linked to the God spirit ... When this linkage is in place it might appear that Supernatural forces can be released', but what really happens is that 'forces already present in the natural world can be harvested in a way that the logical mind has not yet been able to fathom'. For this man the 'logical mind' was of this world, but intuitive or creative abilities arose only to the degree that our souls were 'linked to the God spirit'.[48] Marion Phillips may have occasionally been paralysed by awesome encounters with God, but she also wrote poems - or rather, she explained, they came to her: ' "I" don't do this. This hits me anywhere – I always carry a biro and a paper. ... I hear something ... If someone interrupts the thread stops unwinding and cuts off'.[49] Fred Donovan was a retired building worker who lived 'in a totally cocooned spiritual world which most people I come into contact with know nothing about. To them this other more vibrant world does not exist'. He did not mix with his neighbours, people 'without grace or sensitivity' who invested their lives in the materialist rat race and saw the world 'with dead eyes'. The one place where he found a culture with which he could feel at ease was on holiday in Andalusia: 'I become consumed by the gardens, the architecture, the spiritual light ... that the Moorish Arabs were crazy about – they thought they had found paradise and they were a very spiritual people.' Since the 1960s he had expressed his spirituality in hundreds of songs which, like Marion Phillip's poems, flowed to him from 'some unknown source'.[50]

III

One thing missing from Laski's survey of transcendent ecstasy was the phenomenon of out-of-body experiences. Thomas Partridge drew no religious conclusions from the beauty of nature, but he did find evidence for his faith, as we have seen, in the fact that even an atheist like A. J. Ayer testified to the reality of near-death experiences. Some of the other Christians were also, like the Quaker, Marion Phillips, 'comforted by people's recorded experiences which I have read about. Those who have been very close to death and survived have apparently never wanted to return and never again feared death. Also by the stories of people who have seen dead relatives coming to meet them. If this is only a trick of the mind', she added, 'it is a kind one'.[51] Rose Worley, a retired professional woman, was persuaded 'that this life is not all there is' by what she had read or been told about such experiences:

> People who have 'near death experiences' say that their life is changed as a result ... these are I suppose, religious experiences talking – in its widest sense ... What the near death experience seems to have in common is that the person feels great love and understanding and compassion. It seems there must be spiritual beings who are there to help, and perhaps 'guardian angels' are real in a sense.[52]

Jenny Brown, a liberal-minded Catholic, was similarly impressed by accounts of near-death experiences:

> They describe leaving their bodies and going through a tunnel towards a bright light. Some get further to a garden or similar heaven-type place, often meeting loved ones who've died, always experiencing peace and being forced to return to their bodies – to 'Life', with great reluctance.[53]

An elderly retired nurse, who had responded, aged seventeen, to her mother's death by turning to the church 'for something permanent in my life that would sustain me while I reached adulthood' and remained a 'staunch Catholic' all her life, described a vision she had during an illness: 'I thought I was entering a long tunnel which had a bright light at the end ... By the side of the tunnel I saw a figure dressed in white and I could have gone towards it but somehow I "came to" and was in my hospital bed'.[54]

Jenny Brown dismissed the idea that such experiences were merely 'a brain activity caused by oxygen starvation' on the grounds that so many people told similar stories. The common story line could, of course, point to a quite different conclusion. Jans Schlieter, investigating the history of near-death experiences, points out that it was only in the late 19th century that the notion of moving through a 'tunnel' towards a bright light first entered the stories people told, suggesting that railways and especially underground trains may have had as much to do with the experience as divine revelation.[55] More generally he shows how a stereotypical narrative of the near-death experience became culturally established, especially after the publication of Raymond Moody's best-selling book *Life after Life* in 1975.[56] The upsurge of such experiences since the 1960s was clearly related to advances in medical technology, which resulted in many more people being brought back from the brink of death.[57] But whatever the role played by medical technology, and by culturally available stereotypes, the experiences themselves remained powerful and meaningful. As William James remarked of reductive accounts of religious experiences,

> when other people criticize our own more exalted soul-flights by calling them 'nothing but' expressions of our organic disposition, we feel outraged and hurt, for we know that, whatever be our organism's peculiarities, our mental states have their substantive value as revelations of the living truth; and we wish that all this medical materialism could be made to hold its tongue.[58]

Two weeks after being close to death following a miscarriage, Emma Trelawney, the Anglican magistrate, had what she took to be 'a flash-back', and one close to the accounts summarized by Jenny Brown:

> Going up through a dark tunnel and coming out on to a mossy bank with a low stone wall. My best friend who had died at 13 years was waiting for me with hands out saying 'not yet, not yet', and my mother's parents were walking towards me with a few others behind them. Also behind them I saw what I thought was a huge bonfire – bright light and people dancing and so happy. I felt so warm and longed to stay.[59]

The experience stayed with her, a treasured feeling of having been given a privileged glimpse of the afterlife.[60] Like Emma, Pauline Clark, a born-again Baptist, interpreted her 'wonderful experience of love ... beyond description' as positive proof of life after death.⁶¹ But this was unusual. Of the nineteen mass observers, many of them practising Christians, who testified to near-death or other out-of-body experiences, only four understood their experience in religious terms. The others attributed it to dreaming, drug-induced hallucination, or to 'workings of our brains that we do not yet understand'.⁶² But even in these cases the experience itself could remain profoundly meaningful.⁶³

One of the most vivid accounts of a near-death experience was given by Laura Jefferies, a left-wing middle-aged 'business analyst' who, after a serious engagement with Christianity in her twenties and thirties, had 'shaken off' religion and become an atheist: 'Religion', she remarked in 1985, 'is a prop I needed for a time and don't anymore'.⁶⁴ In her later years she identified with the New Atheism associated with Richard Dawkins, dismissing religion as 'the biggest con trick ever', designed to 'keep the plebs in their place'.⁶⁵ In her MO writing, despite feeling (in her mid-forties) 'happy, confident and in charge of my life', she displayed a curiously positive attitude towards death: 'All my life', she wrote in 1994, 'I have wished I wasn't here, that life is too much aggravation, impatiently wondering what I was doing here, what was it all about, why do I have to stay.'⁶⁶ Underpinning those feelings was something that had occurred when she was nine years old, sick and with a high temperature: an out-of-body experience that she wrote about for MO on at least three separate occasions, in 1996, 2009 and 2013:

> My grandmother came for me. She beckoned for me to come. I knew she had died, I could see her smiling face, it was surrounded by a brilliant, though not glaring, light, and I wanted to go to her. [2009] I could see her face looking through the top window pane, we had like a conversation in my head, she said 'come with me' I said 'but I don't know you very well' she said 'I looked after your mother and I will look after you' and I said 'but what will mum say' and with that I was lying back heavily in bed, I had been floating towards her and now she was gone. Whenever after I have thought about it I curse myself for saying 'but …', and even now still wish I had gone with her'. [2013] 'I felt so heavy, desolate at losing the peace and tranquillity that was almost mine. I still feel the loss now that I have to continue with this world. It gave me a desire for knowledge. I'd felt inadequate about going because I didn't know anything. I'm sure it was my hesitation that lost me the chance to go. [1996]

Central though this experience was to her attitude towards life, she did not see it as indicative of anything supernatural. 'The mind', she wrote, 'can play games.' And while believers might use such experiences to reassure themselves about the reality of the afterlife, for Laura the reassurance lay in the fact that 'a mind trying to make sense of shutting down, being over heated and in stress' could produce such 'peace and tranquility'.[67]

Justine Hammond, who placed an out-of-body experience at the heart of her account of successfully remaking herself in middle age, was similarly disinclined to understand the experience in religious terms. As a child in the 1920s she had been something of a tom boy, 'climbing trees and playing at cowboys and Indians, as well as knights and robbers with the dustbin lid in one hand and a stick for a sword in the other'. Her parents – a shopkeeper and a professional pianist – shook their heads and said, 'She ought to have been a boy', but knowing that her destiny was marriage, they did not offer her the educational advantages of her brothers. Leaving school at fifteen she scrimped and saved, bought a car and learned to drive, so that when war broke out she found work as an ambulance driver, at first the only woman in the team. 'Lovely!! … I talked men's talk and found out how to get men's attention was to talk about things that interested them and not about myself. I was known as a good sport, despising women's idle chatter about clothes, shopping, food and children.' When the superintendent's back was turned she joined the men in competitive 'tear-ups' along the local bypass. Her heroine was Amy Johnson, pioneer aviator and the first woman to fly solo to Australia.[68]

All this was driven underground when, in 1943, she married a man ten years her senior who surprised her by being far more 'Victorian' in his attitudes than her own parents (who enjoyed a relatively equal partnership, her mother having been 'on the fringes of the suffragette movement'). Within five years of marrying, in 1943, she realized she had made a mistake, but by then she had two sons and was economically dependent on her husband. So, overriding her husband's objections to her going out to work, she 'determined to build a career and leave him when my youngest was eighteen, by which time I reckoned I could earn enough to keep myself'. Successfully combining motherhood with a full-time job, she established herself as a school secretary in the local grammar school. As her son's eighteenth birthday approached, however, she discovered to her dismay that due to reorganization of the local educational system 'the job I loved would fold up, so I was faced with being a "nobody" again for the rest of my life. … My life … turned into dust and ashes. I began to sleep badly, waking very early and not being able to return to sleep'.[69]

At 2.00 am one morning, sitting in the kitchen, she had 'what I can only describe as a mystical experience':

> The room faded from view and I was out in the universe (without a body) among the stars. To get there I had followed a great white enveloping light and I knew

such a happiness I hadn't experienced for years. I then noticed the universe was vibrating as if it was alive with electricity and I was vibrating in time with it. Later on in my thoughts I likened this experience to an electric light bulb which vibrates and flickers as it burns itself out. I then thought it's my soul out there and I want to stay there forever for never have I known such peace. There followed a dialogue with myself and I argued against coming back until a voice said to me 'but there is work for you to do' and I immediately ceased arguing and the room swam back into view.[70]

This sounds remarkable like the near-death experiences reported by other mass observers, but in this case induced by psychological depression rather than physical illness or drugs. (Later on she checked with her doctor that she had not been taking any drugs at the time.) Looking back, thirty years later, she wondered whether it had been no more than a dream. But whatever its ontological status the experience remained vivid in her memory and she insisted that it had transformed her life, comparing it to St Paul's conversion on the road to Damascus.

At first her depression only intensified and for a year or more she entered 'a period of what I described as "living under the earth rather than on it", fighting all the way to regain confidence in myself again'.[71] In retrospect she came to see this period 'as one of mourning for the lost "me" – now dead'.[72] Eventually she realized that what she needed was not tranquilizers but to make herself useful to people less fortunate than herself. With her doctor's help she found a job as a ward maid in a geriatric hospital where, face to face with death, she discovered a talent for relating cheerfully with the dying. 'My self-imposed cure worked and about 3 or 4 months later I took up the threads of my life again.'[73] But the woman who emerged felt herself to be very different from the wife who had spent eighteen years silently planning her escape. Rather than leaving her husband she set out to force him to accept her as an equal, something she felt she had achieved by the time he died in 1978. Meanwhile, rediscovering the 'creative urge I once had in childhood', she found the 'courage … to go forward and explore new pastures'.[74]

Employed as a temporary secretary she broadened her experience of the world in a wide variety of different kinds of organizations. To get to grips with what had gone wrong in her life she read Jung, Freud, Gurdjieff, Laing, Maslow and Eysenck, and finding her way into psychology, sociology and comparative religion 'became the ruling passion of my life'.[75] In the 1980s, now a happy widow, she resumed her formal education culminating in a degree in literature which, she wrote in 1991, finally put paid to 'my feelings of inferiority and [I] became what I am today – myself!'[76] Responding in the same year to an MO directive on gender, she declared herself 'a liberated woman', while adding (with reference to Jung) that 'I could equally claim to be a liberated man for now I see no division between the sexes'. No longer repressing her tomboy youth – or, as she put it, 'integrating my "animus" (male side) into conscious life' – she could now accept that 'we are all just human beings and any need to compete I had in the past has disappeared'.[77]

Clearly there was a great deal more to this woman's transformation than the road-to-Damascus mystical experience that she herself placed at its core. Religion does not appear to have played any part in her life prior to this experience, and although after her husband's death she tried going to church, the experiment was short-lived. She was impressed by the clergymen she met, but found her fellow worshippers 'narrow-minded and bigoted and much addicted to gossip ... they wore their Christianity like an outdoor coat'. While studying for her degree she befriended a young Hindu woman who 'was delighted to find that I'd tried to read and understand the Bhagavad Gita' and assured her that 'you are more "Hindu" than many Hindus I've met'. Later she discovered and joined the Council of All Faiths 'where nobody ran down other faiths', but had to abandon it when she left London for her retirement home in the countryside. Her interest in religion had less to do with any search for a transcendental spirit than for what religious ideas could tell her about the earth-bound human condition: 'I am of no definite religious persuasion', she wrote in 1996; and six years earlier, she had declared herself 'inclined towards existentialism and humanism'.[78]

Religion was central to our final account of an out-of-body experience. Hannah Cohen was born in 1954 to a middle-class professional Jewish family. Around the age of ten, on holiday in France with her family, she found herself transported into the presence of God. With what she later described as 'the arrogance of a child' she was unsurprised by the event, assuming it to be 'normal' and feeling herself 'enclosed by love and understanding and kindness and patience and other such superlatives, as if these were only to be expected'. Not knowing 'what to do with the experience', she told no one at the time and then forgot about it completely. It was not until her early twenties, after graduating in anthropology, that the experience 'came to mind once more'. After that, however, it remained 'a reality in my life'. Although she married 'out', her children were brought up in the faith and she took an active role in Jewish religious life. By the time she wrote about her childhood experience for MO, in 1996, the family had moved to Israel, where they felt safer than they had as middle-class professionals living in a run-down working-class area in the UK. Her account reads as follows:

> We were spending the day by a river with sandy banks and nearby grassland with some trees. The light was sparkling and the place had a particular intensity. I was absorbed in a solitary game – I had wandered off slightly apart from the others, when suddenly I was 'transported' high to a place – it sounds crazy, but I seemed to have a conversation in the Divine Presence. There were no words as such, but I expressed things that were worrying me – such as how G-d[79] who was so mighty and powerful could know or care about me and how it could be that this power crossed boundaries of space and time. I received some answers. I was told to look and it was as if I was looking down on the sky and clouds moved apart to show the sea, and France and down and beyond across the continent and beyond all in an instant and it was over then I realised I had been 'gone' a long time – forever – and my family would worry about me and once again I was told to look, and I saw the river bank and myself standing there, and others of my family. ... I can still vividly recall each of the sensations even though they were not physically transmitted. I saw and recognised my T shirt and shorts and sandals on the bank nearby. ... I didn't want to go back, I wanted to stay but was told I had to return. The place was infinitely silent and utterly peaceful, but behind me there was the sound of amazing ... music which I didn't hear but knew it was there. In slight despair at being sent back I began to ask more questions – what about all the bad things that happen in the world, the injuries etc. As I asked (no words) I knew I was being greedy and yet received the response 'I am' – i.e. despite appearances of wrong in the world etc. etc. fundamentally I did not need to worry for I knew that G-d is and was and that He is Good. And then I was back on the ground rather quiet and stunned.[80]

Attempting to assess how the memory of this event had affected her life, she worried 'that I have not done enough to justify the privilege of having received such an experience ... I feel guilty as if ... I should be a better person than I am'. Nevertheless it had served to reinforce her faith – 'I feel I not only believe, but I know'. It also made her 'more able to accept that contradictions can both be true', given her the feeling that she could 'trust my hunches and that still inner voice' and the strength to cope with, among other things, a period of severe depression.

When the memory first came back to her, in her early twenties, she had 'found it very hard to talk about ... I felt as if I might be offending in some way, or as if the telling were an important gift which I could donate but only at the right time'. Eventually she did tell her husband, her children and, with surprising consequences, her mother:

> I found many years after the event that my mother had had a spiritual experience at the same time, in the same place. It was different in kind – she felt as if she was suddenly in a trance. She had recently been preoccupied with thoughts about the existence of G-d and she said that during that afternoon she suddenly knew that he was a reality and that she had to move from a fairly secular state towards greater religious knowledge and observance … She made good her resolution and for the rest of her life continued to learn and develop this side of herself.[81]

What are we to make of this complex story of forgetting, remembering and sharing? How far was the original experience reshaped in the telling? In adulthood Hannah found echoes of her experience in accounts of near-death experiences, and, more precisely, in the prophet Ezekiel's ascent (also from a riverbank) into the presence of God: 'The wind lifted me and I heard behind me a sound of great rushing of those who uttered praises and said "Blessed is the glory of the Lord from this place … the abode of his Divine Presence"'.[82] Was she reconstructing her childhood memory to accord with biblical and other accounts discovered later in life? Did her mother really have a simultaneous spiritual experience, or was this a 'memory' constructed in response to the story gifted to her by her daughter? Could Hannah's childhood experience itself have been a response to religious doubts and anxieties unconsciously communicated to her by her mother? However such questions are answered, we are left with the original experience itself and Hannah's testimony about the long-term effects it had on her life.

IV

According to a recent British survey,

> psychic and mystic experiences are frequent even in modern urban industrial society. The majority of the population has had some such experience, a substantial minority has had more than just an occasional experience, and a respectable proportion of the population has such experiences frequently.[83]

Although fully fledged mystical experiences are rare, many of the mass observers reported being brought up short by something that seemed to take them into a dimension quite distinct from ordinary life. And these moments in which we step outside the mundane taken-for-granted reality of the world and our practical engagement with it may well be important to our psychological well-being.

Crucial to William James's understanding of religious experience was that it changed you. Putting to one side the ultimate sources of such experiences, he argued that their 'truth' lay in their effects, and he piled up evidence (mainly from the writings of mystics) of lives transformed by such experiences. Writing in an altogether more secular vein in the 1960s, Marghanita Laski described the beneficial effects of moments of 'ecstasy': 'Improved mental organisation, whether this takes the form of replacing uneasiness and dissatisfaction with ease and satisfaction, or of appearing to confirm a sought belief, or of inspiring to moral action or of enabling the expression of a new mental creation'.[84] At the same time Abraham Maslow, one of the founders of humanistic psychology, extolled the therapeutic value of what he described as 'peak experiences' – intense, timeless moments approximating to experiences normally categorized as 'religious'. Such moments, he argued, make the world seem 'beautiful, good, desirable, worthwhile'; they prove that life is meaningful and give us the capacity to resist the existential emptiness, the anomie of modern life. 'Joy exists, can be experienced and feels very good indeed and one can always hope that it will be experienced again.'[85]

And there is testimony to that effect from the mass observers. Whatever their ontological status, the experiences reviewed in this chapter mattered – they had an effect on how people lived, and how they understood the meaning of their lives. For some they were pivotal, life-transforming events. For others, less dramatically, they made a positive contribution to their psychological well-being. The briefness of the glimpse stood in inverse relationship to its intensity, and such moments were long remembered. They provided a standard of joy, calm, peace, harmony against which to balance the troubles of everyday living and, for some, to make those troubles easier to bear. It was only for a minute or less that Cynthia Rawlinson, visiting the ruins of Fountains Abbey, felt the presence of a monk standing beside her, but the 'exquisite … sensation of spiritual peace' that she glimpsed, or conjured up, in that moment had not faded when she wrote about it twelve years later.[86]

Christian writers understand such experiences as implicitly religious, 'signals of transcendence', pointing beyond material existence to a supernatural reality.[87] Others, like MO's Rachel Harriman see them as evoking a spirituality that exists 'only in our minds while we're alive'. For her, as for several of the atheists, spirituality was a mental event, a transient awareness of something profoundly meaningful which required no metaphysical rationalization.[88] The American philosopher, Jane Bennett, claims such experiences for a 'secular spirituality'. Enchanted, immobilized, spellbound, transfixed in a 'state of wonder', she writes, we experience simultaneously 'a pleasurable feeling of being charmed by the novel and as yet unprocessed encounter and a more unheimlich (uncanny) feeling of being disrupted or torn out of one's default sensory-psychic-intellectual disposition'. Such 'moments out of time', she argues, contribute powerfully to our psychological well-being, generating 'a mood of fullness, plenitude, or liveliness, a sense of having had one's nerves or circulation or concentration powers tuned up or recharged – a shot in the arm, a fleeting return to childlike excitement about life'.[89] Nietzsche had certainly heard the news that God was dead, but his evocation of the power of the ecstatic moment could hardly be bettered:

> If we affirm one single moment, we thus affirm not only ourselves but all existence. For nothing is self-sufficient, neither in us ourselves nor in things; and if our soul has trembled with happiness and sounded like a harp string just once, all eternity was needed to produce this one event – and in this single moment of affirmation all eternity was called good, redeemed, justified, and affirmed.[90]

Science may enable us to explain a great deal that previously appeared mysterious, inexplicable or beyond the realm of science to understand, but to explain is not to explain away. However perfect our understanding might become of the material processes underlying 'spiritual' experiences, the experiences themselves remain: vividly real, unforgettable. There is ultimately no way of knowing whether the physical, chemical, biological, psychological and social processes involved are sufficient causes of the experience or merely necessary ones. Even if a neurologist could map exactly what is going on in the brain during an altered state of consciousness, would that 'explain' the altered state, or merely describe its material manifestation?

To the religiously minded, the profound spiritual experiences claimed by atheists may well appear as no more than 'an ersatz sort of transcendence in a world from which spiritual values have been largely banished'.[91] For all his generous understanding of secular wonder in the face of great art, music or natural beauty and complexity, Charles Taylor insists that an authentic experience of human 'fullness' – the sensation that 'life is fuller, richer, deeper, more worth while, more admirable, more what it should be' – is only possible in a theistic framework.[92] Beyond the 'ordinary human flourishing' provided by family life and a worthwhile job, Taylor argues, we are troubled by a metaphysical itch, a need to find some larger meaning or purpose to existence: and for those who reject the reality of the transcendent, this need remains forever unassuaged.[93]

It is clear from the evidence reviewed in this chapter that many atheists would dispute this claim. Their lives could also be enhanced by feelings of awe and wonder and long-remembered ecstatic moments. When atheists lay claim to their own sense of fullness and profundity, by what logic can theists dispute the authenticity of their experiences?

Which brings us back to the phenomenology of the experiences themselves. The evidence of the mass observers confirms and supplements what we know from other studies of 'religious', 'transcendent', 'spiritual', 'ecstatic' experiences. Regardless of the labels, these experiences share common features, and they have common effects. By serving to articulate the ineffable, they fortify and sustain our sense that life is meaningful. In a pluralistic and secular society, where people with very different beliefs coexist, there are many ways of assuaging the metaphysical itch, and the best that anyone can claim for their preferred way is that it works for themselves.

7

A pagan priestess

Throughout this book I have tried, where sources allowed, to provide biographical context for the beliefs and experiences described by the mass observers. This final chapter gives full rein to the biographical approach, focussing on a single mass observer in an attempt to understand how her spirituality was embedded in her broader experience of life. Rosemary Burroughs was a pagan priestess with a PhD in philosophy. Her reply to the 1996 directive on the supernatural was the longest, the most comprehensive and the most clearly argued of all 279 responses to that directive. At the end of her lucid account of a multitude of paranormal phenomena and of her spiritual journey into paganism, Rosemary addressed readers inclined to dismiss her experiences as 'a lot of superstitious nonsense':

> Can I really be having these weird experiences, and could I be deluded in some way? ... I am a sane person, and an intelligent one, and the experiences I have described here really did happen to me. ... I am not a silly person ... I have been academically trained to be rational and discriminating.[1]

I first read her response when doing research for *Seven Lives*, and it brought me up short. Intending to include her in that book, I interviewed her early in 2014. Physically crippled by the rheumatoid arthritis which was shortly to kill her, she talked about her spiritual life with a force, honesty and moral strength which compelled respect. How could such an intelligent person believe such bizarre things? By forcing me to listen seriously to what I had always dismissed – along with religion and spirituality in general – as so much 'superstitious nonsense', Rosemary set me the challenge that, in the end, provoked this book.

I

While much late 20th-century spirituality drew on Eastern religions, pagans sought inspiration closer to home: witchcraft, Druidry, and the gods, and especially goddesses, of the pre-Christian Mediterranean.[2] Themes common to these various manifestations of paganism include a sense of kinship with the natural world; a rejection of patriarchy, whether embodied in an exclusively male divinity or the authoritarian structures of a church; and an embrace of disciplines designed to enable each individual to access their true spiritual nature. While clearly reflecting broader shifts in late 20th-century culture – towards ecological thinking, feminism and individual self-making – paganism offered its adherents a modernity rooted in an imagined ancient past. Wiccans, understanding the early modern European witch-craze as an assault by Christianity on pagan beliefs surviving from the ancient world, claimed to be heir to an underground tradition of witchcraft which had survived the 'burning times'. Originating in England during the 1940s, Wicca took off in the 1960s and 1970s, and by the end of the century as many as ten thousand British people, female and male, had been initiated as witches. Exported to the United States, Wicca flourished among radical feminists who seized on the witch as 'one of the very few images of independent female power which western civilisation has offered to modernity'.[3] Druidry, whose roots were in freemasonry and the Celtic revival of late 18th-century romanticism, expanded rapidly from the 1980s, partly under the leadership of ex-Wiccans. In the late 19th century James Frazer's *Golden Bough* (1890) had helped to establish the idea of the original deity as a goddess, a notion later popularized by Robert Graves's *White Goddess* (1948).

Among the groups advocating worship of the Goddess the Fellowship of Isis was particularly influential. The Fellowship was founded in 1976 by members of a wealthy Irish family who, with the aid of a medieval legend about the foundation of Scotland by a princess from ancient Egypt, traced their ancestry back to Isis herself.[4] As the Divine Mother of 'every human, animal, bird, tree', Isis spoke to contemporary values of both feminism and ecology, serving to 'bring balance to our endangered earth, threatened by over-emphasis on male technology and power'.[5] Membership was free and open to anyone, male or female, who respected these values. Communion with Isis did not prevent adherents from worshiping other goddesses or gods. By the early 1990s the membership – over 11,000 in 73 different countries – included Catholics, Protestants, Hindus, Buddhists, Spiritualists, Rosicrucians, Druids, Sufis, Taoists and Nigerians reviving an ancient African religion. The Fellowship recommended rituals of worship based on ancient practices, but – apart from a prohibition of sacrifice, which the mother of all living things would certainly not approve of – there were no vows, no dogmas and no attempt to tell people how they should live their lives.

The claims to ancient lineage made by these various pagan organizations were, no doubt, taken literally by some of their members. For others, however, adopting a similar position to that propounded by liberal Anglicans in the 1960s, historical accuracy was beside the point. Whether or not religious myths reflected real events, their purpose was to embody spiritual and psychological truths: truths to live by and rituals to sustain their adherents in their own spiritual journeys.[6] Understood as useful myth, paganism had an appeal and an impact well beyond that of its devotional adherents. Janet Warman, a south London teacher, was an atheist (her full story is told in *Seven Lives*). Inspired by American radical feminist writers during the 1970s who were 'saying things out loud that I thought all my life' she enlivened her sociology classes with ideas about 'the original robbery, that of women having power and control over their own fertility and having a mother goddess to worship'.[7] 'Belief in a powerful goddess', she wrote with characteristic verve, 'might be more useful for a young female than a father bully prick in the sky; not just the fertility and sexuality of the goddess, but also her capacity for control of her life and the earth around her.'[8] But while Janet evoked the Goddess in aid of a secular feminism, Rosemary Burroughs's encounter with Isis was altogether more profound.

II

Born in 1956, Rosemary was a shy and nervous child. From the start she felt odd, a misfit. She was a late child, born when her mother was forty, and her only sibling, a sister, had left home to marry by the time Rosemary was five years old. Arriving in infant school she found it hard to relate to other children. She sat underneath the table and refused to participate: 'No one had ever spoken to me in a group of people before, so when the teacher spoke to the class as a whole, I didn't realise that I was included.' Although eventually she did well academically, and made a few friends, her difficulties persisted throughout her years at school:

> Reading through my old school reports [she wrote in 1991] the one consistent remark made by all my teachers right from infants' school until the end of the sixth form was that I never spoke in class, was extremely shy, lacking confidence in my own ability and finding any attempt at participation in group work, sporting or social activities painfully distressing.[9]

The inner life that she recalled was one of turmoil and anguish. The slightest setback filled her with 'feelings of shame and self-hatred, of resentment, of nothingness and self-annihilation, the brooding disgust, the feeling that one was not fit to live and not fit to move among decent people'. Baptist Sunday school, where she learned about sainthood and sin, only served to foster these feelings of guilt and self-disgust. Agoraphobic and frightened to go to church, she assumed that God would punish her for her absence, and it was to appease His wrath that at the age of eight or nine she improvised an altar at which she could say her prayers in the garden, and followed this up by making 'a portable, folding altar to take to school so that I could pray with my friends at play time'. Her parents worried about her behaviour and nervous disposition, but, firmly wedded to the values of an earlier era, they were of little help to her in finding her feet in the rapidly changing world of the 1960s and 1970s, seeking, rather, 'to cultivate in me the virtues of humility, obedience, modesty and submissiveness, which they considered appropriate to a middle-class girl'.[10] Her mother, herself socially insecure, having married 'up' to a man who became a senior executive in the gas industry, 'was always telling me that I was odd and silly, that I had silly ideas and silly ways and that people would think I was strange'.[11] When Rosemary complained about her 'feelings' – the hold-all term she used in her childhood diaries to register her inner turmoil – she was told by her parents to keep them to herself: 'I had too many feelings and I ought to think about others more often, instead of thinking of myself.'

As a teenager she was given to existential speculation and tied herself in moral knots: 'I kept feeling I should do good deeds, but then I thought that because I was doing them only to be good, so that I would go to Heaven, then I wasn't really a good person at all, because my motives were selfish.'[12] Even her friends thought her peculiar 'because I was always questioning things in an odd way, wondering about everything'.[13] Yearning for a world imbued with moral meaning she discovered *Lord of the Rings*, a book she was to revisit several times in adulthood. Tolkien, writing 'as if trees had spirits, as if there might be elves living in the woods', offered to re-enchant her world:

> Reading *Lord of Rings* is like … having a hallucination and actually entering the magical kingdom, and then when one comes back, one finds that one is still in the magical kingdom, because Middle Earth … is actually this earth, but one couldn't see it that way until then.[14]

It was when she was in the sixth form that she had her first psychic experiences, including a precognitive dream about her grandmother's death, and she gave expression to her sense of a world beyond the mundane in creative writing and in art. By the time she left school, with three A levels, she had made a name for herself as an artist, designing the school Christmas card and posters for the school play. Her teachers wanted her to go to university or to art school, but she lacked the confidence to do so, and her parents, who had only let her stay on at school because she was still so 'shy and immature', saw no purpose in higher education for a girl destined for marriage and domesticity. So her mother found her 'a quiet little office job' as a civil service clerical officer to fill in the time before she got married and had babies.

It was a disaster. Terrified by the journey to work (agoraphobia) and by the need to use the office lift when she got there (claustrophobia), she found the work itself tedious and pernickety. Unable to keep up, she spent a lot of time crying in the lavatory. She tried to quit after the first week, but stuck it out for eleven months, increasingly desperate and depressed, until her parents relented and allowed her to resign. Subsequently her mother took her to see several publishers offering her services as a book illustrator, but there were no takers for a girl without art school training. So she sat at home writing 'very bad, unpublished novels'.[15]

Shortly before leaving school Rosemary had been asked by a fellow pupil to illustrate a fantasy novel with which he had won a school prize. They talked, found they had common attitudes and interests, and fell in love. Edward, luckier than Rosemary, was turned down at the civil service interview that his businessman father organized for him. After months of unemployment and a temporary job cataloguing library books, his father found something more to Edward's taste, introducing him to a business associate, a publisher looking for someone to edit a new science-fiction magazine. Although Edward was only nineteen, the publisher took him on because he was in touch with 'a famous and very successful fantasy writer' who agreed to contribute to the magazine, and he spent most of the next year hard at work soliciting, selecting and copy-editing stories.[16] Rosemary did many of the illustrations and contributed a story of her own. After seven issues, however, the magazine collapsed, because the publisher, who had form as a conman, failed to pay the contributors or, after a bit, Edward himself. Edward lost his job in the autumn of 1978, a week before the date that he and Rosemary had set for their wedding.

Unemployed, attacked by members of both families and even by friends as 'stupid, lazy, irresponsible dreamers', the first year of their marriage was a miserable time. Already upset by the sudden death of her father shortly before the wedding, Rosemary broke down again and sought psychiatric help, but the counselling offered by the NHS only made things worse. To escape unemployment they enrolled on a degree course at the local polytechnic, and this proved to be their salvation. A sympathetic counsellor helped them to dig their way out of self-contempt and depression, and positive feedback from tutors built up their self-confidence. To their delight and amazement they discovered that the 'silly ideas' dismissed by friends and family

> were in fact philosophical ideas – all our thoughts about the nature of perception, of time, of mind, of the existence of God and the material world, of the structure of society and the state, of what makes actions good or bad – they were all philosophical ideas which had been explored by great thinkers for thousands of years ... Suddenly my husband and I were getting first class marks for our essays, one of the tutors told us that we were obviously both 'thinkers'... It was like coming out of a dark, stifling dungeon into the light and air, being able to breath, to see, to feel free after years of darkness and oppression.[17]

In 1982 they both gained first-class degrees in philosophy. The families were unimpressed, particularly when they decided to take up postgraduate places (and grants) at university. Rosemary's mother, with whom they had lived since their marriage, thought Edward would do better to get a proper job, as a postman; and when, four years later they were both awarded PhDs, Edward's grandmother, aware that a PhD in philosophy was hardly the gateway to riches, remarked sadly: 'And we had such high hopes for him, with his brains.'[18] But, as their student careers came to an end, family disapproval was the least of their troubles.

During the 1980s funding cuts saw the closure of half the philosophy departments in British universities. So although Edward's PhD was published by a mainstream academic publisher, there was little prospect of gaining tenured academic posts. For a few years they pieced together a meagre living with private tuition to schoolchildren and classes at the local technical college. When evening classes in philosophy failed to recruit, they found they could drum up more custom by drawing on a shared interest in the paranormal, one of the things they found they had in common when they first got together. Edward had been fascinated by the occult since being given Colin Wilson's book on the subject for his fourteenth birthday. He experimented with tarot card reading while still at school and subsequently showed Rosemary how it was done. Alongside their studies in philosophy during the 1980s the couple read about the paranormal and even set up as professional tarot card readers, visiting clients in their homes. This was an astute use of their skills, given the extent of demand. (In 2013 nearly a quarter of respondents told pollsters that their cards had been read.[19]) Encouraged by enthusiastic attendance at their evening classes, they wrote a beginner's guide to reading the cards and successfully placed it with a mainstream publisher.

This phase of their lives came to an abrupt end when, in March 1990, Rosemary collapsed with necrosis of the femur in her left leg and was admitted to hospital for an emergency hip replacement: 'My left hip and pelvis had been eroded away, my right one was going the same way, and so were both my knees.' Her rheumatoid arthritis, which had started eight years earlier, was proving increasingly hard to cope with: 'We struggled in poverty, worn down by part-time low-paid work ... [our] lives governed by drugs, medical appointments, and constant pain and exhaustion.' Friends proposed various alternative therapies – homeopathy, acupuncture, radionics, hypnosis, Chinese herbal medicine, Bach Flower remedies, naturopathy, osteopathy and faith healing – 'each of which we pursued with a dwindling purse and hopes constantly raised and dashed'.[20] Nothing helped, and 'the awful philosophies of some of the therapists I went to see' only made things worse. Among other things she was told

> that I had got ill through negative thinking, or that I had an unconscious desire to be crippled, that I did not really want to get better ..., that my relationship with my mother had made me ill and that I was only being ill because she wanted me to be, or that I was being ill in order to manipulate my husband ... My body and the state of my health seemed to mark me out as some dreadful sinner whose moral corruption was manifesting physically, and the more crippled I became, the more stigmatised I was with sin, guilt and shame.[21]

Compared to this, the treatment offered by conventional doctors 'who treat me as a body and seem to care nothing for me as a person' was much to be preferred: 'I do not feel so bad, because that is nothing like as horrible as having my very soul judged by those cranks, quacks and vultures who are alternative therapists.'[22]

When she came out of hospital after the hip replacement it was clear that she would need round-the-clock care.[23] Most of the part-time work was abandoned and the couple found, to their surprise, that they were actually better off on benefits – her disability living allowance, his income support and invalid care allowance. But that was the only good news, and facing further operations and a life of pain and permanent disability, she plunged into despair. Twenty years later she described her state of mind at this time:

> It all came tumbling down: the middle-class illusion of security … the modern myth of self-sufficiency, of personal power and personal strength, of never 'giving in'… The flood gates opened and in came another world – a world which most people do not encounter until old age – when in my thirties I experienced hospital wards, hospital consultants, nurses, bedpans; scary drugs and medical technology, the horrific oblivion and faux death of major anaesthesia and the risks of major surgery; rehabilitation, physiotherapy, occupational therapy, the humiliations of the welfare benefit system … and all the helplessness and dependency that goes along with the whole package.[24]

Within weeks of leaving hospital she started writing for MO, partly because she saw it as an opportunity to record the experience of a chronically sick and disabled person: 'I have some experience of "underclass" life and wish to record it for posterity.'[25] More important, however, was her spiritual response to the collapse of her health.

Since Baptist Sunday school Rosemary had an ambivalent relationship with Christianity – unattached to any church, but feeling a need for conventional religious sanction to protect her from the wrath of God. When, for example, she and Edward, both of them virgins, discussed her fear that her initiation into sexual intercourse would be painful, they resolved to see to the matter shortly before their wedding day so as not to spoil their honeymoon. The experiment was not a success. As a child, resistant to playground whispers, Rosemary had firmly believed that women got pregnant by praying for a baby. When, at the age of twelve, her mother told her about periods she convinced herself that one might become pregnant by using the same lavatory or bath as a man, or even sitting in the same chair. She still believed this, aged twenty, in 1977 – an extraordinary act of self-deception in the sexualized culture of the 1970s. But 'what upset me most', she recalled, 'was that the basis of physical life had turned out to be physical and was not to do with praying and religious practices, and this was a terrible blow to me.' The gross physicality of the sexual act offended her spiritual understanding of the world.

Once their union had been blessed by God in a church wedding, however, she found that she could make love without fearing that the angels were watching her with disapproval. But when she became pregnant she felt that her health problems, their poverty and the fact that they were living in her mother's house left her with no alternative but to agree to an abortion. In an extraordinary passage written thirty years after the event she described her feelings at the time:

> I was absolutely incensed and raging with anger ... I felt that the Devil was around me, and there was one occasion when I saw the Devil in the bedroom, and I felt that I was making a pact with the Devil because I was planning to have an abortion. I also felt that the foetus was itself extremely evil. ... I thought that because I did not want to be pregnant the thing that was growing inside me must be something evil and demonic that had broken in against my will, like a burglar, but far worse, because a burglar only breaks into your house and stays for a few minutes, whereas this was something that had invaded my body, made me feel incredibly sick and ill, and intended to stay there for nine months and then hang around in my life like a total parasite for another eighteen years at least, making my existence a complete hell. On top of all this, when I ought to be completely justified in getting rid of this monstrous, evil parasite, everything in the social order was conspiring against me to make it seem that I was the one in the wrong, committing a sin by seeking an abortion, when I was simply the innocent victim of an arrogant, selfish, grasping, invading, parasitical, spiteful, evil-minded, vile demonic thug that had barged in and taken over my body and my whole life. [26]

By projecting her sense of sin onto the foetus she was able to weather the abortion without a nervous breakdown, but the anger never left her. Perhaps what she was really dealing with was the anger she imagined that her mother had felt at the unwanted pregnancy which resulted in her own birth, and her fear that she too was an evil parasite preying on her mother's life.

As a student of philosophy in the 1980s, Rosemary rejected the idea of a personal deity, but she still felt the need for one, and the resulting clash between head and heart contributed to anxieties which at times threatened again to overwhelm her. In 1990, when she joined MO, she was reading the Bible and praying every night, but she 'had no outlet for my spiritual feelings and experiences' and was unsure whether to describe herself as religious.[27] Four years later, having at last found a religion she could understand, she was ordained as a priestess in the Fellowship of Isis.

It was not Rosemary who discovered Isis, she insisted, but Isis who discovered her. In the early 1980s she had a vivid dream 'in which an old woman came to me and said, "I am the Great Goddess. You must wear my dress." '[28] It was only years later that she came to understand this as an instruction from Isis to become her priestess. Struggling to cope with the despair she felt following her operation – 'a dark night of the soul' – she took to reading books on spiritual matters which eventually induced 'a sudden mystical awakening which lasted several weeks'.

She also read that when one was ready for spiritual growth 'a guru will appear'.[29] A year earlier Edward had enrolled briefly in a correspondence course with the Fellowship of Isis, but found it not to his taste. The annual convention of the Fellowship, however, provided an opportunity to sell copies of their book on tarot, and it was there in the autumn of 1991 that Rosemary was approached by her guru. The Fellowship's undoctrinaire combination of mysticism, feminism and deep ecology offered her the spiritual sustenance she had been unable to find in Christianity.

> In Paganism [she wrote later] the material and the spiritual blend into one another, and the psychological merges with the psychic. Nature is venerated and Deity can manifest through humans and animals, for the divine spark is in all aspects of creation.[30]

She signed up for a course of 'daily meditations, visualisation and Goddess-awareness', leading to her initiation into 'the Mysteries' and, by the autumn of 1994, her ordination as a priestess of Isis.[31]

One of the attractions of the Fellowship for Rosemary was that the rituals of worship could be conducted in private. Churches were seen by the Fellowship as intrinsically oppressive institutions:

> When the natural grouping of family was pushed aside by Patriarchy, the home as focus was superseded by meeting-house, church hall. Whereas in a family easy affection and unspoken ways of behaviour bring happiness, hierarchic Churches and Orders were forced to impose rigid laws.[32]

By contrast, the Iseum – the Hearth of the Goddess, the basic unit of the Fellowship – was an intimate grouping meeting in private, each Iseum cultivating its own particular ethos, beliefs and practices: a group of like-minded friends psychically attuned to one another. After her ordination Rosemary established her own Iseum, consisting of herself, Edward and two friends, meeting in her own home to perform rites of worship on the eight festivals each year designated by the Fellowship.

In the course of her training, Rosemary read widely about the pagan deities, ritual and magic. She learned the mystical and psychological disciplines of 'high magic' (not to be confused with low magic as 'the uninitiated person might suppose', although she practiced that too now and then). She became familiar with astral travel, explaining that

> to speak of believing or not believing in it does not make that much sense — it is just something I do, but whether it is a meditational practice or a psychic

phenomenon is hard to say, as these concepts often merge into one another within occultism.[33]

Similarly with 'channelling' which she undertook not, like spiritualist mediums, to invoke the voices of dead loved ones, but 'to allow the deity to "overshadow" me when I am in an altered state of consciousness':

> It is hard for me to describe this however, without making myself sound like a crank. It is a very personal, intimate, spiritual experience, and part of my religious practice. It probably sounds ludicrous to people who know nothing about it, but it is nevertheless a common practice among people I am in contact with.[34]

Responding to the 1996 directive on the supernatural she reviewed a wide variety of apparently paranormal phenomena, dismissing some as fantasy (werewolves, vampires) or fraud (spoon-bending, ectoplasm), agnostic about others (reincarnation, life after death), but in many cases convinced by her own experience (which she described in detail) that the phenomena were genuine. The latter category included out-of-body experience, doppelganger apparitions, precognitive dreams and haunting 'experienced as a feeling of being touched or pushed by a disembodied entity'.[35]

The Fellowship gave Rosemary a new purpose in life. Five years after her first encounter with the organization she was not only a priestess in charge of her own (tiny) Iseum but also a 'hierophant' (a higher qualification) empowered to initiate others into the worship of the Goddess. To this end she wrote a sixty-thousand-word correspondence course and advertised her services in pagan journals. She does not explain why she needed to devise her own course rather than use an existing one, but the proliferation of idiosyncratic paths to the Goddess was characteristic of the Fellowship's undoctrinaire ethos, as it was of New Age spirituality in general. She offered 'a sort of therapy' to her students, whose detailed monthly accounts of their meditations revealed all kinds of 'unconscious feelings and imagery'. She made no money from this activity, but it 'makes me feel that I am doing something worthwhile … helping people … doing some good in the world … even if it's only on a tiny scale'.[36] Later she self-published several books on Egyptian paganism.

In her communion with Isis, Rosemary found a path to stoic acceptance of her physical disability and pain:[37]

> I learnt the hard way that sometimes you have to give up fighting – give up and give in and say I am nothing, I have nothing, I never was, I never had, because

this is the bottom line, that it all comes from God, Goddess, Fate, whatever you like to call it, beyond our control. No one asked to be born, none of us chose to be a success or a failure, rich or poor, strong or weak, healthy or diseased, able-bodied or disabled.[38]

But Isis offered Rosemary something more: her physical problems were not just a fate to be born but part of the divine plan, a 'dark gift' from the Goddess. Writing in 2010 she portrayed the Goddess as 'the Black Isis … the Screecher and the Wailer on behalf of those who suffer and rage' and 'the strangely transformational alchemy that', with her aid, 'the trials of life can bring':

> Patience, courage, loyalty, tolerance, understanding, forgiveness, endurance, strength of will, a generous heart, hopefulness, faith – every virtue, all these and more, are the many gifts of the spirit that grow in us through a hard life, and only through a hard life. With Divine grace, we have the chance to become the heroes and heroines of our own struggling, flawed lives. Suffering is like that bit of grit around which the pearl forms in the oyster, but these are spiritual pearls, and personally I believe that we take them with us into the next life, which is the realm of spirit from which we came. Deity is forging in us spirits like shining steel, but before we can shine, we must be plunged into the fiery furnace and be beaten on the bitter anvil of this life. … In the end, Black Isis says to me, in a world without suffering, could there even be love? That understanding is the gift that she has given to me, and that is why her gift is not a curse: through the eyes of faith, I shall always strive to see it as a blessing.[39]

Suffering was central to Rosemary's faith from the start. In 1993, at the time of her initiation into the Fellowship, Brighid – a Celtic goddess – 'appeared to me in visions during meditation, telling me that I was going to be initiated by fire'. A few days later, during an act of worship, a candle set her hair on fire. Unable, because of her arthritis, to raise her arms above her head she suffered second-degree burns. 'Some people', she wrote addressing sceptical MO readers, 'would say it is only to be expected that things like this will happen when candles are about', but the precognition, and her later discovery that her instructor had also set her hair on fire at about the same time, provided Rosemary with painful and unforgettable evidence 'that the [supernatural] forces I have experienced are not purely subjective and imaginary'.[40]

Although Rosemary came to understand her suffering as a process of forging a spirit of 'shining steel' for the next world, she was far from indifferent to the affairs of this world. As a member of Campaign for Nuclear Disarmament (CND) she had participated in the London demonstration against cruise missiles in the autumn of 1983, marching all the way despite her arthritis, the thrilling feeling of solidarity in a huge, festive and purposeful crowd for once overcoming her agoraphobia.[41] Saddam Hussein's invasion of Kuwait and the subsequent Gulf War coincided with her own 'dark night of the soul' preceding her discovery of the Fellowship, and the MO diary that she kept during the crisis reflects her spiritual torment at the time. Suggestions that the crisis had been predicted by the prophets and foreshadowed the coming of Armageddon worried her deeply: 'the night the war broke out I was in a terrible state, because I thought it may be the end of the world.'[42] But she also had a more prosaic understanding of events, outraged particularly by the way that shifting *realpolitik* meant that the Allies were confronted with weapons they themselves had sold to Saddam. She started to wear her CND badge again and wrote to her MP protesting against British involvement.

Issues nearer home touched her more directly, especially the brutality of Conservative governments' attacks on the poor. She had voted Conservative in 1979, but very soon changed her mind. There were times in the 1980s

> when my husband and I were literally afraid to read the newspaper because we dared not face the latest personal blow that was going to be inflicted on us, and it happened again and again and again. ... The Conservative government's policies hurt me personally, financially and even physically with real physical pain as well as financial hardship and the frustration of my hopes and ambitions.[43]

Thatcher's 'barbaric values', lauding 'selfish, competitive attitudes and voracious greed', had created a poisonous victim-blaming atmosphere in which the unemployed were attacked as parasites and the chronically sick and disabled were vilified as frauds and scroungers.[44] At the same time as she was being inducted into the mysteries of the Goddess, she was actively involved in a local campaign to allow disabled people to bring their cars into a pedestrianized town centre planned by the local authority which they would otherwise have no effective way of accessing. Although she only attended one meeting, she and Edward drafted questionnaires, corresponded with councillors and the MP, and did most of the paperwork for the campaign's leader, a not-very-well-educated retired traffic warden. When she set her hair on fire they had to drop out, and in subsequent years her health prevented her from taking an active part in political life. But intellectually she remained engaged.

In face of 'a hard cynical capitalist culture' and the ecological catastrophe it was leading to, Rosemary invested her hope in the spread of gentler New

Age values, a post-materialist, environmentally friendly culture. But the slow processes of cultural change were not in themselves sufficient. She was impatient with those who relied solely on changes in individual lifestyle. Ill-considered New Age talk of 'raising the energies', adopting a 'positive attitude' or 'tuning in the right vibrations' served only to burden individuals with responsibility for social and economic forces beyond their control.[45] As for green consumerism, she and Edward, living near the breadline, could do little to reduce their own consumption. And, however valuable as propaganda for a new life, countercultural alternative living by a minority of dedicated drop-outs would not in itself be enough to reverse the rampant engines of capitalism. The scale and urgency of the ecological challenge meant that solutions would have to come from above: only those in power could seriously address these issues. Politically she was inclined to the centre left, joining the Social Democratic Party in the early 1980s and the Labour Party by the end of the decade. Like many others, she was disappointed in her belief that Blair's 1997 victory would fundamentally reverse the evils of Thatcherism, and she transferred her allegiance to the Liberal Democrats when it became apparent locally that they had a chance of defeating the sitting Tory MP. But it was, she acknowledged, a slim hope that politicians of whatever party would show the decisiveness and vision needed to tackle climate change. Nothing exposed more nakedly the short-term horizons of the existing political elite than the contrast between the architectural achievements of her beloved ancient Egypt and the Blair government's pathetic plan to mark two thousand years of the Christian era with a 'millennium dome' scheduled to last for thirty years.

One way of understanding Rosemary's engagement with pagan beliefs and practices, and her experiences of the paranormal, would be to see them as ways of coping with her physical and mental suffering. However illusory others might judge her beliefs to be, they nevertheless enabled her to find meaning and purpose in a life that might otherwise have been hard to bear. But one could also see things the other way around, reverse the causation. In Rosemary's view it was precisely her mental and physical fragility, and the suffering that it entailed, that opened her up to a spiritual realm largely inaccessible to more 'normal' people. 'Dark Isis' delivered her 'gifts of the spirit … through a hard life, and only through a hard life'. Whichever way one chooses to approach it, Rosemary's engagement with paganism is of cultural and sociological, not merely psychological, interest.

New Age beliefs were one response to the destructive materialism of late 20th-century capitalism. Left-wing rationalists are inclined to deplore this response as a retreat from politics, a relapse into superstition and an abandonment of the positive achievements of science and reason. For Rosemary, however, embracing the mystical did not mean abandoning either this-worldly politics or Enlightenment rationality. Afflicted by feelings of fear and panic, she clung to her faith in reason 'almost with desperation. ... If God is not rational, then where are we?'[46] She was never happier than when immersed in the academic study of philosophy – 'a place of light and air, rational argument and intellectual challenge' – and she was fiercely hostile towards what she saw as the quackery of the practitioners of alternative medicine whose ministrations had sapped her spirit and emptied her pocket during the later 1980s.[47] Nothing could have been more 'Enlightened' than her conviction that one day 'it will be proved that rheumatoid arthritis is a physical disease and not "weakness of will" or "karma" or any of the other nonsense that has been said to me over the years; and when that happens, the forces of darkness will have to take a good few steps back and let the light of reason come in'.[48]

But pushing back the forces of darkness and letting in the light of reason was not, in itself, enough. Somewhere, she was convinced that a balance needed to be struck between reason and faith, and it was with a foot firmly planted in each camp that she chose to confront the problems of her life and times. While the rationalist in her was confident that 'much which is now seen as supernatural will eventually be explained by science', her vision of an enchanted world behind appearances made her disinclined to engage with the evidence already accumulated by modern neurological and psychological research that many of the apparently paranormal experiences that she describes could have natural causes.[49] In the face of debilitating physical and mental suffering, a mean and victim-blaming welfare system, and a materialist culture driving relentlessly towards ecological catastrophe, it was the values embodied in her pagan spirituality which did most to sustain her and provide her with a viable way of living on the margin.

III

Rosemary was, on any account, a most unusual person. But she was also a creature of her times, and some of the themes illustrated by her life can be supplemented by the story of another woman who also embraced paganism in middle age. Kirsty Parsons was the daughter of a Sheffield toolmaker. Born in 1948, she went to university in the late 1960s, and, in her mid-forties, quit her job as an education officer in a national museum in London to work full-time as a spiritual healer.

Her embrace of New Age values had begun in the late 1970s during a life crisis in which spiritual questions were closely bound up with issues of class identity. Writing for MO in 1990 she described herself as 'transclassual' – a proudly working-class person in a middle-class job – and extremely class conscious. Angrily dismissing the notion that art and culture were a middle-class preserve, she wrote passionately about the values of the skilled artisan milieu into which she had been born. Her parents both left school at thirteen but they 'are probably the best educated people I know', autodidacts who filled the house with books and paintings.[50] They were also strongly anticlerical and she grew up with no religious beliefs.

When she was twenty-four she married an old school friend with whom she had been living for some years. Her husband did well in the 1970s oil business and she found herself in a milieu of nouveau-riche middle-class people, philistine, acquisitive, materialistic, selfish and 'trivial'. The marriage was childless and she felt a 'growing dissatisfaction with the meaninglessness of life ... I looked around at my worked-for home and its lovely furnishings and realised I had striven for it but it didn't make me happy'.[51] When, in 1978, she discovered that her husband was having an affair, she divorced him 'and entered life as a transclassual'.[52] But the end of her marriage also triggered 'a dramatic spiritual awakening' in which she questioned not only the moral bankruptcy of middle-class materialism but also the atheism she had inherited from her childhood. Deeply moved by a priestly oration at the funeral service for a friend who had died of cancer, she realized that in rejecting religion she had 'thrown out the baby with the bathwater'. Not that established religion itself had anything much to offer. While it was 'Christ who knocked at the overgrown door of my soul', her attempt 'to fit into Christianity as a spiritual structure' was short-lived: 'I was quite unable to accept its patriarchal bureaucracy ... or to find much spirit in its practice.'

Grieving for her friend, and now convinced that the spirit survives death, she made an appointment with a medium at the College of Psychic Studies. The friend did not 'come through', but instead she encountered the spirit of her dead grandmother. 'I left the College trembling with shock and awe', and in subsequent sessions grandmother became 'a warm and loving presence in my life'. It was characteristic of her spiritual journey that she sought out the most prestigious practitioners. A session with Liz Greene, who combines astrology with Jungian psychoanalysis, was equally impressive, but she could not afford repeat visits and 'it has not seemed worthwhile to go to lesser practitioners'. Nor, as a 'non-joiner', was she attracted to any existing cults or sects: 'I like to think for myself, and am completely unable to be obedient ... I am basically a mystic, proceeding by individual meditation, study, prayer and pilgrimage.'

Central to her 'spiritual awakening' was a belief in reincarnation: the journey of the spirit through successive incarnations made sense of life and of suffering in a way that her previous belief in the 'blind forces of evolution' had not. She started to keep a 'reincarnation notebook' noting intimations of past lives 'most particularly in ancient Egypt', and this helped her not only to 'understand some of my own complexity' but also to compensate for current disappointments: she became convinced, as reported in Chapter 3, that she had in previous incarnations experienced 'deep love and the fulfilment of motherhood, although these joys have eluded me in this life.'[53] Although attracted by Buddhism, she felt more at home with 'the pantheons of ancient Egypt, Greece and Rome'; with Druidry (which she studied at the Bardic grade); and with North American native cultures whose shamanistic sense of the spirituality of natural things offered a powerful resource in the struggle against 'the massive arrogance and destructiveness of Western science.'[54] Sometime in the early 1990s she came (like Jung, whom she cites[55]) to *know*, rather than merely *believe*, that God existed:

> A vision of the Goddess Isis came to me and she has visited me many times since. As a result the Goddess became a living reality for me, as She is doing worldwide for many other individuals. I believe the timing and arrival of that vision were no accident.[56]

The revival of paganism was putting women back in touch with ancient spiritual traditions destroyed in the witch hunts of early modern Europe. 'I am one of a few people who are trying to find their way back to the lost wisdom. It is a lonely occupation and concrete covers so many of the tracks.'[57]

Her own contribution lay in her practice as a spiritual healer. Touching her patients lightly on the shoulders to induce relaxation she encouraged them to visualize 'their ideal healing place, perhaps a tropical island or a forest glade', and then, passing her hands about two inches above the whole body, she channelled an energy which helped to trigger the recipient's own natural capacity for self-healing. Praying 'to both male and female aspects of the divine for permission to channel healing to the patient', she visualized 'light flowing down over myself and the patient – filling our entire bodies and flowing into the earth below. I visualise strong green energy flowing up from the earth and flowing through us to the sky above'. Since the divine was itself 'deeply part of nature' there was, she insisted, nothing supernatural about this process. The energies she channelled and released were entirely natural, despite the fact that 'scientists have not yet identified or measured this energy and certain churches reject healing as witchcraft'.[58] In line with the National Federation of Spiritual Healers, with which she was affiliated, she did not discuss her spiritual beliefs with her patients, but stressed instead that the therapy was complementary not alternative, that patients should keep in contact with their own GPs, and that there were no 'arcane mysteries' involved and no faith required to benefit from the process.[59] In this way, safely anchored in a secular world, the therapy could work its spiritual magic without troubling its recipients with the beliefs that underpinned it. 'We must always be down to earth,' she wrote, citing a favourite motto: 'Trust in Allah, but tether your camel first.'[60]

Pagans shared many of the characteristics of the broader currents of late 20th-century New Age spirituality – rejection of scriptural or ecclesiastical authority, eclectic sources of spiritual inspiration, a holistic attitude to the unity of mind, body and the cosmos. But they saw themselves as having achieved a more profound spiritual awakening than most of those who subscribed to New Age ideas.[61] They would certainly have agreed with the only other practising pagan among the mass observers – Selina Field, a thirty-year-old artist/writer/poet – who was insistent on distinguishing herself from the 'superstitions and/or fanciful rubbish' that passed for much 'so-called New Age thinking'. People like her, 'who are really into the Occult/New Age thinking', dismissed most popular New Age literature as 'just junk … re-digested waffle [copied] from other equally silly books'.[62]

For both Rosemary and Kirsty, it was a vision of the Goddess which opened the way to their 'higher spiritual development', transforming the way they lived; both sustained their new faith with disciplined ritual, Rosemary in her Iseum and Kirsty in her activity as a healer. And they were not, as Rosemary put it, 'silly' people. Rosemary was dismissive of some of the sillier paranormal beliefs and was scathing about the charlatanism of New Age acquaintances who suggested that the solution to her physical difficulties lay in 'positive thinking'. She valued rationality and scientific method, and, like Kirsty, understood holistic spirituality as complementary rather than antagonistic to orthodox medical practice. And while embracing the mystical she also kept her camel tethered, actively engaging (as much as her health would allow) with politics and down-to-earth local campaigning.

By reconstructing these two women's spiritual journeys we are reminded of the ways in which spirituality was embedded in life experience more generally. Rosemary's spiritual journey was played out against the background of the middle-class philistinism of both her own and her husband's families, and the contrasting delight of the intellectual world they had encountered as university students. Kirsty rejected the atheism of her working-class parents, but her fierce pride in their autodidact culture informed her dissatisfaction with the philistine materialism of her husband's milieu and her consequent search for some more meaningful approach to life. Charles Taylor suggests that 'ordinary human flourishing' – fulfilment in family life and a worthwhile job – dulls the need for spiritual exploration.[63] The absence of such anchorage clearly played a role in both Rosemary's and Kirsty's spiritual journeys. Pushed to the margins from childhood by unsympathetic parents, disbarred from employment by both mental and physical health, Rosemary found fulfilment in a marriage built not around bringing up children but around intellectual and spiritual exploration. Kirsty had a worthwhile job, but her marriage was also childless – an absence that she attempted to fill with memories of a previous life – and, unlike Rosemary's, deeply unfulfilling. It was when the marriage collapsed that she found herself turning to the spiritual dimensions of life. It would, however, be wrong to view these two women's deep investment in spirituality merely as compensation for a lack of 'ordinary human flourishing'. What they gained, both would have insisted, was far greater than what a more conventional life could have provided. And, compared with life in the narrow, materialistic, philistine milieus against which they revolted, they were surely right.

IV

Dark Isis delivered her gifts to Rosemary through suffering. And the spiritual crisis that led Kirsty to embrace the Goddess was driven by a failed marriage and the death of a close friend. By way of contrast we can end this chapter with Dorothy Hyde, who also found spirituality in middle age, although in her case it took the form of Hindu, not pagan, belief and practice. There was no lack of 'ordinary human flourishing' in Dorothy's life, and suffering appears to have played no part in her spiritual journey. Throughout her writing for MO she presents herself as cheerful and well adjusted, her life purposeful and fulfilling, whether writing as an atheist in the 1980s or, by the mid-1990s, as a devotee of Hare Krishna.[64]

Growing up post-war in a working-class district of a badly bombed town, Dorothy was the treasured only child of parents who had abandoned faith in God along with an inherited habit of Methodist chapel-going during the horrors of the Blitz. She went to Sunday school and read religious tracts 'but was never able to accept the existence of a God, even during those adolescent years of religious questioning when I wanted desperately to have a "faith"... I have always been an atheist', she wrote in 1985, 'but live a life which is basically a "Christian" one. ... My parents are two of the kindest, happiest people I know and lead quiet, fulfilled lives. I hope I can live up to their standards'.[65] Her adolescent curiosity about the supernatural had been fed by a spiritualist grandfather and tales of a great-uncle, well known as a medium, who, unable to bear the pain of foreseeing future unhappy events in other peoples' lives, had committed suicide. To discourage such dangerous interests, her parents, who had entertained themselves with Ouija boards in their youth, indulged her with a couple of sessions in which the upturned glass 'launched up into the air and hit me across the forehead. ... I always assumed my parents did this deliberately to put me off, but I don't know how they managed it'.[66]

Like Rosemary, Dorothy first met her future husband as a schoolgirl. But he was five years older than her and it may have been the close ties that she formed with his sisters that enabled the relationship to survive her student years, when she was studying for an external London university degree. She loved being a student in the tail end of the long '1960s', 'when youth was idolised ... a time', as she remembered it, 'of love and peace and pleasure seeking'. It was probably at this time that she first encountered her Hare Krishna friends among the 'young people who advocated free love', and 'travelled to exotic places to "find" themselves and "tune in, turn on and drop out" – generally with a charming naivete and gentleness'.[67] But she kept faith with her childhood sweetheart, married him, had two children and, as they grew up, combined a part-time job as a supervisor in a large department store with an increasingly active community role, as a school governor, a volunteer for Social Services with 'problem' families and chair of her local community centre. In her late thirties she made contact again with her Hare Krishna friends, took up vegetarianism and Tai Chi. But her induction was gradual. As late as 1994 (aged forty-one) she remained unconvinced that the soul survived the body and still saw herself as holding 'no strong religious views' and having no 'clear philosophy of life and death'.[68]

A key moment came three years later, when, abandoning the decaying working-class neighbourhood in which they had lived for the previous twenty-three years, the family moved upmarket into 'a large Art Deco' house with 'a secluded garden and "nice" neighbours'. Embarrassed by the materialistic acquisitiveness of the move, she comforted herself with the feeling that 'we were just meant to have this house', a perfect location in which she and her husband could pursue their spiritual development. 'I try to live according to the principles of the Krishna movement', she wrote at this time, 'I am not this body, I am a spirit, soul. ... I chant daily, offer food and read religious literature.'[69] Soon, with their daughter away at university, the couple were able to offer accommodation to visiting devotees. By the end of the century she had met her spiritual teacher – 'through a series of coincidences', she explains (echoing Rosemary's account of how she found her teacher) – and had come to understand 'this beautiful, fun-loving, approachable version of the Lord of Creation'. In one of her last contributions to MO, now aged fifty-six, she wrote of her aspiration 'to improve my standard of prayer and practices as set down in the scriptures and associate more with devotees and qualified gurus who can guide me. Not a day goes by when I don't consider ... my spiritual development. It's a brilliant exciting quest, full of music, celebration and joy, not some dry as dust intellectual project'.[70]

The implied opposition between spiritual joy and intellectual sterility is significant. Rosemary was able to straddle the spiritual and the scientific, her mystical encounters with Isis by no means cancelling out her respect for scientific enquiry or the pleasure she took in 'the light and air' of 'rational argument and intellectual challenge'. By contrast, Dorothy's joyous Krishna consciousness seems to have left no space for other ways of knowing the world. Scientists, she explained, expressing profound scepticism about the value of scientific rationality, were imperfect beings, like the rest of us, and yesterday's proven 'facts' often turn out to be wrong. 'If we want to know more about our universe', she concluded, 'we can simply go to the relevant scriptures in submissive and respectful mood, under the guidance of realised gurus, and all knowledge will be found there.'[71]

The contrast between these two women, both of whom embraced religious beliefs and practices on the exotic margins of late 20th-century British culture, points to a more general conclusion. Believers in the supernatural could, as in Dorothy's case, close their minds to naturalistic ways of understanding existence. But they did not necessarily do so. Rosemary represents an extreme example of the capacity to combine belief in supernatural forces with rational and scientific modes of thought, but, as we have seen, many other mass observers sought to reconcile these divergent ways of knowing themselves and the world. And if Dorothy closed her mind to science, some rationalists could be equally blind to the imaginative work performed by religion and belief in the supernatural. The making of meaning is a work of the imagination for believers and non-believers alike. The Goddess Isis played a crucial role – and a positive one – in Rosemary's life, whether or not she actually existed.

8

Conclusion

I

When the marine biologist Alister Hardy started to collect testimony about people's religious experiences he felt that he was discovering a hidden world, comparing his research to that of the early collectors of plankton – 'dipping our little nets in the sea from a rowing boat and marvelling at the variety of life brought forth'.[1] Mass Observation's (MO's) directives on the supernatural, religion, nature, death, heaven and spiritualism yield a similar harvest. What is remarkable about this material is not just the variety of beliefs and experiences reported but also the quality of the reporting. There is a freshness, openness and trust in the mass observers' writings which compels attention. Stirred by directives which posed some of life's most puzzling questions, respondents dug deeply into themselves to formulate their convictions and, frequently, their perplexities.

Coming to this material as a convinced atheist who had never given much thought to either religion or notions of the supernatural more generally, all I could do, at first, was to marvel. How could so many people believe so much bizarre nonsense? It has taken me a long time and much reading in the relevant scholarly literature to understand that the important question posed by these marvellous products of the human imagination is not whether they are 'true' or 'false' but what intimations of meaning in a life they serve to express. All attempts to find meaning in human life are works of the imagination, exercises in our ability to see what is not there until, by believing, we create it. The challenge posed by religion to the atheist is not 'where did the world come from?', 'Where did life come from?' – those are questions science can tackle – but 'where does the meaning come from?' No amount of scientific investigation is going to establish whether or not supernatural forces exist. To the cradle Catholic, like Charles Taylor, the ontological issue seems clear. But so it does to the cradle atheist like myself. Many people suspend judgement, or hover uncertainly around a porous ontological frontier between a purely secular spirituality that exists 'only in our minds while we're alive' and irrepressible whispers of transcendence like those haunting the mass observer whose 'acquired scepticism' was 'just hung on to against a background of accessibility to the supernatural'.[2] For all the sophistication of philosophical reasoning, where one situates oneself seems to be largely a matter of inherited traditions of belief or of disbelief. And, in so far as we choose our religious or philosophical beliefs, we are influenced as much by the promptings of intuition, by predispositions buried deep in the unconscious, as we are by the finer points of rational argument. Our intuitions, distilled in the unconscious from upbringing and life experience, are as powerful as logic or the evidence of our senses in driving our reasoning.

Our secular culture has difficulty in getting to grips with the idea that we are no more than a cosmic accident. It is not easy to accept that any meaning there might be during humanity's probably brief presence in the universe can only be derived from meanings we ourselves create. In the absence of the dignified resignation of the stoic, the appeal to some supernatural force or purpose, to the existence of 'something else', serves to assuage the metaphysical itch, the psychological need for something over and above the mundane fulfilments of work and family life. The materialist who dismisses such appeals to the supernatural as symptomatic of nothing more than gullibility and ignorance forgets the role played by imagination in the way that all of us, believers and non-believers alike, construct our identities and with them our sense that life is meaningful. To the extent that we can gain awareness of the subconscious roots of our beliefs we should be able to suspend them, and their matching disbeliefs, sufficiently to listen to the meanings encoded in the beliefs of others. Rather than worrying about which of us has access to the truth – truth is not a property of the myths by which we live – we should approach each other's beliefs with empathy, looking for human meanings transcending divergent ontological standpoints.

The pain of bereavement might destroy religious faith – how could one believe in so cruel a God? – but it was still difficult for some to resist a lingering nostalgia for the comfort offered by belief in an afterlife. In the face of death, belief or disbelief in the supernatural had less impact on the mass observers' attitudes than the places they tended to look for meaning in their lives – in the warmth of family commitment, in the urgency of their individual journeys or in a more detached and reflective stance. The experience of those rare life-affirming moments 'out of time' which William James understood as the central 'religious experience' was by no means limited to those who believed them to be of supernatural provenance. Near-death experiences might convince some of the reality of the afterlife, but they could also be deeply meaningful for people who had no religious belief. The apparently paranormal inspired a good deal of nonsense, but much of it was playful, expressive of irrepressible intellectual curiosity and a creative resistance to the merely instrumental reason of Weber's iron cage. And most of those who played with the paranormal were nevertheless keen to find ways of reconciling the delight they took in the uncanny and the unexplained with their acceptance of the procedures of modern science as the most reliable path to positive knowledge. Reconciliation was not always easy. While scientific explanations could be found for sensations of awe, wonder, joy, ecstasy, the feelings themselves rested on intuitive modes of cognition which threatened to destabilize atheist identities centred on belief in the power of reason. And while there were believers who admitted to privileging their intuitive knowledge of God over the findings of modern science, there were also atheists who confessed disappointment that science could offer no answers to life's deeper mysteries.

II

The MO material provides a snapshot of the range of beliefs current towards the end of the 20th century, but it is not easy to locate this picture in its larger historical context. The scholarly literature on the place of religion and the process of secularization in modern Western societies is something of a battlefield, polarized between proponents of irreversible secularization and those who, while not disputing the evidence of Christian decline, detect signs of post-secular re-enchantment.[3] Charles Taylor belongs to the latter school, and it may seem perverse that, despite my own atheist beliefs, I have used him as my guide to unfamiliar terrain. Research in this area tends to be framed by stories which play out the beliefs of researchers.[4] Those with religious faith accuse atheist writers of being deaf to matters spiritual; atheists accuse believers, in a phrase calculated to raise the temperature, of 'secularization denial'. I have tried to resist this polarisation. While I do not share Taylor's view that religious belief is likely to make a comeback, I am equally sceptical about the way in which some of the leading historians of secularization characterize the secular mind.

The narrative of secularization established by sociologists in the 1960s has its roots in what one historian describes as 'the era of post-war social democratic confidence, foregrounding the power of rationality and social science to deliver sustained solutions to the problems that were besetting the world.'[5] According to the sociologist Bryan Wilson, defining secularization in 1966: 'Men act less and less in response to religious motivation: they assess the world in empirical and rational terms.'[6] Rehearsing Wilson's argument half a century later Steve Bruce, Britain's most determined defender of the secularization paradigm, defined the process of secularization as involving, among other things, 'the replacement of a specifically religious consciousness ... by an empirical, rational, instrumental orientation'.[7] This formulation seems to me to be doubly deficient. First, it neglects the degree to which human beings have always combined imaginative constructions of their place in the cosmos with instrumental reason – the practical intelligence which underpinned technology from the domestication of fire, Neolithic tool-making or the invention of the wheel. And second, it neglects the inability of instrumental reason to address the search for meaning in life, which, as Bryan Wilson acknowledged, remains central to 'the emotional aspects of man's nature' even in the absence of religion.[8]

Proponents of the secularization paradigm tend to throw out the baby of meaning with the bathwater of religion. While religion is not hardwired into the human mind, the search for meaning does seem to be an essential part of the human condition. Narrowly focussed on the decline of religion, Bruce's account of secularization fails to engage with the operations of the imagination. In a similarly prosaic spirit, an anonymous reader of an earlier version of this book dismissed the mass observers' existential puzzlement as evidence of their own unrepresentativeness, asserting that 'the majority of the population cannot be arsed giving five minutes thought to such concerns'. One does not have to accept Charles Taylor's religious convictions to appreciate his sensitivity to the ways in which, alongside the triumphs of instrumental rationality, modern secular people – all of them – remain meaning-making animals.

At the turn of the century Callum Brown shifted the debate about secularization by locating *The Death of Christian Britain* in the cultural revolution of the 1960s. It was, he argued, the assertion, especially by women, of a liberated autonomous selfhood which fatally undermined the authority of a patriarchal, authoritarian and sexually repressive religious establishment. In a more recent study of atheist humanists living in several Western countries Brown offers a powerful narrative of a post-war generation in transition. Many of his respondents lost religion in childhood; remained silent or indifferent about their unbelief during early adulthood (or in some cases flirted with notions of spirituality); and finally 'came out' as atheists in middle age or later. At the time he interviewed them, most were active members of humanist organizations, campaigning on issues of personal freedom, human rights and 'the whole gamut of modern equality issues', while caring for fellow non-believers by inventing humanist alternatives to Christian rites of passage (weddings and funerals). Brown tells this as a story, not of loss, but of gain: his atheists were pioneering a purely secular culture, in which they could live 'as if God does not exist', observing moral codes that required no supernatural legitimation. Although these caring, activist, atheist humanists were a tiny group, he sees them as prefigurative of human progress towards a fully secular society in which religion will have disappeared.[9]

While it is easy to share Brown's enthusiasm for his respondents, it is more difficult to accept his attribution of their admirable behaviour to their atheism. That there is no necessary relationship between atheism and liberal ideas of autonomous selfhood and human rights is clear enough from the history of atheist regimes during the last hundred years. Moreover, activists campaigning on issues of personal freedom and human rights can also be found among groups of liberal-minded Christians. A closer look at the relationship between Christianity and the cultural revolution of the 1960s tells a more complicated story than the equation Brown offers between female emancipation, individual autonomy, social justice and atheism. Feminist revolt against a patriarchal church was as likely to lead to campaigns for the ordination of women as to atheism. Many of the 1960s reforms – abolition of the death penalty, decriminalization of homosexuality, introduction of no-guilt divorce and even abortion law reform – owed a good deal to progressive Christians.[10] And in breaking the link between conservative morality and the church these Christians were also accepting the reality of secularization. The early 1960s saw a decisive shift among Christian leaders away from insisting that the only alternative to a Christian culture was an amoral and regressive paganism, and towards embracing a tolerant pluralism in which values derived from Christianity could be shared by believers and non-believers alike. It has been argued that this shift in Christian discourse played a key role in triggering the tidal wave of secularization which undermined the churches in the later 1960s and beyond.[11] If so, it provides a local example of a more general process. The secularization of modern Western societies, as Charles Taylor argues at length, has been deeply rooted in the evolution of Christianity since the Reformation.

Callum Brown will have none of this. Taylor's book, he writes, 'defines, not a secular condition, but merely the latest manifestation of the religious one'.[12] Genuine secularity has no place for Christian leftovers, he insists, and the values of his atheist humanists owe nothing to Christianity. But he does note a contrast between a minority whose atheism rested firmly on 'the sovereignty of reason' and a larger number who spoke movingly to him about 'the dignity yet the smallness of human life; the awe they felt on beholding the night sky and its billions of stars, and their sensation of humankind's fragility as just another animal, but an animal with special responsibilities on our planet'.[13] Among the latter, he reports, many resorted to the language of 'spirituality' to describe their feelings. While this may not be evidence of Christian leftovers, it certainly suggests that something more than the exercise of reason underpinned their sense of their place in the cosmos. Those who embraced 'the sovereignty of reason' would, presumably, have endorsed Richard Dawkins's strictly rationalist sense of wonder, seeing it as arising not from contemplating rainbows but from the human ability to 'unweave' them.[14] The object of wonder, for Dawkins, is not nature or the cosmos but the human mind itself. Most of Brown's respondents, however, seem to have had more in common with the feelings described by David Attenborough when recalling the first time he dived on a coral reef: his sense of awe and wonder at being able 'to move among a world of *unrevealed complexity*'.[15] The naturalist's humility in the face of nature stands in sharp contrast to the biologist's hubristic claim that wonder belonged exclusively to the achievements of reason itself.

Brown, anxious to deny the existence among his respondents of any 'enduring religious sentiment', explains that their sense of wonder served to 'induce a rationality that overcomes religion'.[16] This is a very curious assertion. The feelings they describe are, in fact, entirely compatible with religion, just as they are with atheism. What is in play here is not a contest between rationality and religion but a human need to imagine existential meaning, which is common to believers and unbelievers alike. Brown rejects Taylor's account of modern secularity because Taylor insists that the 'exclusive humanism' of the atheist cannot provide the depth and 'fullness' of meaning to which human beings aspire. My own response to this, as outlined in Chapter One, is simply to say that I disagree: there is no objective position from which to judge whether believers live richer, deeper, more fulfilling lives than atheists. Brown, however, wants to go further, dismissing Taylor's evocation of 'transcendence, fullness, or other neo-religious characteristics' as phantasms which 'the secular social scientist has difficulty calibrating'.[17] Phantasms they may be, but Brown's refusal to engage with the religious imagination would have surprised the founding fathers of social science – Marx, Durkheim, Weber – all of whom sought not to dismiss religious emotions but to understand them in secular terms. The purpose of 'calibration' is to allow comparison between different data sets. One does not have to believe in the transcendent reality of experiences reported by religious believers in order to compare them with similar experiences reported by non-believers. Among the mass observers, testimony to feelings of awe and wonder or to moments of heightened emotion when life seemed more than usually meaningful occurs across the whole spectrum of belief and unbelief. Because such feelings transcend the ontological divide, the secular social scientist – or historian – needs to understand them as belonging neither to religion nor (as Brown improbably suggests) to atheism but to a human need for meaning which cannot be satisfied by the exercise of reason alone.

So how to locate the snapshot provided by the mass observers in its historical context? It is quite possible to fit them into a narrative of irreversible secularization. The atheists among them would represent the vanguard; the appeal of spirituality to some could be read as a halfway house in the transition to a thoroughgoing secular outlook; and the doubts and uncertainties expressed by many of those who clung to religion bore witness to its declining hold. But we do not actually know where history is going. And, whether or not the mass observers turn out to have lived during a transition to a purely secular society, they themselves did not live in one. These individuals lived in a here and now that offered no final destination, and my concern has been to observe, contrast and compare their imaginative constructions of their place in the cosmos rather than to calibrate them on an arbitrary scale derived from my own preferred historical outcome. And for this purpose Charles Taylor's picture of an open-ended pluralist society in which the future of supernatural beliefs remains unknown provides a more useful overview of the late 20th-century world than the metanarrative of irreversible secularization.

III

If it is the case that it is only through the imagination that we can find the meaning that we crave, then we should treat each other's imaginative constructions with respect. Dogmatic rationalists building their self-esteem on contempt for the irrational superstitions of the ignorant masses were to be found on both sides of the ontological divide, the religious no less than the atheist. But nothing is gained by claiming that our own deepest convictions are so irrefutable that all reasonable people must embrace them. It is possible, as Charles Taylor shows, to believe in God, and at the same time to have empathy and respect for atheists. And it is also possible to be quite convinced that there is no such thing as the supernatural and, yet, acknowledging that there are limits to human understanding, to respect those who choose to fill the resulting chasms of the unknown with supernatural forces. It is also possible, and perfectly rational, to be uncertain about these issues, to be puzzled.

More important than what we believe is how, in a pluralist society, we handle our beliefs. Since the 1960s the term 'spirituality' has come increasingly into popular parlance as a way of describing our profounder feelings which renders fuzzy and unclear the boundary between the power of imagination, and something which can properly be described as an experience of the transcendental. This extended use of the term worries the fundamentalist Christian and the New Atheist alike. Clinging to their respective existential certainties, feeding off each other's dogmatism, they have more in common that either would like to admit. But outside these embattled camps most people settle for a degree of uncertainty. Divided as they were about the ultimate nature of reality, many of the mass observers were united in their readiness to puzzle about the feelings evoked by death, about their experiences of ecstatic 'moments out of time', about apparently paranormal events, and about the relationship between these feelings and scientific rationality. In analysing their attitudes towards the supernatural, my aim has been to bring divergent ways of finding meaning in human life into dialogue with one another. In the end, irreconcilable differences about the ontological basis of existence may be less important than equivalences of experience obscured by the apologists of belief and unbelief.

Appendix

The supernatural: What do you believe?
MO Directive 47a, 24 May 1996

We have called this section the 'supernatural' but it's quite hard finding a word that is broad enough to cover everything that everyone might think of as supernatural, and their beliefs in it. Do you believe in supernatural occurrences? The first task, then, is to ask you to list everything you can think of that might come under this heading, and the next task is to comment on your own experiences and views. For each item on your list, could you please provide the following information:

(1) Give your definitions of what it is. So if 'ghosts' is the first thing on your list, for example, you should explain what you think a ghost is (or what you think other people believe in if you personally don't believe in ghosts).

(2) If this is something you believe in yourself, please describe when you first heard about it. Was it through stories from your parents or other family members? Through books or films? Through some kind of special experience? Can you recall? Details please.
Do you enjoy reading about the supernatural? Please describe books, magazines etc. which you read. Can you explain why you like them?
Do you watch films, videos or television programmes with a supernatural theme? Please describe. Can you explain why you like them?
Finally, if you do believe in the supernatural, or some elements of the supernatural, can you describe how this is important to your outlook on life? How does it affect your behaviour? How does it relate to your other beliefs, especially any religious beliefs that you may hold? Do you feel they have a special meaning to you because of some experience in your life? Please take this opportunity to write as fully as you can on the question. There is no need to apologise for rambling as we want to hear from you in as much detail and depth as you have time for.

Notes

Preface

1 Charles Taylor, *A Secular Age* (London: Belknap, 2007), 17, 356.
2 Charles Taylor, *Varieties of Religion Today: William James Revisited* (London: Harvard University Press, 2003), 57.
3 Clifford Geertz, *The Interpretation of Cultures* (New York: Basic Books, 1973), 123.
4 Taylor, *Secular Age*, 428.

1 Introduction

1 A hankering, as Weber wrote, 'driven not by material need but by an inner compulsion to understand the world as a meaningful cosmos and to take up a position towards it' (Max Weber, *The Sociology of Religion* (London: Methuen, 1965), 117).
2 Clifford Geertz, *The Interpretation of Cultures*, 5, summarizing Weber.
3 William James formulated the notion that intuitive impressions occurring on the fringe of consciousness play a role in the subjective experience of meaning, a 'feeling of rightness'. For recent discussion building on James's insights see Samantha J. Heintzelman and Laura of A. King, 'On Knowing More Than We Can Tell: Intuitive Processes and the Experience of Meaning', *The Journal of Positive Psychology*, 8, no. 6 (2013): 471–82; Bruce Mangan, 'Meaning, God, Volition, and Art: How Rightness and the Fringe Bring It All Together', *Journal of Consciousness Studies*, 21, nos. 3–4 (2014): 754–67; Eugene Taylor, 'Metaphysics and Consciousness in James' Varieties', in Jeremy Carrette (ed.), *William James and the Varieties of Religious Experience* (London: Routledge, 2005).
4 Ludwig Wittgenstein, *Culture and Value*, edited by G. H. Von Wright (Oxford: Blackwell, 1984), 85.
5 As critics of Charles Taylor have pointed out: J. Butler, 'Disquieted History in *A Secular Age*', in Michael Warner, Jonathan VanAntwerpen and Craig Calhoun (eds), *Varieties of Secularism in a Secular Age* (London: Harvard University Press,

2013), 193–216; Callum Brown, 'The Necessity of Atheism: Making Sense of Secularisation', *Journal of Religious History*, 41, no. 4 (2017): 439–56.

6 R. Gill et al., 'Is Religious Belief Declining in Britain?', *Journal for the Scientific Study of Religion*, 37, no. 3 (1998): 509; Ben Clements, *Religion and Public Opinion: Continuity and Change* (New York: Palgrave Macmillan, 2015), 14.

7 British Social Attitudes, http://www.natcen.ac.uk/news-media/press-releases/2017/september/british-social-attitudes-record-number-of-brits-with-no-religion/ (accessed 27 August 2021).

8 Clive D. Field, BRIN Working Paper Religion in Great Britain, 1939–99: A Compendium of Gallup Poll Data, http://www.brin.ac.uk/wp-content/uploads/2011/12/Religion-in-Great-Britain-1939-99-A-Compendium-of-Gallup-Poll-Data.pdf (accessed 27 August 2021), Table 14: Belief in God, 1947–93; see also Mark Abrams et al., *Values and Social Change in Britain* (Basingstoke: Macmillan, 1985), 60.

9 Hugh McLeod, *The Religious Crisis of the 1960s* (Oxford: Oxford University Press, 2007), 1, 265.

10 Gill et al., 'Is Religious Belief Declining in Britain?', 513. For more up-to-date figures see Madeleine Castro et al., 'The Paranormal Is (Still) Normal: The Sociological Implications of a Survey of Paranormal Experiences in Great Britain', *Sociological Research Online*, 19, no. 3 (2014): 16.

11 Clive D. Field, *British Religion in Numbers* (Manchester: University of Manchester, 2010).

12 Gillian Bennett, *'Alas, Poor Ghost!': Traditions of Belief in Story and Discourse* (Logan: Utah State University Press, 1999), 3. For a more recent elaboration of the argument see Nadia Bartolini, Robert Chris, Sara MacKian and Steve Pile, 'The Place of Spirit: Modernity and the Geographies of Spirituality', *Progress in Human Geography*, 41, no. 3 (2017): 338–54.

13 YouGov, University of Lancaster, Faith Matters, 30 January 2013 (accessed 27 August 2021).

14 Gill et al., 'Is Religious Belief Declining in Britain?', 509; YouGov, University of Lancaster, Faith Matters, 30 January 2013.

15 Linda Woodhead, 'Introduction', in Linda Woodhead and Rebecca Catto (eds), *Religion and Change in Modern Britain* (Abingdon: Routledge, 2012), 6; YouGov, 'Atheism', *The Times*, 12 February 2015.

16 As Callum Brown points out, 'people rarely find a negative position attractive or useful for personal identity', and many of his atheist respondents had reservations about 'the tenor of Dawkins' style' (*Becoming Atheist: Humanism and the Secular West* (London: Bloomsbury Academic, 2017), 72, 127). 'I'm an atheist but I don't like Richard Dawkins', one respondent told Lois Lee, while another explained that 'calling yourself an "atheist" in company, can occasionally seem like holding up a big sign saying, "if any of you are anything other than atheists, I think you're all

fucking morons". Um, which is disrespectful, in the extreme. Obviously' (Lois Lee, *Recognizing the Non-Religious, Reimagining the Secular* (Oxford: Oxford University Press, 2015), 135–6).

17 Jacques Monod, *Chance and Necessity: An Essay on the Natural Philosophy of Modern Biology* (New York: Alfred A. Knopf, 1971), 180.
18 Charles Taylor, *Sources of the Self: The Making of the Modern Identity* (Cambridge: Cambridge University Press, 1989), 404, 94.
19 Peter Berger, *A Rumour of Angels: Modern Society and the Rediscovery of the Supernatural* (Harmondsworth: Penguin, 1971), 83.
20 Bertrand Russell, *Philosophical Essays*, 1910, 60, cited in Nicholas Humphrey, *Soul Searching: Human Nature and Supernatural Belief* (London: Chatto & Windus, 1995), 38.
21 Jean-Paul Sartre, *Nausea* (London: Penguin Books, 1969).
22 Max Weber, *The Protestant Ethic and the Spirit of Capitalism* (London: Penguin, 2002).
23 Douglas Litowitz, 'Max Weber and Franz Kafka: A Shared Vision of Modern Law', *Law, Culture and the Humanities*, 7, no. 1 (2011): 48–65.
24 As Zuckerman convincingly argues on the basis of interviews with people in two of the least religious countries in the world (Denmark and Sweden). But one doesn't need to be religious to doubt his assertion that a concern with existential meaning beyond that to be found in family, work and (in Sweden) shooting elk is confined to 'a very small, select proportion of humanity' (Phil Zuckerman, *Society without God: What the Least Religious Nations Can Tell Us about Contentment* (New York: New York University Press, 2020), 91–2).
25 William James, *The Varieties of Religious Experience: A Study in Human Nature: Being the Gifford Lectures on Natural Religion Delivered at Edinburgh in 1901–1902*, e-book (New York: Modern Library, 1929), 71.
26 For the literature on this see the Wikipedia entry on 'confirmation bias'.
27 Emile Durkheim, *The Elementary Forms of the Religious Life* (New Orleans, LA: Quid Pro Books, [1915] 2012), 431.
28 Richard Dawkins, *Unweaving the Rainbow: Science, Delusion and the Appetite for Wonder* (London: Allen Lane, 1998), 176–9.
29 Cf. Gordon Lynch:
> 'Attention to the sacred may help to clarify forms of sacralised value that transcend the boundaries of the religious and non-religious. … At a time in which both religious and non-religious assertions are made about the irreducible and irreconcilable differences between religious and non-religious life-worlds, understanding forms of sacralised values that are shared across those differences is helpful for problematising unhelpfully simplistic identity claims. ('Researching the Religious Dimensions of Social Life', in Luke

Dogett and Alp Arat, *Foundations and Futures in the Sociology of Religion* (London: Routledge, 2017), 160)

See also Timothy Stacey, *Myth and Solidarity in the Modern World, beyond Religious and Political Division* (London: Routledge, 2018).

30 This is a major theme of Charles Taylor's account of *A Secular Age*.
31 Terry Eagleton, *Reason, Faith and Revolution: Reflections on the God Debate* (London: Yale University Press, 2009), 84.
32 Peter E. Gordon, 'The Place of the Sacred in the Absence of God: Charles Taylor's "A Secular Age"', *Journal of the History of Ideas*, 69, no. 4 (2008): 647–73. For a telling critique of Taylor's argument that our deepest human attachments – love – necessarily involve a yearning for the transcendent, see Thomas A. Carlson, 'Secular Affection Moods: Exploring Temporality with *A Secular Age*', in Florian Zemmin, Colin Jager and Guido Vanheeswijck (eds.), *Working with a Secular Age: Interdisciplinary Perspectives on Charles Taylor's Master Narrative* (Berlin: De Gruyter, 2016), 245–62.
33 'The term nature often refers to the physical universe and supernatural to the metaphysical. This leaves a lot of territory unmentioned, e.g. the shared imaginative world of the social and cultural' (Simon Dein, 'The Category of the Supernatural: A Valid Anthropological Term?', *Religion Compass*, 10, no. 2 (2016): 42).
34 Maurice Bloch, 'Why Religion Is Nothing Special but Is Central', *Philosophical Transactions Royal Society London B Biol Sci*, 363, no. 1499 (2008): 2055–61. Bloch offers an evolutionary explanation of the ability of human beings 'to live very largely in the imagination' (p. 2058), and suggests that the separation of religion from the 'social transcendent' is, in evolutionary terms, a recent, superficial and probably transient phenomenon. It was, argues Marcel Gauchet, the development of the world religions during Karl Jasper's 'axial age' that first separated the supernatural from the secular state ('Give unto Caesar that which is Caesar's'), opening the way, in the long term, for the eventual sidelining of the supernatural in the social imaginary (Marcel Gauchet, *The Disenchantment of the World: A Political History of Religion* (Princeton: Princeton University Press, 1999).
35 Mary Midgley, *The Myths We Live By* (Abingdon: Routledge, 2004). The salience of the mythical in modern culture has recently been explored by several US literary scholars: Matthew Sterenberg, *Mythic Thinking in Twentieth-Century Britain: Meaning for Modernity* (Basingstoke: Palgrave Macmillan, 2013); Joshua Landy and Michael Saler (eds), *The Re-Enchantment of the World: Secular Magic in a Rational Age* (Stanford: Stanford University Press, 2009); Jo Carruthers and Andrew Tate, *Spiritual Identities: Literature and the Post-Secular Imagination* (Oxford: Peter Lang, 2010).
36 Erik Erikson, *Identity, Youth and Crisis* (London: Faber & Faber, 1968); Alasdair MacIntyre, *After Virtue, a Study in Moral Theory* (London: Duckworth, 1981);

Taylor, *Sources of the Self*; Dan P. McAdams, *The Stories We Live By* (New York: W. Morrow, 1993).

37 For similar arguments see Lois Lee, *Recognizing the Non-Religious*; Ann Taves et al., 'Psychology, Meaning Making and the Study of Worldviews: Beyond Religion and Non-Religion', *Psychology of Religion and Spirituality*, 10, no. 3 (2018): 207–17; Thomas J. Coleman III et al., 'Focusing on Horizontal Transcendence: Much More than a "Non-Belief"', *Essays in the Philosophy of Humanism*, 21, no. 2 (2013): 1–18; William E. Connolly, 'Belief, Spirituality and Time', in Warner et al. (eds), *Varieties of Secularism in a Secular Age* (London: Harvard University Press, 2013), 126–44.

38 James Hinton, *The Mass Observers: A History, 1937–1949* (Oxford: Oxford University Press, 2013).

39 These rough totals are derived from calculations based on information in the online catalogue. Nearly 3,500 are listed there, but 900 of them failed to respond to any directives after registering with the MO Project.

40 Religion and Morality (1985); Death and Bereavement (1992); Nature (1994); Heaven and Hell (2009); Spiritualism (2013).

41 These figures have been calculated for the online catalogue of the MO Project at The Keep.

42 By the time they wrote for MO, many of the mass observers were retired. These generalizations reflect their occupational status before retirement.

43 'Age Structure of UK Population', *Social Trends*, 41, no. 1 (2011): 11. The regional distribution of the 1996 respondents (as of the panel more generally) was skewed between north and south – Northern Ireland, Wales, Scotland, the North East, North West Yorkshire and the East Midlands were under-represented (30 per cent compared with 45 per cent of the UK population); the rest of country was only slightly over-represented, with the exception of the South East which had nearly twice as many respondents as its share of the population – probably because the archive is situated in Sussex and local publicity and word of mouth attracted a disproportionate number of volunteers from the surrounding area.

44 Gill et al., 'Is Religious Belief Declining in Britain?', table 1.

45 There are some educational differences between the three groups: the Christians were the most likely to have left school at the minimum age, but they had almost as many graduates as the atheists. More of the believers in a non-religious spirituality were graduates than in the other two groups, but the difference was not great.

46 David Voas and Siobhan McAndrew, 'Three Puzzles of Non-Religion in Britain', *Journal of Contemporary Religion*, 27, no. 1 (2012): 36–41; Richard Dawkins, *The God Delusion* (London: Black Swan, 2007), 128–9.

47 Non-believers were more likely than Christians to have stayed on at school beyond the school-leaving age, but the proportion of graduates among the two groups was

roughly the same. Believers in a non-religious spirituality were rather more likely to be graduates.
48 Gill et al., 'Is Religious Belief Declining in Britain?', table 1.
49 Paul Heelas, *New Age Movement: The Celebration of the Self and the Sacralization of Modernity* (Oxford: Blackwell, 1996), 88, 119, 124, 162.
50 Three respondents self-identified as Jewish, two of them atheists.
51 Annebella Pollen, 'A Hybrid Heterogeneity Hard to Contain: Research Methods and Methodology in the Post-1981 Mass Observation Project', *History Workshop Journal*, 75 (Spring 2013): 213–35.
52 This is something that the leaders of the first phase of MO had well understood in the 1940s. Hinton, *Mass Observers*, 289.

2 Belief and disbelief

1 Taylor, *A Secular Age*, 3.
2 C602 1996 Supernatural.
3 Taylor, *Secular Age*, 437.
4 Cited in Hinton, *Seven Lives from Mass Observation: Britain in the Late Twentieth Century* (Oxford: Oxford University Press, 2016), 121.
5 W1813 2009 Heaven.
6 The best account is McLeod, *Religious Crisis*. Their failure to do so was a major reason for their decline (Linda Woodhead, 'The Rise of "No Religion" in Britain: The Emergence of a New Cultural Majority', *Journal of the British Academy* 4 (2016): 245–61; Linda Woodhead, 'Secularism with Added Agency', in Luke Dogett and Alp Arat, *Foundations and Futures in the Sociology of Religion* (Abingdon: Routledge, 2017).
7 R2144 1994 Death. The British Social Attitudes survey in 2008 showed only 7 per cent of Anglicans as biblical literalists; 57 per cent thought that although the Bible was the 'inspired word of God … not everything [was] to be taken literally'; and 33 per cent agreed that 'scripture is an ancient book of fables, legends, history'.
8 W1813 1990 Divisions.
9 C2142 1994 Death.
10 G1416 1994 Death.
11 S2207 2009 Heaven.
12 M388 1985 Religion.
13 G1148 1985 Religion.
14 F2090 1985 Religion.
15 Christopher H. Partridge, *Encyclopaedia of New Religions* (Oxford: Lion Hudson, 2004), 140–1.
16 W640 1985 Religion.

17 Taylor, *Secular Age*, 303–4, 531–2; Berger, *A Rumour of Angels*, 43–4.
18 McLeod, *Religious Crisis*, 11–12.
19 B2240 2009 Heaven.
20 N1592 1996 Supernatural.
21 William James, *Varieties of Religious Experience* (New York: Modern Library, 1902), 94.
22 Alex Owen, *The Place of Enchantment, British Occultism and the Culture of the Modern* (London: University of Chicago Press, 2004); Andrew Rawlinson, *The Book of Enlightened Masters: Western Teachers in Easter Traditions* (Chicago: Open Court, 1997), 28, 37, 39, 194–6; Ronald Hutton, 'Modern Pagan Witchcraft', in Blécourt et al. (eds), *Witchcraft and Magic in Europe: The Twentieth Century* (London: Athlone Press, 1999), 10, 18; John Gray, *The Immortalization Commission: Science and the Strange Quest to Cheat Death* (London: Allen Lane, 2011).
23 McLeod, *Religious Crisis*, 18, 265; Callum Brown, *The Death of Christian Britain: Understanding Secularisation 1800–2000* (London: Routledge, 2001).
24 Graham Harvey and Giselle Vincett, 'Alternative Spiritualities: Marginal and Mainstream', in Linda Woodhead and Rebecca Catto (eds), *Religion and Change in Modern Britain* (Abingdon: Routledge, 2012), 167–8; Heelas, *New Age Movement*, 88, 119, 162.
25 Heelas, *New Age Movement*; Paul Heelas and Linda Woodhead, *The Spiritual Revolution: Why Religion Is Giving Way to Spirituality* (Oxford: Blackwell, 2005). While Tony Glendinning and Steve Bruce point out that most users of these therapies had little interest in their spiritual origins, the challenge they represented to conventional medicine remains symptomatic of resistance to a materialist world view ('New Ways of Believing or Belonging: Is Religion Giving Way to Spirituality?', *British Journal of Sociology*, 57, no. 3 (2006): 399–414.
26 James, *Varieties*, 92.
27 Anyone who has sampled the spiritual self-help shelves of their local bookshop will sympathize with William James's complaint that much of this literature 'is so moonstruck with optimism and so vaguely expressed that an academically trained intellect finds it almost impossible to read it at all' (James, *Varieties*, 94).
28 Heelas, *New Age Movement*, 21, 40, 82–3; Christopher H. Partridge, 'Truth, Authority and Epistemological Individualism in New Age Thought', *Journal of Contemporary Religion*, 14, no. 1 (1999): 77–95.
29 Even those who attached themselves to spiritual teachers did so as individuals freely choosing in a spiritual marketplace, and the competition for clientele among purveyors of different Eastern traditions produced spiritual ideas adapted to Western sensibilities and quite distinct from anything that had ever existed in the East (Andrew Rawlinson, *The Book of Enlightened Masters*, 35, 62–3, 95). See also Richard King, 'Asian Religions and Mysticism', in Jeremy Carrette (ed.), *William*

James and The Varieties of Religious Experience (London: Routledge, 2005). King argues that the Eastern Religions which influenced Western spirituality had already been transformed in colonial encounters with the European Enlightenment.

30 G1483 1994 Death.
31 T2582 1994 Death.
32 A1706 1990 Social Divisions.
33 A1706 1996 Supernatural.
34 Heelas, *New Age Movement*, 163, 169. See also Jeremy Carrette and Richard King, *Selling Spirituality: The Silent Takeover of Religion* (London: Routledge, 2004).
35 Grace Davie, *Religion in Britain: A Persistent Paradox* (Chichester: Wiley-Blackwell, 2015), 159.
36 W571 1994 Death; 1992 Nature.
37 M1171 1996 Supernatural.
38 C1939 1992 Nature; 1994 Death.
39 H276 1992 Nature. His beliefs are discussed in Chapter 7.
40 T2543 1992 Nature; 1994 Death; 1996 Supernatural.
41 British Household Panel Survey 1991, ESRC data archive, University of Essex. Grace Davie notes a sharp fall off of church attendance on leaving school (*Religion in Britain since 1945: Believing without Belonging* (Oxford: Blackwell, 1994), 117, 121).
42 David Voas, 'The Mysteries of Religion and the Lifecourse', Centre for Longitudinal Studies, University College, London, Working Paper 1, 2015, 25.
43 E174 1985 Religion.
44 R1025 1985 Religion. For many years she continued going to church, partly because she wanted a church wedding, but she refrained from repeating sections of the creed with which she disagreed – e.g. life after death. And once married, she dropped the church altogether.
45 D996 1993 Growing Up.
46 D996 1985 Religion.
47 H260 1985 Religion.
48 D996 1985 Religion.
49 D996 1990 Close Relationships; 1993 Pleasure.
50 A1292 1985 Religion.
51 W632 1994 Death.
52 C110, cited in Hinton, *Seven Lives*, 152.
53 P1906 1985 Religion.
54 F1634 1996 Supernatural; C2600 1992 Nature.
55 P1637 1994 Death. But she added: – 'and yet, and yet – can this really be all there is?'
56 K310 1985 Religion.
57 K310 1994 Death.

58 B2605 1994 Death.
59 P1906 1985 Religion.
60 G1041 1992 Nature.
61 R470, cited in Hinton, *Seven Lives*, 120.
62 R1468 2009 Heaven.
63 R1468 1996 Supernatural.
64 E1510 1996 Supernatural.
65 R1760 2009 Heaven.
66 R1760 1996 Supernatural. On her education see Teresa Cairns, 'Class, Gender and Education in the 20th Century: An Exploration of Educational Life Histories of Correspondents to the Mass Observation Archive', University of Sussex, PhD thesis, 2007.
67 P2759 1996 Supernatural.
68 H266 1996 Supernatural. See also the responses to the 1996 Supernatural directive by P1500, P2759, H2784.
69 H2784 1996 Supernatural.
70 T1285 1996 Supernatural; 1990 Close Relationships.
71 H266 1996 Supernatural.
72 S2220 1996 Supernatural.
73 Berger, *A Rumour of Angels*, 61.
74 Researching non-belief, Coleman et al. found 'a great reluctance' among their respondents to speak about 'experiences that were profoundly meaningful' because, in the absence of any unambiguously secular language, they feared being understood as professing religious or spiritual beliefs (Coleman et al., 'Focusing on Horizontal Transcendence', 5).

3 Death and afterwards

1 S2207 2009 Heaven.
2 R2144 2009 Heaven. Another one – a 'very deeply religious' Anglican woman, working as a receptionist, thought there *would* be a library: 'Sometimes I think that when I die I will be in a sort of huge library. My ongoing task will be to find pieces of writing which will help people cope' (C1713 1994 Death).
3 S496 2009 Heaven.
4 Sarah Williams found a similar pattern of belief among the working-class people she interviewed in London: S. C. Williams, *Religious Belief and Popular Culture in Southwark, c.1880–1939* (Oxford: Oxford University Press, 1999), 101–2.

5 S496 1985 Religion. Cf. a 65-year-old typist:

> Although I support the teachings of Christ and am ostensibly a Christian, I do not go to church except for baptisms, weddings and funerals. Another rule perpetrated by some vicars is that they won't baptise a baby unless his/her parents go to church regularly. The child is penalised for the parents' so-called transgression as if he/she is a sort of appendage of the parents instead of a separate little individual entitled to humane justice in his/her own right. The vicar is playing God; that 'holier than thou' attitude is really pure arrogance. (B89 1985 Religion)

6 C108 1992 Nature; 2009 Heaven. And so did Marion Phillips, a Quaker: 'An afterlife means to me that lives have not been wasted. It means reunion with those we love and miss. I include animals and birds in this idea' (H2410 2009 Heaven). Another woman, who, though no longer seeing herself as religious, had been brought up Catholic and felt that this 'developed in me a sensitivity to spirituality', wrote:

> During my life-time I have grieved very much for my pets that died. Swearing that I won't have any more to hurt me by their short lives I continue to do so. A rapport with an animal is a very strong emotion for both. I had to stay with my dog when he was put to sleep, and that night I looked up to the vast sky and spoke to him as if he were still alive, as well he may be. Why should it be only humans who be victors over death? The body may die, but the essence of the animal's rapport with you existed, and maybe continues to do so in another dimension. (G1843 1994 Death)

See also B1215 1994 Death.

7 C108 2009 Heaven.
8 Gillian Bennett, *Traditions of Belief: Women and the Supernatural* (Harmondsworth: Penguin, 1987), 32, 35.
9 B2710 2009 Heaven.
10 Williams, *Religious Belief and Popular Culture*, 165. Jens Schlieter, comparing modern with pre-modern accounts of near-death experiences, makes a similar point: in the 20th century encounters with dead relatives replace the encounters with Jesus, angels (or Satan), which dominated earlier accounts of such experiences; 'in contrast to extensive "otherworldly journeys" of premodern deathbed visions, many modern near-death accounts combine personal "life-world" experiences – reported, however, from the "beyond"– with only some supernatural elements' (*What Is It Like to Be Dead?: Near-Death Experiences, Christianity, and the Occult* (New York: Oxford University Press, 2018), 33–4).
11 Emile Durkheim, *The Elementary Forms of the Religious Life* (London: Allen & Unwin, 1915), 206–9, 16–17.
12 Abby Day, *Believing in Belonging: Belief and Social Identity in the Modern World* (Oxford: Oxford University Press, 2011), 202–3.

13 S496 1994 Death; 1996 Supernatural.
14 B2109 1996 Supernatural.
15 W1813 1994 Death.
16 W1813 2013 Spiritualism.
17 Bennett, 'Alas, Poor Ghost!' Traditions of Belief in Story and Discourse, 65.
18 Bennett, Traditions of Belief, 66.
19 C1713 1994 Death.
20 B1180 1996 Supernatural. Geraldine Reynolds, a retired headmistress who had lost her Christian faith at teacher training college, had no belief in the survival of the spirit until, six months after her father's death, her mother told her that she felt his presence beside her in bed and, at the same time, objects began to move unaccountably around in Geraldine's bathroom. Instructed by her lover (who seems to have understood the needs of unquiet spirits) she placed an object which had belonged to her father in the bathroom, and his visits to both his daughter and his wife promptly ceased (E174 1996 Supernatural). Unaccountable movement of objects seems to be one way in which spirits get in touch. One young woman (D2664 1996 Supernatural) told a story about her boyfriend's grandmother, who had died. His mother visited a medium who assured her that granny would get in touch via a domestic appliance. Later, when her iron unaccountably fell to the floor, the boyfriend's mother said: 'Don't worry, son, it's your gran.'
21 H2410 1994 Death. She also had 'a very definite mental image of my aunt', who had no surviving children to worry about, 'shaking off her former life and squaring herself up and walking on into the distance'.
22 R1468 1994 Death.
23 G1563 1996 Supernatural.
24 T534 1996 Supernatural.
25 St. Thomas Aquinas, Summa Theologica, part one, question 113: 'As guardians are appointed for men who have to pass by an unsafe road, so an angel guardian is assigned to each man as long as he is a wayfarer.'
26 Gwen Halliday, who treasured a childhood memory of being visited by her dead brother, felt that her father and her husband (both deceased) offered practical help whenever she asked (S496 1996 Supernatural).
27 E.g. C2142 1996 Supernatural; R1532 1996 Supernatural; Z583 1996 Supernatural.
28 K1515 1996 Supernatural.
29 D1602 2013 Spiritualism.
30 H277 1996 Supernatural.
31 W1813 2013 Spiritualism.
32 W2790 1996 Supernatural.
33 M2164 1996 Supernatural.
34 R470 1996 Supernatural.

35 L1290 1985 Religion.
36 B2605 2009 Heaven.
37 B1533 1994 Death.
38 E1510 1994 Death.
39 I have recounted two other examples of this phenomenon in *Seven Lives*, 30, 83.
40 R1418 1996 Supernatural; 1990 Close Relationships; 2009 Heaven.
41 S2311 1996 Supernatural.
42 H1806 1996 Supernatural. Paula Harrison's grandfather told her that he was only able to stop crying after the death of his wife when, one night, she joined him in bed:

> He said she was just the same as always. She got in, settled down, giving him a sharp dig in the ribs with her elbow as she did so. It didn't seem at all strange and after that he fell asleep. When he woke she was gone, [and] he felt such comfort that she was still there that he didn't cry any more after that. (W1813 1994 Death)

43 W853 1996 Supernatural.
44 H1806 1996 Supernatural.
45 H1806 2013 Spiritualism.
46 In the 1990s, according to Gallup only 14 per cent of the population believed in the possibility of 'exchanging messages with the dead', a figure which, in contrast to ghost belief, had increased only slightly since the 1960s. But the question was badly phrased: spiritualists believed that the dead could send messages to the living, but not vice versa. MO's 30 per cent may well be closer to the truth.
47 C1883 1996 Supernatural; R1025 2013 Spiritualism.
48 J2187 1996 Supernatural.
49 W1813 2013 Spiritualism.
50 T2582 1996 Supernatural.
51 B2760 1996 Supernatural. Gillian Bennett's women had no time for spiritualism: 'If the dead can be summoned at will by strangers and have no purpose for their appearance but to answer foolish questions at the whim of a medium, then they cannot be the sort of intuitively apprehended community of carers that present-day believers envisage' (Bennett, *Traditions of Belief*, 104).
52 D2585 2013 Spiritualism; Peter Brierley and Heather Wright, *UK Christian Handbook* (London: Christian Research, 1996/7), 280.
53 D2585 1996 Supernatural.
54 D2585 1994 Death.
55 H277 1996 Supernatural.
56 A1733 1996 Supernatural.
57 H260 1996 Supernatural.

58 H260 2013 Spiritualism.
59 SAGB, http://www.sagb.org.uk/history.htm (accessed 5 December 2017).
60 H276 1994 Death. Janice Ranger, who also combined spiritualism with Labour Party activism, was equally hostile towards multiculturalism, expressing views which might have been at home in the National Front.
61 H276 1992 Nature.
62 H276 1994 Death. These views closely echo those of the SAGB, which spoke not of God but of 'an Infinite Intelligence', and asserted that 'in the Hereafter, all must account for their actions on earth and will judge themselves accordingly', http://www.sagb.org.uk/teachings.htm (accessed 5 December 2017).
63 R. Gill et al., 'Is Religious Belief Declining in Britain?', 512.
64 B2710 1994 Death.
65 G1416 Death.
66 T2582 1996 Supernatural.
67 H1745 1996 Supernatural.
68 S1534 1996 Supernatural.
69 See note 62 above.
70 Although Gillian Bennett found that many of the elderly Christians she interviewed in the 1980s accepted the idea (Bennett, 'Alas, Poor Ghost!' Traditions of Belief in Story and Discourse, 15, 33), a representative survey conducted in the early 1990s found that only 14 per cent of Anglicans and 11 per cent of Catholics endorsed the view that 'we come back as someone or something else' (Douglas Davies and Alastair Shaw, Reusing Old Graves: A Report on Popular British Attitudes (Crayford: Shaw & Sons, 1995), 94). The number of MO's Christians who were inclined to believe in reincarnation was roughly in line with those figures.
71 W1835 1996 Supernatural.
72 G2583 1994 Death.
73 H2161 1990 Social Divisions. She had worked as an unordained deacon until her retirement in 1976 and was still, twenty years later, taking services (1997 Unpaid Work).
74 H2161 1994 Death.
75 G1416 1994 Death.
76 J2799 1996 Supernatural; 1997 Doing a Job; 1997 Unpaid Work.
77 N1592 1996 Supernatural.
78 T2582 1994 Death.
79 H2161 1994 Death.
80 S2662 1996 Supernatural.
81 S2487 1994 Death.
82 L2669 1996 Supernatural.
83 H1745 1996 Supernatural.

84 N1592 2009 Heaven.
85 D1602 2009 Heaven.
86 R2247 1996 Supernatural.
87 H1705 1994 Death.
88 C1405 1994 Death.
89 L2794 1996 Supernatural.
90 R2247 1996 Supernatural.
91 W2790 1996 Supernatural.
92 N1592 2009 Heaven, cited in Hinton, *Seven Lives*, 78. She was quoting from memory a line from Edward Fitzgerald's translation of the *Rubaiyat of Omar Khayyam*: 'Myself when young did eagerly frequent/Doctor and Saint, and heard great Argument/About it and about: but evermore/Came out by the same Door as in I went.'
93 C1878 1996 Supernatural.
94 C1405 1994 Death.
95 S2207 2009 Heaven.
96 T540 1994 Death. It was not the divorce that caused her break from the Catholic church but the behaviour of her priest who, after her terminally ill mother had killed herself, insisted that suicides were destined for hell.
97 S2207 2009 Heaven.
98 Omitting the 14 per cent who either couldn't decide or didn't answer the question.
99 Though some had been terrorized in childhood: 'Hell was a very real place when I was a child. Sermons were full of it and I was scared of some fiery place where I could end up for even the most petty misdemeanours' (S2207 2009 Heaven). 'When I was young I believed in a cloud in the sky heaven and hell fires' (C108 2009 Heaven).
100 Some atheists found it incomprehensible that people could believe in God without believing in an afterlife: 'My mother', wrote Elizabeth Redmond, 'believed in God, but not in life after death … strange, her God must have been a nasty person if he made us with a hope for eternal life and then didn't give us it' (B1665 1994 Death).
101 P1743 1994 Death.
102 B2710 1994 Death. Compare Felicity Davidson who wondered, at funerals, whether either the vicar or the public actually believed in the 'sure and certain resurrection', or whether they have the same doubts as I do' (T2543 1994 Death). Lloyd, from a working-class background, had a career as a librarian before taking religious orders in his mid-thirties.
103 P1009 1994 Death.
104 P1009 2009 Heaven.
105 E.g. R1321 2009 Heaven; H2639 1994 Death; 2009 Heaven.
106 W729 2009 Heaven.

107 C2142 1994 Death.
108 C2142 1992 Nature; 1991 Women; 1996 Supernatural.
109 Another woman observed that her mother, who had 'a very literal idea of meeting all your loved ones ... wondered how she would face her first husband who was killed in the war and how he would feel about her re-marriage' (S2207 2009 Heaven).
110 B2710 1994 Death; 1990 Relationships.
111 S2246 1996 Supernatural.
112 P2175 1990 Social Divisions.
113 P2175 1992 Nature.
114 P2175 1994 Death. Among the non-religious believers, several expressed a spiritualized version of this view: when we die the life force – 'the spirit that animates the body ... the power that laughs in your eyes' – is 'subsumed into the universal spirit' (W2720 1996 Supernatural), or as another mass observer put it, the 'small spark of spirit ... returns to the great ocean' (S2574 1994 Death).
115 R1418 1996 Supernatural.
116 T1843 1994 Death.
117 R2692 1994 Death.
118 C2600 1994 Death.
119 S2487 1994 Death.
120 C2761 1996 Supernatural.
121 C2722 1994 Death.

4 Religion and science

1 Stephen Jay Gould, *Rock of Ages: Science and Religion in the Fullness of Life* (London: Vintage Digital, 2011).
2 R2144 2009 Heaven.
3 H1543 2009 Heaven.
4 P1326 1992 Nature.
5 Being in the second half of the alphabet she was sent the extended version.
6 P1326 1996 Supernatural.
7 P1743 1996 Supernatural.
8 W1893 1992 Nature.
9 G1803 1994 Death.
10 R2144 2009 Heaven.
11 R2143 1996 Supernatural.
12 B1989 2009 Heaven. Although one or two of the mass observers found it hard to break the habit. Gwen Halliday, the lapsed Wesleyan whose vision of the afterlife

was 'clouds and meeting people who have gone before you', puzzled about 'where do [sic] the sky start and where does it end?' (L1504 1992 Nature), and Sally Thompson, the shopkeeper with a spiritualist daughter, confessed that she found it difficult to take seriously scientific theories of the universe, preferring her childhood understanding of 'the wonders of space' as 'God's kingdom … the spiritual world. Maybe in my heart that's all I want to believe is in the sky above' (H260 2005 Universe).

13 D944 1996 Supernatural.
14 G1803 1992 Nature.
15 B2238 1996 Supernatural.
16 S2207 2009 Heaven.
17 Pierre Teilhard de Chardin, *The Phenomenon of Man* (London: Fount Paperbacks, 1977). For a discussion of similar ideas among scientists in Britain see Peter J. Bowler, *Reconciling Science and Religion: The Debate in Early Twentieth-Century Britain* (London: University of Chicago Press, 2001).
18 Several others also objected to this passage in the directive, particularly its curious suggestion that belief in God implied fatalism about the capacity of humanity to avert catastrophic environmental change: 'Many people believe that nature was created by an all-powerful God or deity. Some also think that it is still controlled by supernatural forces. If we are subject to such forces it may be that the human race can do little to influence or change the non-human world. Perhaps we should surrender to fate?'
19 P1743 1992 Nature.
20 H2410 1996 Supernatural.
21 Z53 1992 Nature.
22 Taylor, *Secular Age*.
23 W2322 1992 Nature.
24 P1326 1992 Nature.
25 K1515 1992 Nature.
26 L1504 1996 Supernatural.
27 T540 1992 Nature.
28 D2092 1992 Nature.
29 B2240 1992 Nature.
30 C2570 1994 Death.
31 D944 1996 Supernatural.
32 R4143 1996 Supernatural; 1992 Nature; 2009 Heaven.
33 S2246 1994 Death.
34 J1692 1992 Nature.
35 H1705 1992 Nature.
36 'Creative evolution' is Henri Bergson's term, prefiguring the arguments advanced by Teilhard de Chardin.

37 Simon Schaffer, 'Newtonian Angels', in Joad Raymond (ed.), *Conversations with Angels: Essays towards a History of Spiritual Communication, 1100–1700* (Basingstoke: Palgrave Macmillan, 2011).
38 Peter J. Bowler and Iwan Rhys Morus, *Making Modern Science: A Historical Survey* (Chicago: University of Chicago Press, 2005), 89–91.
39 M388 1996 Supernatural.
40 J2799 1996 Supernatural.
41 W729 1994 Death.
42 B2710 1994 Death.
43 S2207 2009 Heaven.
44 W1813 1994 Death.
45 B1989 1994 Death.
46 G2583 1992 Nature.
47 B2710 1994 Death. Bevan wrote: 'My imagination of the act of dying and the state of the dead owes more in fact to wide reading about Spiritualism/the occult rather than to my by-nomeans-nominal-and-yet-not-totally-convinced-and-certainly-(God-forbid!)-not-fanatical Christian belief' (G2583 1994 Death).
48 G1416 1996 Supernatural.
49 *Church Times*, 2 November 2007, 29.
50 J1692 1996 Supernatural.
51 A1706 1996 Supernatural.
52 B2240 1992 Nature; Danah Zohar, *The Quantum Self: Consciousness, Physics and the New World View* (London: Bloomsbury, 1990), 218–20.
53 Source withheld to protect her anonymity.
54 As well as her husband, both the men with whom she had previously had relationships had died shortly after the relationship ended.
55 HI1745 2007 Age.
56 H1745 2009 Heaven.
57 The guru (Edwin Courtenay) sees '"dead people" all over the place and gives this as one reason why he does not drive – they are around him all the time and would probably be constantly stepping in front of his car!' Perhaps her father's death in a road accident had something to do with Fiona's attraction to this man. On Courtenay see http://www.edwincourtenay.co.uk/aboutedwin.php (accessed 3 March 2017).
58 H1745 2013 Spiritualism.
59 H1745 2005 Universe.
60 H1745 1994 Death.
61 Source withheld to protect her anonymity.
62 H1745 1996 Supernatural.

63 Gwyn Hocking, Professor of Materials Chemistry, University of London, in 2001. In 2016, Hocking was national secretary of the Theosophical Society.
64 H1745 2013 Spiritualism.
65 https://explore.scimednet.org/index.php/wiki/peter-fenwick/ (accessed 3 March 2017).
66 https://explore.scimednet.org/index.php/about/ (accessed 3 March 2017).
67 Mike King, *Postsecularism: The Hidden Challenge to Extremism* (Cambridge, UK: James Clarke, 2009), 140–1. For an extended exposition of such views see Mike King, *Secularism: The Hidden Origins of Disbelief* (Cambridge, UK: James Clarke, 2007).
68 Fritjof Capra and Pier Luigi Luisi, *The Systems View of Life: A Unifying Vision* (Cambridge: Cambridge University Press, 2014), 14, 70. For a similar view, claiming William James as an ancestor of such thinking, see Eugene Taylor, 'Metaphysics and Consciousness in James' *Varieties*', in Jeremy Carrette (ed.), *William James and The Varieties of Religious Experience* (London: Routledge, 2005). It would, however, be easy to exaggerate the novelty of such thinking. As Logie Barrow points out, discussing the uses to which Newton's 'imponderables' were put by 19th-century spiritualists: They provided 'a licence … to proliferate forces which often remained even more mysterious than the phenomena that they had been invented to explain' (*Independent Spirits: Spiritualism and the English Plebeians, 1850–1910* (London: Routledge & Kegan Paul, 1986), 73).
69 The existence of such esoteric conspiracies on the fringes of British intellectual life in the early years of the 20th century is well documented, e.g. John Gray's account of Gerald Balfour (brother of the prime minister) fathering a child with an upper-class medium in the belief that between them they could produce a baby scientifically programmed to become the next saviour of humanity. Balfour's esoteric circle was unconvinced of the credentials of a young Indian who had been selected for this role by the Theosophist, Annie Besant (Gray, *The Immortalisation Commission*, 82–6). More generally see Owen, *The Place of Enchantment*; Pamela Thurschwell, *Literature, Technology, and Magical Thinking* (Cambridge: Cambridge University Press, 2001); P. J. Bowler, *Reconciling Science and Religion*; Jason A. Josephson-Storm, *The Myth of Disenchantment: Magic, Modernity, and the Birth of the Human Sciences* (Chicago: University of Chicago Press, 2018).
70 Peter Leggett, *The Sacred Quest: By Experiment and Experience – The Next Step* (Ipswich: Pilgrim Books, 1987); Peter Leggett and Max Payne, *A Forgotten Truth: A Spiritual Vision for Modern Man* (Ipswich: Pilgrims Book Services, 1986). The following information is from an obituary of Israel (Leslie Price, 'Martin Israel and the Parting of Friends', *Psypioneer Journal*, 3, no. 11 (2007):

> He withdrew from a private circle (called 'Light and Science') which met at the flat of Margaret Brice-Smith to listen to a high entity (thought by some to be

the Master D.K.) who spoke through the mediumship of Helen Greaves. Paul Beard [president of the College of Psychic Studies] has referred to this group in his tribute to one of the participants, Dr Leggett. (Other members included Bill Blewett College of Psychic Studies (CPS) vice-president, Dr Edward Aubert of Burrswood, Commander Martin Pares, and Jean Sydney of the CFPSS Mysticism Committee.) Beard wrote in LIGHT Winter 1994, p. 104: *'We shared membership of a small group, of which most members played an active part in some other spiritual organisation, which met to receive spiritual teaching given through Helen Greaves.'* So far as I am aware this is the only published reference to the circle, of which Martin was possibly the last surviving member.

71 Another mass observer, Alistair Bevan (G2583 1996 Supernatural), cited Martin Israel as his authority for asserting that there was no contradiction between Christian doctrine and the idea of reincarnation. Israel was a Jewish scientist who had lectured in pathology at the Royal College of Surgeons before becoming an Anglican priest (Obituary in *Daily Telegraph*, 26 October 2007).

72 For the details see Hinton, *Seven Lives*, 67.

73 N1592 1996 Supernatural c.f. Sally Noonan, the no-nonsense atheist impatient with the 'irrational' behaviour of the recently bereaved, had no problem with the 'body auras', which some claimed to be able to perceive: 'As we give off heat, water vapour and gases, in certain lights we might shimmer interestingly but not supernaturally' (S2311 1996 Supernatural).

74 Amy Wallace and Bill Henkin, *The Physic Healing Book* (New York: Delacorte Press, 1981).

75 N1592 1996 Supernatural.

76 N1592 1996 Supernatural. She attributed this image to Somerset Maugham, although she could not remember where he had written it. A Google search produces nothing from Maugham but several similar statements by both Christian and Jewish writers.

77 N1592 2009 Heaven.

78 N1592 2009 Heaven.

79 R2770 1996 Supernatural.

80 B2728 1996 Supernatural.

81 M2164 1996 Supernatural.

82 M2164 2009 Heaven.

83 G2776 1996 Supernatural.

84 C2600 1996 Supernatural.

85 G2776 1996 Supernatural; Marc Bloch, *The Historian's Craft* (Manchester: Manchester University Press, 1984), 133–7.

86 'Already we have in the practice of science the prototype for all human common action ... In its endeavour, science is communism' (J. D. Bernal, *The Social Function*

of Science (London: Routledge, 1939), 415). More generally, see Mary Midgley, *Science as Salvation: A Modern Myth and Its Meaning* (Abingdon: Routledge, 1992).

87 R2065 2005 Universe.
88 C2600 1996 Supernatural.
89 R1418 2005 Universe.
90 M2164 2009 Heaven.
91 R2065 1992 Nature.
92 R2065 1990 Close Relationships; 1990 Organisations.
93 Gary Sloan, 'George Bernard Shaw: Mystic or Atheist?', http://www.liberator.net/articles/SloanGary/Shaw.html (accessed 25 May 2016).
94 R2065 1996 Supernatural.
95 R2065 1990 Organisations; Kathleen Komar, 'Rilke: Metaphysics in a New Age', in Sigrid Bauschinger and Susan Cocalis (eds), *Rilke-Rezeptionen: Rilke Reconsidered* (Tübingen/Basel: Franke, 1995); Kathleen Komar, 'Rethinking Rilke's *Duisiner Elegien* at the End of the Millennium', in Erika A. Metzger (ed.), *A Companion to the Works of Rainer Maria Rilke* (Rochester, NY: Camden House, 2004).

5 Uses of the paranormal

1 Dawkins, *Unweaving the Rainbow*, 28–9.
2 W2720 1996 Supernatural.
3 L796 1996 Supernatural.
4 Bennett, *Traditions of Belief*, 122–4, 128–32.
5 S496 2013 Spiritualism.
6 G1148 1996 Supernatural.
7 W633 1996 Supernatural.
8 B2760 1996 Supernatural.
9 R1760 1996 Supernatural.
10 Bennett, *'Alas, Poor Ghost!'*, 24.
11 B1180 1996 Supernatural.
12 W2322 1996 Supernatural.
13 B2760 1996 Supernatural.
14 C1713 1996 Supernatural.
15 H260 1996 Supernatural.
16 N403 2013 Spiritualism.
17 W571 1996 Supernatural.
18 B36 1996 Supernatural.
19 S2442 1996 Supernatural.

20 Berger, *Rumour of Angels*, 33, 59 following Nietzsche, argues that our capacity for 'play' opens us up to the transcendental. André Droogers (*Religion at Play* (Cambridge: Lutterworth Press, 2015), 8, 10, 11) argues that common ground between religious and secular world views can be found once we embrace the playful approach – 'the human capacity to deal simultaneously … with two or more ways of classifying reality…, referring to "as if" in contrast with the indicative "as is"… Believers should learn to wink, playing the religious game in a serious way'.
21 J2187 1996 Supernatural.
22 Jane Bennett, *The Enchantment of Modern Life: Attachments, Crossings, and Ethics* (Princeton: Princeton University Press, 2001), 132, 138–9.
23 M381 1996 Supernatural.
24 B1665 1996 Supernatural.
25 C2722 1996 Supernatural.
26 K2721 1994 Death.
27 H2410 1992 Nature.
28 H2410 1996 Supernatural; 1992 Nature.
29 C1832 1996 Supernatural.
30 G2776 1996 Supernatural.
31 G2134 1996 Supernatural.
32 T2543 1996 Supernatural.
33 T2543 2013 Spiritualism.
34 Rebecca Hurley (B2605) also mentions ghosts who warn drivers of danger of road accidents. There had been sightings of ghosts around Edgehill ever since a month after the battle (Owen Davies, *The Haunted: A Social History of Ghosts* (Basingstoke: Palgrave Macmillan, 2009), 46). On the prevalence of superstition among miners see Davies, *The Haunted*, 69, and among other risky occupation groups (sportsmen, actors, gamblers) see Stuart A. Vyse, *Believing in Magic: The Psychology of Superstition* (Oxford: Oxford University Press, 1997), 25–6.
35 R470 cited in Hinton, *Seven Lives*, 115–6.
36 H266 1996 Supernatural.
37 G2769 1996 Supernatural.
38 H2410 1996 Supernatural. Several others agreed.
39 C1878 1996 Supernatural.
40 W2782 1996 Supernatural.
41 K1515 1996 Supernatural, reporting his daughter's experience.
42 R2692 1996 Supernatural; W2782 1996 Supernatural.
43 W1813 1996 Supernatural.
44 S2487 1994 Death.
45 S2487 1994 Death.
46 R2065 1994 Death.

47 R2065 1994 Death.
48 S2207 1996 Supernatural.
49 W1813 1996 Supernatural.
50 Cf. Rhodri Hayward, *Resisting History: Religious Transcendence and the Invention of the Unconscious* (Manchester: Manchester University Press, 2007).
51 B2109 1996 Supernatural.
52 James Hinton, *Nine Wartime Lives: Mass-Observation and the Making of the Modern Self* (Oxford: Oxford University Press, 2010), 66.
53 F1634 1996 Supernatural; 1994 Death.
54 T2150 1996 Supernatural.
55 C41 1996 Supernatural.
56 I have relied on the very extensive Wikipedia entry: notable critics include Susan Blackmore and Lewis Wolpert.
57 H2784 1996 Supernatural.
58 J931 1996 Supernatural; 1994 Death.
59 G2776 1996 Supernatural.
60 Peter Brugger, 'From Haunted Brain to Haunted Science, a Cognitive Neuroscience View of Paranormal and Pseudoscientific Thought'; W. G. Roll and M. A. Persinger, 'Investigations of Poltergeists and Haunts: A Review and Interpretation', both in J. Houran and R. Lange (eds), *Hauntings and Poltergeists: Multidisciplinary Perspectives* (London: McFarland, 2001), 149–52, 154, 161–3, 195–6; Richard Wiseman, *Paranormality: Why We See What Isn't There* (London: Macmillan, 2011).
61 C2722 1996 Supernatural.
62 Bennett, *Traditions of Belief*, 85–8.
63 Oliver Sacks, *Hallucinations* (London: Picador, 2012).
64 Cited in Davies, *The Haunted*, 150.
65 Robert C. Fuller, 'Minds of Their Own: Psychological Substrates of the Spiritual but Not Religious Sensibility', in William B. Parsons (ed.), *Being Spiritual but Not Religious: Past, Present, Future(s)* (London: Routledge, 2018), 89–109; Maarten Boudry, 'The Cultural Buck Stops Somewhere: The Origin of Supernatural Belief and the Role of Agency Detection', *Religion, Brain & Behavior*, 99, no. 3 (2019): 253–5.
66 Andrew McNeillie, 'Homage to Patagonia', cited in Marina Warner, *Phantasmaoria: Spirit Visions, Metaphors, and Media into the Twenty-First Century* (Oxford: Oxford University Press, 2006), xixx.
67 M2132 1996 Supernatural.
68 B1509 1996 Supernatural.
69 E1510 1996 Supernatural.
70 M381 1996 Supernatural.
71 C2722 1996 Supernatural.

72 Thurschwell, *Literature, Technology and Magical Thinking*.
73 C108 1996 Supernatural.
74 R470 1996 Supernatural.
75 W1813 2013 Spiritualism.
76 H1745 2013 Spiritualism.
77 R1321 1996 Supernatural.
78 C110 1996 Supernatural.
79 Many such experiences had been recorded in the Society for Psychical Research's 1886 report *Phantasms of the Living*. See Thurschwell, *Literature, Technology and Magical Thinking*, 24.
80 W2529 1996 Supernatural.
81 C2600 1996 Supernatural.
82 B2240 1996 Supernatural.
83 G2776 1996 Supernatural.
84 D944 1996 Supernatural. Myers saw telepathy as a progressive evolutionary step rather than a movement back towards a lost atavistic sense: 'Telepathy is surely a step in evolution. To learn the thoughts of other minds, without the mediation of the special senses, manifestly indicates the possibility of a vast extension of psychical powers' (quoted in Thurschwell, *Literature, Technology, and Magical Thinking*, 27).
85 B1509 1996 Supernatural,
86 T2582 1996 Supernatural.
87 H1745 2013 Spiritualism. As Fiona Evans pointed out, if animals did indeed communicate telepathically, that would definitely place telepathy in the realm of nature, not the supernatural. None of the Christians (many of whom believed in telepathy) suggested primitive origins for telepathy, but some of the atheists did, as had Freud (Thurschwell, *Literature, Technology, and Magical Thinking*, 119ff.).
88 C2722 1996 Supernatural.
89 Roger Luckhurst, *The Invention of Telepathy* (Oxford: Oxford University Press, 2002).

6 Moments out of time

1 In contrast, Weber put less weight on the 'irrational element' common to all religious experience than on the belief systems 'that capture and mould' that experience. Weber, *The Protestant Ethic*, 232–3; Wilhelm Hennis, 'The Spiritualist Foundation of Max Weber's "Interpretative Sociology"', *History of the Human Sciences*, 11, no. 2 (1998): 83–106; Peter Ghosh, 'Max Weber and William James: "Pragmatism", Psychology, Religion', *Max Weber Studies*, 5.2/6.1 (2005–6): 243–80.

2 Richard King, 'Asian Religions and Mysticism', in Jeremy Carrette (ed.), *William James and* The Varieties of Religious Experience.
3 E. D. Starbuck, *The Psychology of Religion: An Empirical Study of the Growth of Religious Consciousness* (London: Walter Scott, 1899).
4 Alister Hardy, *The Spiritual Nature of Man: A Study of Contemporary Religious Experience* (Oxford: Clarendon Press, 1979), 1; David Hay, *God's Biologist: A Life of Alister Hardy* (London: Darton, Longman and Todd, 2011), 230–64.
5 David Hay and Kate Hunt, 'Understanding the Spirituality of People Who Don't Go to Church', A report on the findings of the Adults' Spirituality Project at the University of Nottingham, 2000, https://www.spiritualjourneys.org.uk/look/look_essays.php (accessed 29 August 2021), 1; David Hay, *Religious Experience Today: Studying the Facts* (London: Mowbray, 1990); David Hay, *Exploring Inner Space: Is God Still Possible in the 20th Century?* (Harmondsworth: Penguin, 1982).
6 C.f. Abraham H. Maslow, *Religions, Values, and Peak Experiences* (Columbus: Ohio State University Press, 1964), 61–2:

> Practically everything that, for example, Rudolf Otto defines as characteristic of the religious experience – the holy; the sacred; creature feeling; humility; gratitude and oblation; thanksgiving; awe before the *mysterium tremendum*; the sense of the divine, the ineffable; the sense of littleness before mystery; the quality of exaltedness and sublimity; the awareness of limits and even of powerlessness; the impulse to surrender and to kneel; a sense of the eternal and of fusion with the whole of the universe; even the experience of heaven and hell – all of these experiences can be accepted as real by clergymen and atheists alike.

7 Marghanita Laski, *Ecstasy in Secular and Religious Experience* (London: Cresset Press, 1961), 9, 24n; David Hay and Ann Morisy, 'Reports of Ecstatic, Paranormal, or Religious Experience in Great Britain and the United States – a Comparison of Trends', *Journal for the Scientific Study of Religion*, 17, no. 3 (1978): 266.
8 Laski, *Ecstasy*, 5.
9 Laski, *Ecstasy*, 344. For more recent collection of such experiences (in the United States) among people who did not see them as belonging to religion or spirituality, see Coleman III et al., 'Focusing on Horizontal Transcendence: Much More Than a "Non-Belief"', *Essays in the Philosophy of Humanism*, 21, no. 2 (2013): 1–18.
10 G1483 1996 Supernatural.
11 G1416 1996 Supernatural.
12 H2410 1992 Nature.
13 H2410 1996 Supernatural.
14 The phrase is from Charles William, writer of Christian fantasy novels, and a member of the Inklings alongside C. S. Lewis and Tolkien.

15 H2410 1996 Supernatural.
16 Lord Byron, 'Childe Harold's Pilgrimage', canto iii, stanza lxxii, 1816, http://knarf.english.upenn.edu/Byron/charold3.html(accessed 13 February 2018)
17 Maurice Cranston, *The Romantic Movement* (Oxford: Blackwell, 1994), 16, 76.
18 William Wordsworth, 'Tintern Abbey', 1798, https://www.poetryfoundation.org/poems/45527/lines-composed-a-few-miles-above-tintern-abbey-on-revisiting-the-banks-of-the-wye-during-a-tour-july-13-1798(accessed 29 August 2021).
19 Cited by Hay, *Religious Experience Today*, 25.
20 N1484 1996 Supernatural; 1992 Nature.
21 D2123 1992 Nature.
22 R860 1992 Nature.
23 H1705 1992 Nature.
24 S2246 1992 Nature.
25 R1452 1985 Religion.
26 M1395 1992 Nature.
27 W1813 1990 Social Divisions. Len Smith, the mechanic whose story is told in *Seven Lives*, expressed a similar sense of loss when younger members started to move his Methodist church 'in the direction of happy-clappy services. Not my cup of tea at all'. After his son died in a motor cycle accident he gave up churchgoing altogether finding comfort and a more private communication with God during weekly visits with his wife to the grave of their son (H1543 2010 Belonging).
28 B653 1985 Religion.
29 W1835 2009 Heaven.
30 W633 1985 Religion.
31 M2629 1996 Supernatural.
32 B2240 2009 Heaven. The power of cathedrals to inspire a sense of the sacred even among those with no religious belief is noted by several of Hay's informants (David Hay and Kate Hunt, *Understanding the Spirituality of People Who Don't Go to Church* (Nottingham: University of Nottingham, 2000), 25–6; David Hay, *Exploring Inner Space*, 202) and by Grace Davie, *Religion in Britain since 1945: Believing without Belonging* (Oxford: Blackwell, 1994), 55; Grace Davie, *Religion in Britain: A Persistent Paradox*, 143. The same phenomenon, though interpreted differently, is noted by Callum Brown, *Becoming Atheist*, 107. As Davie notes (138), cathedrals also cater to the religious needs of believers who, for whatever reason, prefer the anonymity of a city-centre place of worship to the community of a parish church.
33 J1407 1996 Supernatural.
34 T1843 1993 Pleasure.
35 T. S. Eliot, *Four Quartets* (London: Faber & Faber, 1959), 44.
36 Eric Hobsbawm, *The Age of Capital* (London: Weidenfeld and Nicolson, 1977), 333–4, 349–50; Taylor, *Secular Age*, 354–6, 360; Oane Reitsma, 'Musical Works as Higher

Culture in a Secular Age', in Florian Zemmin et al. (eds), *Working with a Secular Age: Interdisciplinary Perspectives on Charles Taylor's Master Narrative.*

37 M2164 1996 Supernatural.
38 M2164 1992 Nature.
39 M2164 2009 Heaven; 1991 Education.
40 M2164 1993 Pleasure.
41 H. H. Gerth and C. Wright Mills (eds), *From Max Weber, Essays in Sociology* (London: Routledge, 1991), 345.
42 N1592, cited in Hinton, *Seven Lives*, 78.
43 D996 1990 Close Relationships.
44 D996 1993 Pleasure.
45 T1843 2001 Courting.
46 Laski, *Ecstasy*, 26, 486, 439–44. See also David M. Wulff, 'Mystical Experience', in Cardena et al.(eds), *Varieties of Anomalous Experience: Examining the Scientific Evidence* (Washington, DC: American Psychological Association, 2000), 410; Hardy, *Spiritual Nature*, 1-2: c.f. Bennett, *Traditions of Belief*, 62: 'that commonplace, but yet perplexing, experience of the surfacing of unconscious into conscious thought – those familiar, involuntary perceptions, intuitions, and recurrent thoughts that seemingly miraculously solve long-standing problems'.
47 B653 1996 Supernatural.
48 W1893 1992 Nature.
49 H2410 1991 Reading and Writing.
50 R450 1996 Supernatural.
51 H2410 1994 Death.
52 C1878 1996 Supernatural.
53 S2207 1994 Death.
54 H1198 1996 Supernatural.
55 Schlieter, *What Is It Like to Be Dead?*, 288.
56 Schlieter, *What Is It Like to Be Dead?*
57 Schlieter, *What Is It Like to Be Dead?*, xviii, 228.
58 James, *Varieties*, 14.
59 R860 2013 Spiritualism.
60 R860 2013 Spiritualism.
61 B36 1994 Death.
62 W1813 2013 Spiritualism.
63 This evidence from the mass observers calls into question Schlieter's argument that the upsurge of near-death experiences since the 1960s 'followed almost exclusively a religious agenda', reflecting the 'strongly felt need of individuals not only to share their near-death experiences, but to assign far-reaching religious significance to them' (Schlieter, *What Is It Like to Be Dead* , xv, 251). While reports

of such experiences may well have served to express resistance to a reductively materialist understanding of the human condition, near-death experiences could be meaningful and life changing without resorting to notions of the afterlife, the soul or the divine. Schlieter's tentative endorsement of a biologically rooted capacity of a consciousness faced with its own imminent extinction to generate a comprehensive life review (Schlieter, *What Is It Like to Be Dead*, part four) is a more promising approach to the 'workings of our brains that we do not yet understand' than his reduction of near-death narratives to discourses of religion.

64 W632 1985 Religion.
65 W632 2009 Heaven.
66 W632 1994 Death.
67 W632 1996 Supernatural; 2009 Heaven; 2013 Spiritualism.
68 W768 1991 Women and Men.
69 W768 1992 Nature.
70 W768 1996 Supernatural.
71 W768 1996 Supernatural.
72 W768 1992 Nature.
73 W768 1994 Death.
74 W768 1992 Nature; 1996 Supernatural.
75 W768 1990 Close Relationships.
76 W768 1991 Education.
77 W768 1991 Women and Men.
78 W768 1996 Supernatural; 1990 Close Relationships.
79 Orthodox Jews avoid writing the name of God.
80 B2197 1996 Supernatural.
81 B2197 1996 Supernatural.
82 Ezekiel 3:12.
83 Castro et al., 'The Paranormal Is (Still) Normal', 16.
84 Laski, *Ecstasy*, 371.
85 Maslow, *Religions Values*, 69, 80. Although everyone, he believed, experienced such moments, some did their best to suppress them, fearful that even a temporary suspension of the ego's struggle for control over the unconscious would tip them into insanity (*Religions Values*, 33). For a discussion of more recent laboratory-based psychological testing of such claims, see Wulff, 'Mystical Experience'.
86 C2142 1996 Supernatural.
87 Berger, *Rumours of Angels*, 70.
88 Coleman et al. (2013) theorize this as 'horizontal transcendence … the experiential dimension to human life of interconnectedness that is profound, exceptional, and wondrous while requiring no religious, spiritual, or theistic framework or narrative in which to force the structure of the discourse'. The philosopher George Santayana

(as summarized by John Gray, *Seven Types of Atheism* (London: Penguin Books, 2018), 131–2) took a similar view of such moments: 'momentary sensations in individual minds, themselves moments in the transformations of matter … Spirit was a flash in the dark, a transient awareness flaring up in matter itself, not a separate metaphysical reality'.

89 Bennett, *The Enchantment of Modern Life*, 5.
90 Friedrich Nietzsche, *The Will to Power* (New York: Random House, 1967), 532–3.
91 Eagleton, *Reason, Faith and Revolution*, 83–4.
92 Taylor, *Secular Age*, 5.
93 Taylor, *Secular Age*, 434–5, 819.

7 A pagan priestess

1 A2212 1996 Supernatural.
2 The following paragraph is largely based on Ronald Hutton, 'Modern Pagan Witchcraft', in Blécourt et al. (eds), *Witchcraft and Magic in Europe: The Twentieth Century* (London: Athlone Press, 1999), 8–79; Ronald Hutton, *The Triumph of the Moon: A History of Modern Pagan Witchcraft* (Oxford: Oxford University Press, 1999).
3 Hutton, 'Modern Pagan Witchcraft', 61. See also Shai Feraro, 'Connecting British Wicca with Radical Feminism and Goddess Spirituality during the 1970s and 1980s: The Case Study of Monica Sjöö', *Journal of Contemporary Religion*, 30, no. 2 (2015): 307–21.
4 Lorraine Evans, *Kingdom of the Ark: The Startling Story of How the Ancient British Race Is Descended from the Pharaohs* (London: Simon & Schuster, 2000); Ralph Ellis, *Scota, Egyptian Queen of Scots: Cleopatra to Christ* (Cheshire: Edfu Books, 2006).
5 Olivia Robertson (ed.), *Handbook of the Fellowship of Isis* (*Clonegal*: Cesara, 1992), 4.
6 Graham Harvey, 'Paganism', in Woodhead et al. (eds), *Religions in the Modern World: Traditions and Transformations* (London: Routledge, 2009).
7 A1292 1991 Women.
8 A1292 1996 Supernatural.
9 A2212 1991 Education.
10 A2212 1993 Growing Up.
11 A2212 2010 Belonging.
12 A2212 1993 Growing Up.
13 A2212 1991 Education.
14 A2212 1993 Pleasure.
15 A2212 1997 Job.

16 S2211 1997 Job. Edward started writing for Mass Observation (MO) at the same time as Rosemary, and continued throughout the 1990s.
17 A2212 1991 Education.
18 A2212 2011 1980s.
19 Theos, *The Spirit of Things Unseen: Belief in Post-Religious Britain*, 2013, www.theosthinktank.co.uk/research (accessed 29 August 2021).
20 Source withheld to protect her anonymity.
21 A2212 1997 NHS.
22 A2212 1997 NHS.
23 Her Day Diary in March 1992 gives a detailed account of her quotidian dependency on her husband – for dressing, washing, being taken to the lavatory, etc.
24 Source withheld to protect her anonymity.
25 A2212 2010 Research.
26 A2212 2005 Sex.
27 A2212 1993 Pleasure.
28 A2212 1996 Supernatural.
29 A2212 1993 Pleasure.
30 A2212 1996 Supernatural.
31 A2212 1993 Pleasure.
32 Robertson (ed.), *Handbook of the Fellowship of Isis*, 6.
33 A2212 1996 Supernatural.
34 A2212 1996 Supernatural.
35 A2212 1996 Supernatural.
36 A2212 2004 Letters. Thirteen years later, having risen to the rank of archpriest, she was training pagan clergy.
37 Edward, as well as supporting her in the worship of Isis, was a practising stoic (he published his own book on the subject), and her words here reflect his own exposition of stoicism.
38 A2212 2010 Election.
39 Source withheld to protect her anonymity. Not that this was an easy task. Her MO writings include moments of panic when, overwhelmed with irrational fears, she felt on the edge of insanity: 'a serious failure of my faith', she wrote after one such attack: 'I should have had faith that everything is in the hands of the deity, and I need to trust him' (A2212 2010 Election).
40 A2212 1996 Supernatural.
41 In 1983, I was chair of the CND committee responsible for organizing that demonstration: a point of contact between two lives that could hardly have been more different from one another.
42 A2212 1991 Gulf War.
43 A2212 1997 Election.

44 A2212 2011 1980s.
45 A2212 1992 Nature.
46 A2212 2010 Election.
47 A2212 2010 Personal Finance.
48 A2212 2010 Childhood and Illness.
49 A2212 1996 Supernatural.
50 R2247 1990 Divisions.
51 R2247 1996 Supernatural.
52 R2247 1990 Divisions.
53 R2247 1996 Supernatural.
54 R2247 1990 Organisations.
55 When asked in a 1959 BBC television interview (Face To Face) whether he believed in God, Jung answered, 'I don't need to believe, I know', https://www.youtube.com/watch?v=2AMu-G51yTY (accessed 29 August 2021).
56 R2247 1996 Supernatural.
57 R2247 1992 Nature.
58 R2247 1996 Supernatural.
59 NFSH, Code of Conduct: 'Healers do not express or discuss their personal beliefs and views with a patient unless invited to do so', www.thehealingtrust.org.uk/ (accessed 15 October 2017).
60 R2247 1996 Supernatural.
61 Giselle Vincett and Linda Woodhead, 'Spirituality', in Woodhead et al. (eds), *Religions in the Modern World: Traditions and Transformations*, 327.
62 B2653 1994 Death. William James would certainly have agreed. First engaging with pagan ideas aged fourteen, Selina had experimented with Wicca covens and spent several years in a Gurdjieff group before taking up Druidry. From Gurdjieff she learned that most of us sleep our way through life, never realizing the potential buried in our subconscious, our real selves (Owen, *The Place of Enchantment, British Occultism and the Culture of the Modern*, 231–6; see also Heelas, *The New Age Movement*, 47–8; Rawlinson, *The Book of Enlightened Masters*, 282–312). Druidry helped her to 'awaken the creative self, to be Conscious (develop higher levels of awareness), to change negatives to positives, therefore becoming not merely a nicer person, but enabling higher, spiritual development to begin' (B2653 1996 Supernatural).
63 Taylor, *Secular Age*, 7, 143, 431.
64 This was a tiny sect, with about 600 members in 18 groups in the UK in 1995 (Brierley and Wright, *UK Christian Handbook*, 282).
65 B1215 1985 Religion.
66 B1215 1994 Death.
67 B1215 1993 Growing Up.

68 B1215 1994 Death; 1994 Autobiography.
69 B1215 1997 Future.
70 B1215 2009 Heaven.
71 B1215 2009 Heaven.

8 Conclusion

1 Hay, *Religious Experience Today*, 32.
2 J1407 1996 Supernatural.
3 To a considerable degree, this conflict is institutionalized in British universities between departments of sociology and departments of religious studies. I was accused by one anonymous referee of an earlier version of this book of being taken in by 'secularization deniers' in religious studies departments, while another thought I had succumbed to atheistic perspectives propagated in departments of sociology.
4 David S. Nash, 'Believing in Secularisation: Stories of Decline, Potential, and Resurgence', *Journal of Religious History*, 41, no. 4 (2017): 505–31.
5 Nash, 'Believing in Secularisation', 510.
6 Bryan Wilson, *Religion in Secular Society, a Sociological Comment* (London: Watts, 1966), xvii.
7 Steve Bruce, *Secularization: In Defence of an Unfashionable Theory* (Oxford: Oxford University Press, 2011), 2, following Bryan Wilson's formulation, *Religion in Sociological Perspective* (Oxford: Oxford University Press, 1982), 149.
8 Wilson, *Religion in Secular Society, a Sociological Comment*, xvii–xviii, 43–4. Bruce does, however, acknowledge that 'it may well be that our sense of mastery over fate is a dangerous illusion of which we will be disabused when the various chickens of modern technology come home to roost in the form of environmental disaster' (Bruce, *Secularization*, 45). For everyone today who thinks that scientific ingenuity will find technological solutions to climate change, there are others who believe that it is the domination of technological thinking and instrumental reason which lies at the root of the ecological crisis.
9 Brown, *Becoming Atheist*.
10 McLeod, *Religious Crisis*, 220–6.
11 Sam Brewitt-Taylor, 'The Invention of a "Secular Society"? Christianity and the Sudden Appearance of Secularization Discourses in the British National Media, 1961-4', *Twentieth Century British History*, 24, no. 3 (2013): 327–50; Sam Brewitt-Taylor, 'Notes toward a Postsecular History of Modern British Secularization', *Journal of British Studies*, 60 (April 2021): 310–33.
12 Brown, 'Necessity of Atheism', 451.
13 Brown, *Becoming Atheist*, 108, 185.

14 Richard Dawkins, *Unweaving the Rainbow: Science, Delusion and the Appetite for Wonder*, London: Allen Lane, 1998
15 Cited by Lee, *Recognizing the Non-Religious*, 176 (emphasis added). See also Lisa H. Sideris, *Consecrating Science, Wonder, Knowledge and the Natural World* (Oakland: University of California, 2017), 46, 169ff.
16 Brown, *Becoming Atheist*, 117.
17 Brown, 'Necessity of Atheism', 449.

Bibliography

'Age Structure of UK Population', *Social Trends* 41, no. 1 (2011): 11.
Barrow, Logie, *Independent Spirits: Spiritualism and the English Plebeians, 1850–1910*, London: Routledge & Kegan Paul, 1986.
Bartolini, Nadia, Robert Chris, Sara MacKian and Steve Pile, 'The Place of Spirit: Modernity and the Geographies of Spirituality', *Progress in Human Geography*, 41, no. 3 (2017): 338–54.
Bennett, Gillian, *'Alas, Poor Ghost!' Traditions of Belief in Story and Discourse*, Logan: Utah State University Press, 1999.
Bennett, Gillian, *Traditions of Belief: Women and the Supernatural*, Harmondsworth: Penguin, 1987.
Bennett, Jane, *The Enchantment of Modern Life: Attachments, Crossings, and Ethics*, Princeton: Princeton University Press, 2001.
Berger, Peter, *A Rumour of Angels: Modern Society and the Rediscovery of the Supernatural*, Harmondsworth: Penguin, 1971.
Bernal, John D., *The Social Function of Science*, London: Routledge, 1939.
Blécourt, Willem de, Ronald Hutton and Jean La Fontaine (eds), *Witchcraft and Magic in Europe: The Twentieth Century*, London: Athlone Press, 1999.
Bloch, Marc, *The Historian's Craft*, Manchester: Manchester University Press, 1984.
Bloch, Maurice, 'Why Religion Is Nothing Special but Is Central', *Philosophical Transactions, Royal Society London B Biol Sci*, 363, no. 1499 (2008): 2055–61.
Boudry, Maarten, 'The Cultural Buck Stops Somewhere: The Origin of Supernatural Belief and the Role of Agency Detection', *Religion, Brain & Behavior*, 99, no. 3 (2019): 253–5.
Bowler, Peter J., *Reconciling Science and Religion: The Debate in Early Twentieth-Century Britain*, London: University of Chicago Press, 2001.
Bowler, Peter J., and Iwan Rhys Morus, *Making Modern Science: A Historical Survey*, Chicago: University of Chicago Press, 2005.
Brewitt-Taylor, Sam, 'The Invention of a "Secular Society"? Christianity and the Sudden Appearance of Secularization Discourses in the British National Media, 1961–4', *Twentieth Century British History*, 24, no. 3 (2013): 327–50.
Brewitt-Taylor, Sam, 'Notes toward a Postsecular History of Modern British Secularization', *Journal of British Studies*, 60, no. 2 (April 2021): 310–33.
Brierley, Peter, and Heather Wright, *UK Christian Handbook*, London: Christian Research, 1996/7.
British Household Panel Survey, ESRC data archive, University of Essex, 1991.

British Social Attitudes Survey, 2008 http://www.brin.ac.uk/figures/the-2008-british-social-attitudes-survey/ (accessed 24 May 2017).
British Social Attitudes, 2017, http://www.natcen.ac.uk/news-media/press-releases/2017/september/british-social-attitudes-record-number-of-brits-with-no-religion/ (accessed 13 July 2018).
Brown, Callum, *Becoming Atheist: Humanism and the Secular West*, London: Bloomsbury Academic, 2017.
Brown, Callum, *The Death of Christian Britain: Understanding Secularisation 1800–2000*, London: Routledge, 2001.
Brown, Callum, 'The Necessity of Atheism: Making Sense of Secularisation', *Journal of Religious History*, 41, no. 4 (2017): 439–56.
Bruce, Steve, *Secularization: In Defence of an Unfashionable Theory*, Oxford: Oxford University Press, 2011.
Brugger, Peter, 'From Haunted Brain to Haunted Science, a Cognitive Neuroscience View of Paranormal and Pseudoscientific Thought', in J. Houran and R. Lange (eds), *Hauntings and Poltergeists: Multidisciplinary Perspectives*, 195–213, London: McFarland, 2001.
Butler, Jon, 'Disquieted History in *A Secular Age*', in Michael Warner, Jonathan VanAntwerpen and Craig Calhoun (eds), *Varieties of Secularism in a Secular Age*, 193–216, London: Harvard University Press, 2013.
Byron, Lord, 'Childe Harold's Pilgrimage', canto iii, stanza lxxii, 1816, http://knarf.english.upenn.edu/Byron/charold3.html (accessed 15 February. 2016).
Cairns, Teresa, 'Class, Gender and Education in the 20th Century: An Exploration of Educational Life Histories of Correspondents to the Mass Observation Archive', University of Sussex, PhD thesis, 2007.
Capra, Fritjof, and Pier Luigi Luisi, *The Systems View of Life: A Unifying Vision*, Cambridge: Cambridge University Press, 2014.
Carlson, Thomas A., 'Secular Affection Moods: Exploring Temporality with A Secular Age', in Florian Zemmin, Colin Jager and Guido Vanheeswijck (eds), *Working with a Secular Age: Interdisciplinary Perspectives on Charles Taylor's Master Narrative*, 245–62, Berlin: De Gruyter, 2016.
Carrette, Jeremy (ed.), *William James and the Varieties of Religious Experience*, London: Routledge, 2005.
Carrette, Jeremy, and Richard King, *Selling Spirituality: The Silent Takeover of Religion*, London: Routledge, 2004.
Carruthers, Jo, and Andrew Tate, *Spiritual Identities: Literature and the Post-Secular Imagination*, Oxford: Peter Lang, 2010.
Castro, Madeleine, RogerBurrows and RobinWooffitt, 'The Paranormal Is (Still) Normal: The Sociological Implications of a Survey of Paranormal Experiences in Great Britain', *Sociological Research Online*, 19, no. 3 (2014): 30–44.
Clements, Ben, *Religion and Public Opinion: Continuity and Change*, New York: Palgrave Macmillan, 2015.

Coleman, Thomas J., Christopher F. Silver and Jenny Holcombe, 'Focusing on Horizontal Transcendence: Much More Than a "Non-Belief"', *Essays in the Philosophy of Humanism*, 21, no. 2 (2013): 1–18.

Connolly, William E., 'Belief, Spirituality and Time', in Warner et al. (eds), *Varieties of Secularism in a Secular Age*, 126–44, London: Harvard University Press, 2013.

Courtenay, Edwin, http://www.edwincourtenay.co.uk/aboutedwin.php (accessed 3 March 2017).

Cranston, Maurice, *The Romantic Movement*, Oxford: Blackwell, 1994.

Davie, Grace, *Religion in Britain: A Persistent Paradox*, Chichester: Wiley-Blackwell, 2015.

Davie, Grace, *Religion in Britain since 1945: Believing without Belonging*, Oxford: Blackwell, 1994.

Davies, Douglas, and AlastairShaw, *Reusing Old Graves: A Report on Popular British Attitudes*, Crayford: Shaw & Sons, 1995.

Davies, Owen, *The Haunted: A Social History of Ghosts*, Basingstoke: Palgrave Macmillan, 2009.

Dawkins, Richard, *The God Delusion*, London: Black Swan, 2007.

Dawkins, Richard, *Unweaving the Rainbow: Science, Delusion and the Appetite for Wonder*, London: Allen Lane, 1998.

Day, Abby, *Believing in Belonging: Belief and Social Identity in the Modern World*, Oxford: Oxford University Press, 2011.

Dein, Simon, 'The Category of the Supernatural: A Valid Anthropological Term?', *Religion Compass*, 10, no. 2 (2016): 35–44.

Dogett, Luke, and AlpArat (eds), *Foundations and Futures in the Sociology of Religion*, London: Routledge, 2018.

Droogers, André, *Religion at Play*, Cambridge: Lutterworth Press, 2015.

Durkheim, Emile, *The Elementary Forms of the Religious Life*, London: Allen & Unwin

Eagleton, Terry, *Reason, Faith and Revolution: Reflections on the God Debate*, London: Yale University Press, 2009.

Eliot, T. S., *Four Quartets*, London: Faber & Faber, 1959.

Ellis, Ralph, *Scota, Egyptian Queen of Scots: Cleopatra to Christ*, Cheshire: Edfu Books, 2006.

Erikson, Erik, *Identity, Youth and Crisis*, London: Faber & Faber, 1968.

Evans, Lorraine, *Kingdom of the Ark: The Startling Story of How the Ancient British Race Is Descended from the Pharaohs*, London: Simon & Schuster, 2000.

Feraro, Shai, 'Connecting British Wicca with Radical Feminism and Goddess Spirituality during the 1970s and 1980s: The Case Study of Monica Sjöö', *Journal of Contemporary Religion*, 30, no. 2 (2015): 307–21.

Field, Clive D., BRIN Working Paper Religion in Great Britain, 1939–99: A Compendium of Gallup Poll Data, http://www.brin.ac.uk/wp-content/uploads/2011/12/

Religion-in-Great-Britain-1939-99-A-Compendium-of-Gallup-Poll-Data.pdf (accessed 27 August 2021).

Field, Clive D. *British Religion in Numbers*, Manchester: University of Manchester, 2010.

Fuller, Robert C., 'Minds of Their Own: Psychological Substrates of the Spiritual but Not Religious Sensibility', in William B. Parsons (ed.), *Being Spiritual but Not Religious: Past, Present, Future(s)*, 89–109, London: Routledge, 2018.

Geertz, Clifford, *The Interpretation of Cultures*, New York: Basic Books, 1973.

Gerard, David, Mark Abrams and Noel Timms, *Values and Social Change in Britain*, Basingstoke: Macmillan, 1985.

Gerth, Hans. H., and Charles Wright Mills (eds), *From Max Weber, Essays in Sociology*, London: Routledge, 1991.

Ghosh, Peter, 'Max Weber and William James: "Pragmatism", Psychology, Religion', *Max Weber Studies*, 5.2/6.1 (2005–6): 243–80.

Gill, Robert, C. Kirk Hadaway and Penny L. Marler, 'Is Religious Belief Declining in Britain?', *Journal for the Scientific Study of Religion*, 37, no. 3 (1998): 507–16.

Glendinning, Tony, and Steve Bruce, 'New Ways of Believing or Belonging: Is Religion Giving Way to Spirituality?' *British Journal of Sociology*, 57, no. 3 (2006): 399–414.

Gordon, Peter E., 'The Place of the Sacred in the Absence of God: Charles Taylor's "A Secular Age"', *Journal of the History of Ideas*, 69, no. 4 (2008): 647–73.

Gould, Stephen Jay, *Rock of Ages: Science and Religion in the Fullness of Life*, London: Vintage Digital, 2011.

Gray, John, *The Immortalization Commission: Science and the Strange Quest to Cheat Death*, London: Allen Lane, 2011.

Gray, John, *Seven Types of Atheism*, London: Penguin Books, 2018.

Hardy, Alister, *The Spiritual Nature of Man: A Study of Contemporary Religious Experience*, Oxford: Clarendon Press, 1979.

Harvey, Graham, 'Paganism', in Linda Woodhead, HirokoKawanami and Christopher Partridge (eds), *Religions in the Modern World: Traditions and Transformations*, 358–78, London: Routledge, 2009.

Harvey, Graham, and GiselleVincett, 'Alternative Spiritualities: Marginal and Mainstream', in Linda Woodhead and Rebecca Catto (eds), *Religion and Change in Modern Britain*, Abingdon: Routledge, 2012.

Hay, David, *Exploring Inner Space, Is God Still Possible in the 20th century?*, Harmondsworth: Penguin, 1982.

Hay, David, *God's Biologist: A Life of Alister Hardy*, London: Darton, Longman and Todd, 2011.

Hay, David, *Religious Experience Today: Studying the Facts*, London: Mowbray, 1990.

Hay, David, and Kate Hunt, *Understanding the Spirituality of People Who Don't Go to Church*, Nottingham: University of Nottingham, 2000.

Hay, David, and Ann Morisy, 'Reports of Ecstatic, Paranormal, or Religious Experience in Great Britain and the United States – A Comparison of Trends', *Journal for the Scientific Study of Religion*, 17, no. 3 (1978): 255–68.

Hayward, Rhodri, *Resisting History: Religious Transcendence and the Invention of the Unconscious*, Manchester: Manchester University Press, 2007.

Heelas, Paul, *The New Age Movement: The Celebration of the Self and the Sacralization of Modernity*, Oxford: Blackwell, 1996.

Heelas, Paul, and Linda Woodhead, *The Spiritual Revolution: Why Religion Is Giving Way to Spirituality*, Oxford: Blackwell, 2005.

Heintzelman, Samantha J., and Laura A. King, 'On Knowing More Than We Can Tell: Intuitive Processes and the Experience of Meaning', *Journal of Positive Psychology*, 8, no. 6 (2013): 471–82.

Hennis, Wilhelm, 'The Spiritualist Foundation of Max Weber's "Interpretative Sociology"', *History of the Human Sciences*, 11, no. 2 (1998): 83–106.

Hinton, James, *The Mass Observers: A History, 1937–1949*, Oxford: Oxford University Press, 2013.

Hinton, James, *Nine Wartime Lives: Mass-Observation and the Making of the Modern Self*, Oxford: Oxford University Press, 2010.

Hinton, James, *Old Men Ought to Be Explorers: A History of My Adolescence*, forthcoming.

Hinton, James, *Seven Lives from Mass Observation: Britain in the Late Twentieth Century*, Oxford: Oxford University Press, 2016.

Hobsbawm, Eric, *The Age of Capital*, London: Weidenfeld and Nicolson, 1977.

Houran, James, and Rense Lange (eds), *Hauntings and Poltergeists: Multidisciplinary Perspectives*, London: McFarland, 2001.

Humphrey, Nicholas, *Soul Searching: Human Nature and Supernatural Belief*, London: Chatto & Windus, 1995.

Hutton, Ronald, *The Triumph of the Moon: A History of Modern Pagan Witchcraft*, Oxford: Oxford University Press, 1999.

James, William, *The Varieties of Religious Experience: A Study in Human Nature: Being the Gifford Lectures on Natural Religion Delivered at Edinburgh in 1901–1902*, New York: Modern Library, 1929.

Josephson-Storm, Jason A., *The Myth of Disenchantment: Magic, Modernity, and the Birth of the Human Sciences*, Chicago: University of Chicago Press, 2018.

King, Mike, *Postsecularism: The Hidden Challenge to Extremism*, Cambridge, UK: James Clarke, 2009.

King, Mike, *Secularism: The Hidden Origins of Disbelief*, Cambridge, UK: James Clarke, 2007.

King, Richard, 'Asian Religions and Mysticism', in Jeremy Carrette (ed.), *William James and* The Varieties of Religious Experience, London: Routledge, 2005.

Komar, Kathleen, 'Rilke: Metaphysics in a New Age', in Sigrid Bauschinger and Susan Cocalis (eds), *Rilke-Rezeptionen: Rilke Reconsidered*, Tübingen/Basel: Franke, 1995.
Komar, Susan, 'Rethinking Rilke's Duisiner Elegien at the End of the Millennium', in Erika A. Metzger (ed.), *A Companion to the Works of Rainer Maria Rilke*, Rochester, NY: Camden House, 2004.
Landy, Joshua, and Michael Saler (eds), *The Re-Enchantment of the World: Secular Magic in a Rational Age*, Stanford: Stanford University Press, 2009.
Laski, Marghanita, *Ecstasy in Secular and Religious Experience*, London: Cresset Press, 1961.
Lee, Lois, *Recognizing the Non-Religious, Reimagining the Secular*, Oxford: Oxford University Press, 2015.
Leggett, Peter, *The Sacred Quest: By Experiment and Experience – the Next Step*, Ipswich: Pilgrim Books, 1987.
Leggett, Peter, and Max Payne, *A Forgotten Truth: A Spiritual Vision for Modern Man*, Ipswich: Pilgrims Book Services, 1986.
Litowitz, Douglas, 'Max Weber and Franz Kafka: A Shared Vision of Modern Law', *Law, Culture and the Humanities*, 7, no. 1 (2011): 48–65.
Luckhurst, Roger, *The Invention of Telepathy*, Oxford: Oxford University Press, 2002.
Lynch, Gordon, 'Researching the Religious Dimensions of Social Life', in Luke Dogett and Alp Arat (eds), *Foundations and Futures in the Sociology of Religion*, London: Routledge, 2018.
MacIntyre, Alasdair, *After Virtue, a Study in Moral Theory*, London: Duckworth, 1981.
Mangan, Bruce, 'Meaning, God, Volition, and Art How Rightness and the Fringe Bring It All Together', *Journal of Consciousness Studies*, 21, nos. 3–4 (2014): 754–67.
Maslow, Abraham H., *Religions Values and Peak Experiences*, Columbus: Ohio State University Press, 1964.
McAdams, Dan P., *The Stories We Live By*, New York: W. Morrow, 1993.
McLeod, Hugh, *The Religious Crisis of the 1960s*, Oxford: Oxford University Press, 2007.
Midgley, Mary, *The Myths We Live By*, Abingdon: Routledge, 2004.
Midgley, Mary, *Science as Salvation: Modern Myth and Its Meaning*, Abingdon: Routledge, 1992.
Monod, Jacques, *Chance and Necessity: An Essay on the Natural Philosophy of Modern Biology*, New York: Alfred A. Knopf, 1971.
Nash, David S., 'Believing in Secularisation: Stories of Decline, Potential, and Resurgence', *Journal of Religious History*, 41, no. 4 (2017): 505–31.
Nietzsche, Friedrich, *The Will to Power*, New York: Random House, 1967.
Owen, Alex, *The Place of Enchantment, British Occultism and the Culture of the Modern*, London: University of Chicago Press, 2004.
Parsons, William B., *Being Spiritual but Not Religious: Past, Present, Future(s)*, London: Routledge, 2018.

Partridge, Christopher H., *Encyclopaedia of New Religions*, Oxford: Lion Hudson, 2004.

Partridge, Christopher H., 'Truth, Authority and Epistemological Individualism in New Age Thought', *Journal of Contemporary Religion*, 14, no. 1 (1999): 77–95.

Pollen, Annebella, 'A Hybrid Heterogeneity Hard to Contain: Research Methods and Methodology in the Post-1981 Mass Observation Project', *History Workshop Journal*, 75 (Spring 2013): 213–35.

Rawlinson, Andrew, *The Book of Enlightened Masters: Western Teachers in Easter Traditions*, Chicago: Open Court, 1997.

Reitsma, Oane, 'Musical Works as Higher Culture in a Secular Age', in Florian Zemmin et al. (eds), *Working with A Secular Age: Interdisciplinary Perspectives on Charles Taylor's Master Narrative*, 229–44, Berlin: De Gruyter, 2016.

Robertson, Olivia (ed.), *Handbook of the Fellowship of Isis*, Clonegal: Cesara, 1992.

Roll, William G., and Michael A. Persinger, 'Investigations of Poltergeists and Haunts: A Review and Interpretation', in James Houran and Rense Lange (eds), *Hauntings and Poltergeists: Multidisciplinary Perspectives*, 123–62, London: McFarland, 2001.

Sacks, Oliver, *Hallucinations*, London: Picador, 2012.

Sartre, Jean-Paul, *Nausea*, London: Penguin Books, 1969.

Schaffer, Simon, 'Newtonian Angels', in Joad Raymond (ed.), *Conversations with Angels: Essays towards a History of Spiritual Communication, 1100–1700*, Basingstoke: Palgrave Macmillan, 2011.

Schlieter, Jens, *What Is It Like to Be Dead?: Near-Death Experiences, Christianity, and the Occult*, New York: Oxford University Press, 2018.

Sideris, Lisa H., *Consecrating Science, Wonder, Knowledge and the Natural World*, Oakland: University of California Press, 2017.

Sloan, Gary, 'George Bernard Shaw: Mystic or Atheist?', http://www.liberator.net/articles/SloanGary/Shaw.html (accessed 25 May 2016).

The Spiritualist Association of Great Britain (SAGBG), http://www.sagb.org.uk/history.htm (accessed 5 December 2017).

Stacey, Timothy, *Myth and Solidarity in the Modern World: Beyond Religious and Political Division*, London: Routledge, 2018.

Sterenberg, Matthew, *Mythic Thinking in Twentieth-Century Britain: Meaning for Modernity*, Basingstoke: Palgrave Macmillan, 2013.

Taves, Ann, Egil Asprem and ElliottIhm, 'Psychology, Meaning Making and the Study of Worldviews: Beyond Religion and Non-Religion', *Psychology of Religion and Spirituality*, 10, no. 3 (2018): 207–17.

Taylor, Charles, *A Secular Age*, London: Belknap, 2007.

Taylor, Charles, *Sources of the Self: The Making of the Modern Identity*, Cambridge: Cambridge University Press, 1989.

Taylor, Charles, *Varieties of Religion Today: William James Revisited*, London: Harvard University Press, 2003.

Taylor, Eugene, 'Metaphysics and Consciousness in James' *Varieties*', in Jeremy Carrette (ed.), *William James and* The Varieties of Religious Experience, London: Routledge, 2005.
Teilhard de Chardin, Pierre, *The Phenomenon of Man*, London: Fount Paperbacks, 1977.
Theos, *The Spirit of Things Unseen: Belief in Post-Religious Britain*, 2013, www.theosthinktank.co.uk (accessed 29 August 2021).
Thurschwell, Pamela, *Literature, Technology, and Magical Thinking, 1880–1920*, Cambridge: Cambridge University Press, 2001.
Voas, David, 'The Mysteries of Religion and the Lifecourse', Centre for Longitudinal Studies, University College, London, Working Paper 1, 2015.
Voas, David, and Siobhan McAndrew, 'Three Puzzles of Non-Religion in Britain', *Journal of Contemporary Religion*, 27, no. 1 (2012): 36–41.
Vyse, Stuart A., *Believing in Magic: The Psychology of Superstition*, Oxford: Oxford University Press, 1997.
Wallace, Amy, and Bill Henkin, *The Physic Healing Book*, New York: Delacorte Press, 1981.
Warner, Marina, *Phantasmaoria: Spirit Visions, Metaphors, and Media into the Twenty-First Century*, Oxford: Oxford University Press, 2006.
Warner, Michael, et al. (eds), *Varieties of Secularism in a Secular Age*, London: Harvard University Press, 2013.
Weber, Max, *The Protestant Ethic and the Spirit of Capitalism*, London: Penguin, 2002.
Weber, Max, *The Sociology of Religion*, London: Methuen, 1965.
Williams, Sarah C., *Religious Belief and Popular Culture in Southwark, c.1880–1939*, Oxford: Oxford University Press, 1999.
Wilson, Bryan, *Religion in Secular Society, a Sociological Comment*, London: Watts, 1966.
Wiseman, Richard, *Paranormality: Why We See What Isn't There*, London: Macmillan, 2011.
Wittgenstein, Ludwig, *Culture and Value*, edited by G. H. Von Wright, Oxford: Blackwell, 1984.
Woodhead, Linda, 'The Rise of "No Religion" in Britain: The Emergence of a New Cultural Majority', *Journal of the British Academy*, 4 (2016): 245–61.
Woodhead, Linda, 'Secularism with Added Agency', in Luke Dogett and Alp Arat (eds), *Foundations and Futures in the Sociology of Religion*, London: Routledge, 2018.
Woodhead, Linda, and Rebecca Catto (eds), *Religion and Change in Modern Britain*, Abingdon: Routledge, 2012.
Woodhead, Linda, Hiroko Kawanami and Christopher Partridge (eds), *Religions in the Modern World: Traditions and Transformations*, London: Routledge, 2009.

Wordsworth, William, 'Tintern Abbey', 1798, https://www.poetryfoundation.org/poems/45527/lines-composed-a-few-miles-above-tintern-abbey-on-revisiting-the-banks-of-the-wye-during-a-tour-july-13-1798 (accessed 29 August 2021).

Wulff, David M., 'Mystical Experience', in Etzel Cardena, Steven Jay Lynn and Stanley Krippner (eds), *Varieties of Anomalous Experience: Examining the Scientific Evidence*, 397–428, Washington, DC: American Psychological Association, 2000.

YouGov, 'Atheism', *The Times*, 12 February 2015.

YouGov, University of Lancaster, Faith Matters, 30 January 2013 (accessed 27 August 2021).

Zemmin, Florian, et al. (eds), *Working with* A Secular Age: *Interdisciplinary Perspectives on Charles Taylor's Master Narrative*, Berlin: De Gruyter, 2016.

Zohar, Danah, *The Quantum Self: Consciousness, Physics and the New World View*, London: Bloomsbury, 1990.

Zuckerman, Phil, *Society without God: What the Least Religious Nations Can Tell Us about Contentment*, New York: New York University Press, 2020.

General Index

1960s cultural revolution 15–16, 18, 136–7

Adler, Margot 49
after-life 29–33, 46–8, 58–9
  of pets 30, 152 n.6
alternative therapies 18–19, 117, 127–8
An Experiment with Time (Dunne) 85
angels 80–1
Armstrong, Karen 16
Association for the Scientific Study of Anomalous Phenomena 61
astrology 61
atheism 4, 5, 21–6, 36–37, 49–50, 66–7, 136–7
Attenborough, David 138
auras 63–4
awe and wonder 7, 17, 92–4, 109, 135, 138–9 (*see also* moments out of time)
Ayer, A. J. 58

Bach, Sebastian 96
Bennett, Gillian 4, 30, 32, 72, 73
Bennett, Jane 108
Berger, Peter 26
Blavatsky, Madame 18, 63
British Humanist Association 67
Broad, C. D. 46
Brown, Callum 136–9
Bruce, Steve 136
Buddhism 3, 40
But That I Can't Believe (Robinson) 16
Byron, Lord 93

Campaign for Nuclear Disarmament 26, 122–3
Capra, Fritjof 62
Chariots of the Gods (Von Däniken) 82
Christian Science 23
Christianity 2–3, 15–18, 26–7, 55, 73–4
  Anglican 16–17, 30, 94–5
  Catholic 95

Churches' Fellowship for Psychical and Spiritual Studies 59, 63
clairvoyance (*see* premonition)
class consciousness 82–3, 126, 128–9
Coleridge, Samuel 84
College of Psychic Studies 126
Council of All Faiths 103

Darwin, Charles 54–7, 68, 88
Dawkins, Richard 4, 71, 101, 138, 144 n.16
Day, Abby 31
death 29–50
Djwhal Khu 63
Druidry 112, 127
Dunne, J. W. 85
Durkheim, Emile 6, 31, 138

ecology 6, 18, 112, 120, 123–5
Eliot, T. S. 96–7
enchantment 114, 123
  disenchantment 5, 58, 75
  re-enchantment 88, 135
Enlightenment (European) 4, 5, 6
epistemological individualism 18–20
Eric Von Däniken 82
evolution 54–7, 68, 127
exorcism 74
Ezekiel 82, 106

Fellowship of Isis 112, 119–22
feminism 18, 40, 48, 112, 120, 137
Fenwick, Peter 62
Fort, Charles 85
Frazer, James 112

Gaia 57
ghosts 3–4, 31–2, 32–6, 77–8, 84
Gould, Stephen Jay 52
Graves, Robert 112
Green Party 20, 67
Greene, Liz 126
Greenham Common 65

Griffiths, Bede 16
guardian angels 33–4

Hardy, Alister 92, 133
Hare Krishna 129–31
Hartnett, Michael 49
Hay, David 92
Heron, John 63
Hinduism 11, 103, 129
Hocking, Gwyn 61–2
horoscopes 3, 71
Humanist Teachers Association 23
humanistic psychology 63

identity 6–7, 25
Iraq War 123
Israel, Rev Dr Martin 59, 63, 160 n.70

James, William 5, 18, 19, 21, 91–2, 100, 107, 134
Joule, James 57
Joyce, James 92
Jung, Carl 103, 127

Kafka, Franz 5
Koestler, Arthur 62

Labour Party 42, 124
Laski, Marghanita 92, 98, 107
Leggett, Peter 62–3
Liberal Democrats 124
Life after Life (Moody) 100
life force 3, 11, 20, 21, 57, 68
Lord of the Rings 114
Lovelock, James 57

Marx, Karl 138
Maslow, Abraham 103, 107, 166 n.6
Mass Observation 8–9, 11–12, 85
Mass Observation directives
 close relationships (1990) 13
 nature and environment (1994) 54, 93, 158 n.18
 social divisions (1990) 13
 supernatural (1996) 9–10, 51, 71
Mass observers 9–12, 13, 133, 147 n.43
McNeillie, Andrew 84
Meaning 1–2, 5–6, 7, 8, 133
 and death 29, 30, 45, 49–50

and imagination 7, 131, 133, 134, 136, 139
and puzzlement 8, 12, 26–7, 65, 69, 136
Medical and Scientific Network 83
moments out of time 91–109
 music 96–7
 natural beauty 93–4
 out of body experiences 99–106, 168 n.63
 religious worship 94–6
 sex 97–8
Monod, Jacques 5
Moody, Raymond 100
Muslims 11
Myers, Frederic 86, 88
myth 7, 134

National Federation of Spiritual Healers 128
New Age 11, 18–20, 123–4, 126, 128
New Atheism 4, 8, 101, 140
Newton, Isaac 57
Nietzsche, Friedrich 108

Open University 25, 42
Otto, Rudolf 93, 166 n.6
Ouija Boards 78–9, 130

paganism 111–29
paranormal 3–4, 71–89, 120–1
 as class assertion 81–2
 and (pseudo-) scientific speculation 58–60, 66, 83–9
 as re-enchantment 75–6, 88
personal God 2–3, 10, 46, 54, 56
poltergeists 78, 85
Portrait of the Artist as a Young Man (Joyce) 92
premonitions, 3, 72–3, 85
Puzzled People (Mass Observation) 12

rationalism 4–5, 25–6, 52–3, 58, 65–6, 136, 138
reincarnation 40–5
religious experiences 91–2, 107, 133, 135, 166 n.6 (*see also* moments out of time)
Rilke, Rainer Maria 68
Robinson, John 16, 18
Romanticism 6–7, 93, 94

Ruskin, John 93
Russell, Bertrand 5, 65

Sacks, Oliver 84
Saddam Hussein 123
Schlieter, Jans 100
Schumacher, E. F. 62
science 5–6
   hostility to 83, 131
   and religion 51–69
   speculative 58–60, 66, 77–8, 83–9
   spiritualization of 59–65
Scientific and Medical Network 62
Second World War 24
secular sacred 6–7
secularization 2, 3, 6, 7, 135–9
Shaw, Bernard 68
Sheldrake, Rupert 83
Snow, C. P. 97
Social Democratic Party 124
Society for Psychical Research 58, 61, 62, 88
Spinoza 48, 57, 94
spiritual healing 127–8
spiritualism 37–40, 61, 73–4
Spiritualist Association of Great Britain 39
spirituality
   non-religious 3, 4, 18–21, 40, 62, 91–2
   secular 27, 48, 96–8, 107–8, 138, 145 n.29
Starbuck, Edwin 92
Starhawk 49
Steiner, Rudolph 16
Subud 17

tarot 116–17
Taylor, Charles 15, 55, 108, 129, 133, 135, 136, 137–9
Teilhard de Chardin, Pierre 54
telepathy 86
Thatcher, Margaret 40, 123, 124
The Death of Christian Britain (Brown) 136
The Fortean Times 85
The Golden Bough (Frazer) 112
The Idea of the Holy (Otto) 93
The Marriage of East and West (Griffiths) 16
The Tao of Physics (Capra) 62
The Varieties of Religious Experience (James) 91
The White Goddess 112
The X-Files 71
Theosophical Society 62, 63
Theosophy 17, 18
Thompson, William 57
Tolkien, J. R. R. 71, 114
Trine, Ralph Waldo 21
Turner, J. M. W. 93

University of the Third Age 65

Weber, Max 5, 46, 93, 97, 134, 138
Wells, H. G. 61
Wicca 112
Williams, Sarah 30
Wilson, Bryan 136
Wilson, Colin 60, 116
Wittgenstein, Ludwig 2
wonder (*see* awe and wonder)
Wordsworth, William 93

Index of Mass Observers

(This index lists all the mass observers who are cited on more than one occasion.)

Baker, Jenny 24, 33
Bevan, Alistair 41, 58
Blake, Gloria 43, 57
Bolton, Harry 36, 49, 67
Brewer, Florence 56–7, 59–60
Brewster, Gerald 53, 56, 87
Brown, Jenny 16, 45, 54, 58, 80, 99, 100
Burroughs, Rosemary 111, 113–25, 128–9
Buxton, Phillip 23, 24

Charlton, Mark 34, 44
Clark, Pauline 74, 100–1
Connell, Pauline 41, 42
Crane, Robert 66, 67–8, 79, 87

Darling, Mark 50, 66, 87
Davidson, Felicity 21, 77
Delaney, Sandra 16, 52, 53
Dilnot, Barbara 16, 72

Edwards, Garry 48, 56, 94
Evans, Fiona 41, 60–2, 86, 87
Evans, Rose 25, 72

Fairbrother, Hugh 36–7
Farleigh, Edward 17, 56, 60, 87, 95–6
Farrow, Elsie 34, 39
Fielding, Emma 20, 60
Forrest, Jill 65–6, 76, 84, 87
Forrester, Mathew 75, 85
Fraser, Adrian 50, 67, 76, 84, 85–6

Gately, Sam 23, 86–7
Geraghty, Samantha 48–9
Grainger, Elsie 19, 38, 41, 42, 87
Gregory, Brian 53–4, 74
Gurney, Eric 25, 36, 85

Halliday, Gwen 30, 31, 72
Hammond, Justine 102–3

Harman, Clare 72, 95
Harriman, Rachel 49–50, 96, 107
Harrison, Paula 15, 16, 31–2, 34, 38, 58,
    78, 86, 94–5
Hartman, Christine 52, 55
Hodges, Sarah 45, 55
Howard, Liz 47, 57–8
Hurley, Rebecca 24, 35–6

Jefferies, Laura 23, 101–2
Jevons, Laetitia 72, 73
Jones, Mary 43, 45

Kirby, Julia 33, 73

Latimer, Gillian 16, 41, 59, 92
Lewis, Harry 26, 83–4
Lloyd, David 30, 40–1, 46, 58, 59

Marshall, Stella 17–18, 42, 43, 44,
    63–5, 69, 97

Palmer, Dorothy 22–3, 97
Parsons, Kirsty 43–4, 125–9
Partridge, Thomas 58, 99
Phillips, Marion 33, 54–5, 76, 78,
    92–3, 98, 99
Ponsonby, Phil 53, 56

Rawlinson, Cynthia 16, 47, 107
Reilly, William 33–4, 55
Reynolds, Geraldine 22,
    153 n.20
Richardson, Veronica 16, 57
Rust, Bob 24, 35, 77, 86

Seymour, Julia 46, 52, 54

Taylor, Mary 19, 92
Terry, Howard 21, 39–40, 41

Thompson, Margaret 35, 67, 97
Thompson, Sally 22, 39, 74
Trelawney, Emma 94, 100

Warman, Janet 23, 112
Woody, Bill 41–2, 57
Worley, Rose 44–5, 78, 99

www.ingramcontent.com/pod-product-compliance
Lightning Source LLC
Chambersburg PA
CBHW061831300426
44115CB00013B/2338